Face the (GCSE) Spanish Inquisition with CGP!

No doubt about it, you'll be asked some difficult questions in Edexcel GCSE Spanish. Luckily, this CGP Revision Guide is bursting with brilliant notes for every topic, plus crystal-clear explanations of all the vocab and grammar you'll need.

But that's not all. We've also packed in plenty of exam-style reading, writing, translation, speaking and listening questions — with **free audio files** available from this page:

www.cgpbooks.co.uk/GCSESpanishAudio

How to access your free Online Edition

You can read this entire book on your PC, Mac or tablet, with handy links to all the online audio files. Just go to **cgpbooks.co.uk/extras** and enter this code:

1013 8336 3348 8899

By the way, this code only works for one person. If somebody else has used this book before you, they might have already claimed the Online Edition.

CGP — still the best! ☺

Our sole aim here at CGP is to produce the highest quality books — carefully written, immaculately presented and dangerously close to being funny.

Then we work our socks off to get them out to you — at the cheapest possible prices.

CONTENTS

CONTENTS

Published by CGP

Editors:
Rose Jones
Jennifer Underwood

Contributors:
Matthew Parkinson
Jacqui Richards

With thanks to Chloe Anderson, Encarna Aparicio-Dominguez, Hannah Roscoe and Glenda Simpson for the proofreading.

With thanks to Ana Pungartnik for the copyright research.

Acknowledgements:
Audio produced by Naomi Laredo of Small Print.
Recorded, edited and mastered by Graham Williams of the Speech Recording Studio,
with the assistance of Andy le Vien at RMS Studios.

Voice Artists:
Jessica Gonzalez Campos
David Martel Santana
Ángela Lobato del Castillo

Edexcel material is reproduced by permission of Edexcel.
With thanks to iStock.com for permission to use the images on pages 29, 48 and 56.
Abridged and adapted extract on page 19 from 'Las inquietudes de Shanti Andía' by Pío Baroja.
Abridged and adapted extract on page 35 from 'Pepita Jiménez' by Juan Valera.
Abridged and adapted extract on page 38 from 'Viajes por Europa y América' by Gorgonio Petano y Mazariegos.

ISBN: 978 1 78294 549 9
Printed by Elanders Ltd, Newcastle upon Tyne.
Clipart from Corel®

Based on the classic CGP style created by Richard Parsons.

Numbers

There are some tricky customers among Spanish numbers so make sure you're first in line for top marks.

Uno, dos, tres — *One, two, three*

0	cero		20	veinte
1	uno (un), una		21	veintiuno
2	dos		22	veintidós
3	tres		23	veintitrés
4	cuatro		30	treinta
5	cinco		31	treinta y uno
6	seis			
7	siete		40	cuarenta
8	ocho		50	cincuenta
9	nueve		60	sesenta
10	diez		70	setenta
11	once		80	ochenta
12	doce		90	noventa
13	trece			
14	catorce			
15	quince			
16	dieciséis			
17	diecisiete			
18	dieciocho			
19	diecinueve			

> All twenty-something numbers are rolled into one — like 'veintiuno' (*twenty-one*).

> After 30, numbers are joined by 'y' (*and*), but written separately — like 'treinta y uno' (*thirty-one*).

Grammar — using 'one' with masculine nouns

When you put 'one' in front of a masculine word, uno becomes 'un'.

veintiún caballos	*21 horses*
treinta y un caballos	*31 horses*

Before a feminine word, the 'o' changes to 'a':

veintiuna galletas	*21 biscuits*

> See p.59 for more on masculine and feminine nouns.

100	cien(to)		700	setecientos/as
101	ciento uno		900	novecientos/as
200	doscientos/as		1000	mil
500	quinientos/as		1 000 000	un millón

> 'Cien' becomes 'ciento' when used in front of another number (except 'mil').

1826	mil ochocientos veintiséis	2000	dos mil
1984	mil novecientos ochenta y cuatro	2005	dos mil cinco

Primero, segundo, tercero — *First, second, third*

These words always end in 'o' for masculine things and 'a' for feminine things.

1st	primero/primera (1º/1ª)		6th	sexto/a
2nd	segundo/a (2º/2ª)		7th	séptimo/a
3rd	tercero/a (3º/3ª)		8th	octavo/a
4th	cuarto/a		9th	noveno/a
5th	quinto/a		10th	décimo/a

Grammar — 'primero', 'tercero' + masculine nouns

When 'primero' or 'tercero' appear in front of a masculine word, they drop the 'o'.

el primer baile	*the first dance*
el tercer cantante	*the third singer*

Other useful number phrases

> el número = number

una docena	*a dozen*	un par	*a couple / pair*	unos/as *some / a few / about*

unas **diez peras**
*about **ten pears***

1st the worst, 2nd the best, 3rd the one with the Spanish test...

*Lee el texto y contesta a las preguntas **en español**.*

> 'Tener' is a radical-changing verb. See p.77.

Marta tiene veintidós años. Su hermana solo tiene diecisiete años, pero su abuelo tiene ochenta y ocho años. Marta vive muy cerca de aquí — en la segunda calle a la derecha.

e.g. ¿Cuántos años tiene Marta? *Tiene veintidós años.*

1. ¿Cuántos años tiene su hermana? [1]
2. ¿Cuántos años tiene su abuelo? [1]
3. ¿Dónde vive Marta? [1]

2

Times and Dates

Time to learn some really useful phrases which are sure to get you good marks in your Spanish GCSE.

¿Qué hora es? — *What time is it?*

1) You'll need to know how to <u>tell the time</u> for lots of topics. It's bound to come up in your exams...

See p.1 for more numbers.

Es la una.	*It's one o'clock.*
Son las dos.	*It's two o'clock.*
Son las cinco y cuarto.	*It's quarter past five.*
Son las dos menos cuarto.	*It's quarter to two.*
Son las siete y media.	*It's half past seven.*
Son las ocho y cinco.	*It's five past eight.*
Son las tres menos veinte.	*It's twenty to three.*

Grammar — at / it's X o'clock

To say '<u>at X o'clock</u>', you need '<u>a</u>':

a <u>la una</u>   *at one o'clock*
a <u>las ocho</u>   *at eight o'clock*

('La' changes to 'las' for anything other than 'one o'clock'.)

To say '<u>it's X o'clock</u>', use '<u>es</u>' or '<u>son</u>':

es la una   *it's one o'clock*
son las ocho   *it's eight o'clock*

('Es changes to 'son' for anything other than 'one o'clock'.)

2) The <u>24-hour clock</u> is also used in many Spanish-speaking countries, so make sure you can tell the time <u>both</u> ways.

The 24-hour clock

(Son) las veintiuna horas treinta minutos.	*(It's) 21.30.*
(Son) las tres horas catorce minutos.	*(It's) 03.14.*
(Son) las diecinueve horas cincuenta y cinco minutos.	*(It's) 19.55.*

Los días de la semana — *The days of the week*

la semana	*the week*
el fin de semana	*(at) the weekend*
lunes	*Monday*
martes	*Tuesday*
miércoles	*Wednesday*
jueves	*Thursday*
viernes	*Friday*
sábado	*Saturday*
domingo	*Sunday*

hoy	*today*
mañana	*tomorrow*
ayer	*yesterday*
anoche	*last night*
pasado mañana	*the day after tomorrow*
anteayer	*the day before yesterday*
el lunes	*on Monday*
los lunes	*on Mondays*
todos los días	*every day*
quince días	*a fortnight*
cada quince días	*every fortnight*
cada tres días	*every three days*

In English, a fortnight is fourteen days, but if you're talking about a fortnight in <u>Spanish</u>, you actually say <u>fifteen days</u>.

Days of the week are always masculine and lower case.

Fui de compras ayer.	*I went shopping yesterday.*
Tengo un examen pasado mañana.	*I have an exam the day after tomorrow.*
Voy al cine los sábados.	*I go to the cinema on Saturdays.*

the day before yesterday — anteayer

tomorrow — mañana

every six days — cada seis días

Section 1 — General Stuff

Times and Dates

Knowing about dates is important — they do tend to crop up every now and then. What's even better is that they can help you sort out your Spanish social life. What's not to love?

More useful time phrases

esta mañana	*this morning*
esta tarde	*this afternoon/evening*
esta noche	*tonight*
mañana por la mañana	*tomorrow morning*
la semana que viene	*next week*
la semana pasada	*last week*

See p.2 for more time phrases.

To say '<u>in</u> the evening', you add '<u>por</u>':

Juego al tenis por la mañana.
I play tennis in the morning.

You don't translate 'at' here — you literally say 'I play tennis the weekend'.

in the afternoon — por la tarde
at the weekend — el fin de semana

Los meses del año — *The months of the year*

Just like the days of the week, the months of the year are all <u>masculine</u> and <u>shouldn't have capital letters</u>.

enero	*January*	julio	*July*	la estación	*season*
febrero	*February*	agosto	*August*	la primavera	*spring*
marzo	*March*	septiembre	*September*	el verano	*summer*
abril	*April*	octubre	*October*	el otoño	*autumn*
mayo	*May*	noviembre	*November*	el invierno	*winter*
junio	*June*	diciembre	*December*		

Voy a la playa todos los años en agosto.   *I go to the beach every year in August.*

En invierno, iremos a esquiar.   *In winter, we will go skiing.*

Bern hoped to impress his date with his alternative choice of transport.

¿Qué fecha es? — *What's the date?*

In English, you say '<u>the third</u> of May' or '<u>the twentieth</u> of December'. In Spanish, you can say either '<u>el primero de</u>' or '<u>el uno de</u>' for the <u>first</u> of the month, but for all the other dates, you say '<u>the three</u> of May' or '<u>the twenty</u> of December'...

el tres de mayo	*(on) the third of May*
el veinte de diciembre	*(on) the twentieth of December*
Es el uno de / el primero de febrero.	*It's the first of February.*
Es el dos de marzo de dos mil dieciocho.	*It's the second of March 2018.*

You <u>don't</u> translate '<u>on</u>' at the start of dates in Spanish, so <u>both</u> 'the third of May' and 'on the third of May' are written '<u>el tres de mayo</u>'.

TRACK LISTENING 01

Sultanas, raisins, dates — *tasty treats for exam revision...*

*Listen to what Carlos, Anabel and Julia have to say, and then answer the questions **in English**.*

e.g. How often does Carlos go to the gym?   **Every day.**

1 a. When was Anabel's birthday meal?   [1]

b. Where did Anabel go yesterday?   [1]

c. When is Julia going to the theatre?   [1]

Questions

Knowing about questions will come in handy in your speaking test — you'll have to understand what you're being asked, and in the role play you'll have to ask your teacher a question or two. Best to be prepared.

Question marks and tone of voice

1) To turn a statement into a question, put an <u>upside down question mark</u> at the <u>beginning</u> and a <u>normal one</u> at the <u>end</u>.

2) When speaking, <u>raise your voice</u> at the <u>end</u> of the sentence to show you're asking a question.

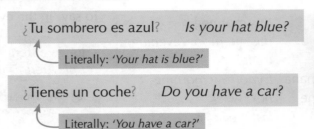

¿Tu sombrero es azul? *Is your hat blue?*

Literally: *'Your hat is blue?'*

¿Tienes un coche? *Do you have a car?*

Literally: *'You have a car?'*

"Of course I have a car — why wouldn't a dog have a car?"

¿Qué... — *What...?*

If your question starts with '<u>What...</u>', you normally need to start it with '<u>¿Qué...</u>' in Spanish.

¿Qué comes por la mañana? *What do you eat in the morning?*

¿Qué quieres hacer el fin de semana? *What do you want to do at the weekend?*

Go back to p.2-3 for more time phrases.

¿Cuál... — *Which one..? What...?*

1) '<u>¿Cuál...</u>' normally means '<u>Which...</u>' or '<u>Which one...</u>':

¿Cuál quieres? *Which (one) do you want?*

2) However, sometimes you might need to use '<u>¿Cuál...</u>' even if you'd use '<u>What...</u>' in English. This is usually when you use the verb '<u>ser</u>' and you're asking for a <u>piece of information</u>, rather than a definition.

¿Cuál es tu problema? *What is your problem?*

¿Cuál es tu dirección? *What is your address?*

¿Cuándo? ¿Por qué? ¿Dónde? — *When? Why? Where?*

Question words like this are known as interrogatives. See p.71.

There are <u>loads of other words</u> you can use to <u>begin a question</u> — get them <u>all</u> learnt.

¿Cuándo?	*When?*
¿Por qué?	*Why?*
¿Dónde?	*Where?*
¿Cómo?	*How?*
¿Cuánto/a?	*How much?*
¿Cuántos/as?	*How many?*
¿Quién(es)?	*Who?*
¿Cuál?	*Which?*
¿Es...?	*Is it...?*

Remember that question words need accents.

¿Cuántos/as tienes?	*How many do you have?*
¿Por qué haces eso?	*Why are you doing that?*
¿De dónde eres?	*Where are you from?*
¿Cuál prefieres?	*Which do you prefer?*
¿Es muy difícil?	*Is it very difficult?*

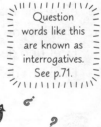

Questions

Now you know how to form questions, you need to get practising them in conversations. If you're asking loads of questions, you might need to be able to say 'please', too — there's more about being polite on p.6.

Tengo una pregunta — *I have a question*

Here are some of the <u>most common ways</u> you can use the <u>question words</u> from p.4.

¿Qué fecha?	*What date?*
¿Qué día?	*What day?*
¿Cuándo es tu cumpleaños?	*When is your birthday?*
¿Cuántos años tienes?	*How old are you?*
¿A qué hora...?	*At what time...?*
¿Qué hora es?	*What time is it?*
¿Por cuánto tiempo?	*For how long?*
¿Cuánto cuesta(n)?	*How much does it / do they cost?*
¿Cuánto vale(n)?	*How much does it / do they cost?*
¿Cuánto es?	*How much is it?*
¿De qué color (es)?	*What colour (is it)?*

Question

¿Cuánto cuesta ir al cine?
How much does it cost to go to the cinema?

Simple Answer

Cuesta siete euros.
It costs seven euros.

Extended Answer

Cuesta siete euros, cincuenta céntimos. Es muy caro.
It costs seven euros, fifty cents. It's very expensive.

 SPEAKING

To learn Spanish or not to learn Spanish, that is the question...

Have a look at the role play that Carla did with her teacher.

Teacher:	¿A qué hora vas al gimnasio, Carla?	Grade 8-9
Carla:	Voy al gimnasio a las cuatro de la tarde.	
Teacher:	¿Cuánto cuesta ir al gimnasio?	
Carla:	Cuesta tres euros cada vez.	
Teacher:	¿Vas al gimnasio todos los días?	
Carla:	No, solo los fines de semana, pero los jueves, juego al **baloncesto**[1] porque me gusta mucho. ¿Te gusta el baloncesto?	
Teacher:	Ah, **vale**[2], muy bien. Sí, me gusta el baloncesto.	
Carla:	Y tú, ¿cuándo practicas **deporte**[3]?	
Teacher:	Juego al fútbol los sábados.	

[1]basketball
[2]OK
[3]sport

Tick list:
- ✓ tenses: present
- ✓ opinion phrase
- ✓ correct time phrases e.g. los jueves
- ✓ correctly formed question

To improve:
+ add a few more complex structures, e.g. cada tres días

Use the instructions on the role play card to prepare your own role play. Address your friend as 'tú' and speak for at least two minutes. [10 marks]

'!' means you'll need to answer a question you haven't prepared. You can have a good guess at what you might be asked though — here, the question is likely to still be on the topic of tennis as the questions before the '!' are about tennis too.

Estás hablando con tu amigo/a español/a. Habláis sobre el deporte.
- *el tenis — la hora*
- *el tenis — la frecuencia*
- *!*
- *? deporte preferido*
- *? la natación — el precio*

When you see '?', you need to ask your teacher a question.

Being Polite

Being polite is an important part of the speaking test — so mind your manners with these tips.

Los saludos — *Greetings*

If you're writing these greetings as exclamations, you need an upside down exclamation mark at the start and a normal one at the end, for example: ¡Hola!

hola	*hello*
buenos días	*good day / good morning*
buenas tardes	*good afternoon / good evening*
buenas noches	*good night*
hasta luego	*see you later*
hasta el lunes	*see you on Monday*
hasta mañana	*see you tomorrow*
hasta pronto	*see you soon*
adiós	*goodbye*

¿Qué tal?	*How are you? (informal)*
¿Cómo estás?	*How are you? (informal)*
¿Cómo está?	*How are you? (formal)*

muy bien	*very well*	great — fenomenal
bien	*well*	so-so — así así
no muy bien	*not very well*	terrible — fatal

Por favor y gracias — *Please and thank you*

You don't want to sound rude in the exam, so learn these charming little words and phrases.

por favor	*please*	Eres muy amable.	*That's very kind of you. (informal)*
gracias	*thank you*	Es muy amable.	*That's very kind of you. (formal)*
muchas gracias	*thank you very much*	De nada.	*You're welcome.*
Lo siento.	*I'm sorry.*	vale	*OK*
Lo siento mucho.	*I'm really sorry.*	¡Claro!	*Of course!*

Le presento a... — *May I introduce... ?*

If you're male, you say 'encantado', and if you're female, it's 'encantada'.

Use 'Esta es...' for introducing someone female.

Le presento a...	*May I introduce... ?*	Encantado/a.	*Pleased to meet you.*
Este es...	*This is...*	Mucho gusto.	*Pleased to meet you.*

Here's how a conversation might go if you wanted to introduce someone:

Señora Valls:	Hola Ana, ¿qué tal?	*Hello Ana, how are you?*
Ana:	Muy bien. ¿Cómo está?	*Very well. How are you?*
Señora Valls:	Así así.	*So-so.*
Ana:	Le presento a Arturo.	*May I introduce Arturo?*
Señora Valls:	Encantada.	*Pleased to meet you.*

Ana uses the formal way to ask how Señora Valls is because Señora Valls is older than her. See p.7 for more information.

If you're talking to someone you call 'tú', you say 'Te presento a...' — it's informal.

Al teléfono — *On the phone*

You'll need a few extra phrases for being polite on the phone. Try these ones for size.

¿Dígame? / ¿Diga?	*Hello?*	Le paso.	*I'll put you through.*
Llámeme.	*Call me.*	Vuelvo enseguida.	*I'll be right back.*
No cuelgue.	*Stay on the line.*	el número equivocado	*wrong number*

Being Polite

And the politeness doesn't end there — here are some more ways to charm the examiner...

Quisiera — *I would like*

1) Don't just say 'I want' — make sure you <u>ask politely</u> for what you would like:

> Quisiera un café.   *I would like a coffee.*

2) And this is how to say that you <u>would like to do</u> something:

> Quisiera hablar.   *I would like to talk.*
> ¿Puedo sentarme? *May I sit down?* ←

'Poder' is a radical-changing verb. See p.77.

> *go to the toilet* — ir al baño
> *have a drink* — beber algo

Tú y usted — *Informal and Formal 'you'*

> ### Grammar — 'tú' and 'usted'
>
> In Spanish, there are <u>four</u> different ways of saying '<u>you</u>'.
>
> **Informal 'you':**
>
> ① 'Tú' — for <u>one person</u> who's your <u>friend</u>, a <u>family member</u> or of a <u>similar age</u>.
>
> ② 'Vosotros/as' — for a group of <u>two or more people</u> that you <u>know</u>. Only use '<u>vosotras</u>' if all the people in the group are <u>female</u>.
>
> **Formal 'you':**
>
> ③ 'Usted' — for <u>one person</u> that is <u>older than you</u> or someone you <u>don't know</u>.
>
> ④ 'Ustedes' — for a group of <u>two or more people</u> that you <u>don't know</u>.
>
> 'Usted' and 'ustedes' <u>don't use the same 'you' part of the verb</u> as 'tú' and 'vosotros'.
>
> - For '<u>usted</u>', use the '<u>he/she/it</u>' part of the verb (see p.76-86).
> - For '<u>ustedes</u>', use the '<u>they</u>' part of the verb.

One does not appreciate being called 'tú'.

'Tú', 'vosotros/as', 'usted' and 'ustedes' are all pronouns — see p.69.

So, here are the <u>four</u> different ways of asking where someone is from:

Tú	Vosotros/as	Usted	Ustedes
¿De dónde eres?	¿De dónde sois?	¿De dónde es?	¿De dónde son?

 WRITING

Argh, so many 'you's — I'm seeing quadruple...

Here, Andrés is introducing his two friends Mateo and Lucía to each other.

Andrés:	¡Buenos días, Mateo! ¿Qué tal?
Mateo:	Muy bien, gracias, ¿y tú?
Andrés:	Sí, bien. Esta es mi amiga, Lucía.
Mateo:	¡Hola Lucía! Encantado.
Lucía:	Mucho gusto.
Mateo:	¿Cómo estás, Lucía?
Lucía:	No muy bien, estoy enferma.
Mateo:	**Ay, ¡qué lástima!**[1]
Lucía:	Sí, es **una pena**[2].
Andrés:	**Pues**[3], hasta luego, Mateo.
Mateo:	¡Adiós!

Grade 4-5

[1]Oh, what a shame!
[2]a pity
[3]Well

Tick list:
- ✓ variety of phrases
- ✓ correct Spanish punctuation
- ✓ gender agreement

To improve:
- + develop each idea a bit further
- + different tenses (add a past or future)
- + use more varied adjectives, e.g. 'fatal' instead of 'no muy bien'

Now have a go yourself:

Escribe tu propio diálogo en el que te presentas.
*Escribe aproximadamente **40** palabras **en español**.*

[8 marks]

Opinions

Having opinions stops you sounding dull — but more importantly, it gets you marks, and lots of them.

¿Qué piensas de...? — *What do you think of...?*

¿Qué piensas?	*What do you think?*
¿Qué piensas de... ?	*What do you think of... ?*
¿Qué te parece... ?	*What do you think of... ?*
¿Cuál es tu opinión de... ?	*What's your opinion of... ?*
¿Le encuentras simpático/a?	*Do you find him/her nice?*
Pienso que / Creo que...	*I think that...*
... me parece...	*I think... is...*
Estoy de acuerdo.	*I agree.*
No estoy de acuerdo.	*I disagree.*
(No) es verdad.	*That's (not) true.*

Urgh. So many questions, so little time.

If you're talking about more than one thing, you need 'me parecen'.

¿Qué piensas de **mi novio**? — What do you think of **my boyfriend**?

Pienso que **es amable.** — I think **he's kind.**

What's your opinion of...? — ¿Cuál es tu opinión de...?

I think — Creo que

See p.14 for more useful describing words.

Las opiniones — *Opinions*

Me gusta... (sing.)	*I like... (singular)*
Me gustan... (pl.)	*I like... (plural)*
Me gusta(n) mucho...	*I really like...*
Me encanta... (sing.)	*I love... (singular)*
Me encantan... (pl.)	*I love... (plural)*
Me interesa(n)...	*I'm interested in...*
Encuentro... fantástico.	*I find... fantastic.*

No me gusta(n)...	*I don't like...*
No me gusta(n)... para nada.	*I don't like... at all.*
... no me interesa(n).	*... doesn't / don't interest me.*
Encuentro... horrible.	*I find... awful.*
Odio...	*I hate...*

Grammar — 'gustar' and 'encantar'

Use '<u>me gusta</u>' and '<u>me encanta</u>' when you want to say you like or love a <u>singular</u> thing.

If you want to say you like or love a <u>plural</u> thing, <u>add</u> an '<u>n</u>' to the end.

Me gusta<u>n</u> las uvas. *I like grapes.*
Me encanta<u>n</u> las películas. *I love films.*

To say you <u>like doing an activity</u>, use an <u>infinitive</u> (see p.76) after the correct form of 'gustar' or 'encantar'.

e.g. **Me gusta** <u>bailar</u>. *I like <u>dancing</u>.*
infinitive

If you <u>don't like</u> something, always try to say what you <u>prefer</u>: Prefiero... *I prefer...*

Grammar — 'preferir' is a radical-changing verb

'<u>Preferir</u>' (*to prefer*) is a <u>radical-changing verb</u> (see p.77 for more). With 'preferir', the second '<u>e</u>' changes to '<u>ie</u>':

prefiero	*I prefer*
prefieres	*you prefer*
prefiere	*he/she/it prefers*
prefieren	*they prefer*

The stem of the 'we' and 'you inf, pl.' forms doesn't change:
'preferimos' = 'we prefer'
'preferís' = 'you (inf, pl.) prefer'

Me gusta el té, pero prefiero el café.
I like tea, but I prefer coffee.

No me gusta cantar — prefiero bailar.
I don't like singing — I prefer dancing.

Opinions

Being able to express your opinion is great — but it's even better if you can justify it. Why? Because it makes you sound great, cool, fabulous, marvellous and definitely not boring...

Porque — *Because*

To start justifying your opinion, you need 'porque' (*because*). Look out, though — 'porque' and '¿por qué?' sound very similar, but they're written differently and mean different things.

¿Por qué te gusta ir al cine?	*Why do you like going to the cinema?*
Me gusta ir al cine porque...	*I like going to the cinema because...*

(No) me gusta porque es... — *I (don't) like it because it's...*

Here's a nice long list of adjectives you can use to justify your opinions and collect some good marks too.

bueno/a	*good*	agradable	*nice, kind*	interesante	*interesting*
estupendo/a	*fantastic*	amable	*friendly*	divertido/a	*amusing, entertaining, fun*
fenomenal	*great*	fabuloso/a	*fabulous*	malo/a	*bad*
genial	*brilliant*	increíble	*incredible*	desagradable	*unpleasant*
guay	*cool*	maravilloso/a	*marvellous*	aburrido/a	*boring*
emocionante	*exciting*	precioso/a	*beautiful*	ridículo/a	*ridiculous*
perfecto/a	*perfect*	bonito/a	*pretty*	decepcionante	*disappointing*
impresionante	*impressive*	entretenido/a	*entertaining*	raro/a	*strange*

These useful little phrases could also help you out:

Me fastidia.	*It annoys me.*
Me aburre.	*It bores me.*
Me hace llorar.	*It makes me cry.*
Me hace reír.	*It makes me laugh.*

Adjectives change to agree with plural nouns too — see p.61 for more on agreement.

Grammar — nouns and adjectives agree

The ending of the adjective must agree with the noun (p.61).

'el cine' is masculine so 'bueno' must end in 'o'.

El cine es bueno.	*The cinema is good.*
La película es buena.	*The film is good.*

'la película' is feminine so the adjective ends in 'a'.

Adjectives that end with other letters like 'interesante' stay the same for both masculine and feminine nouns.

READING

I think, therefore I get good marks in Spanish...

Luis and Elena are discussing the cinema. Read what they say and answer the questions **in English**.

Luis: ¿Te gusta ir al cine, Elena?

Elena: Sí, me encanta ir al cine porque es divertido. Me gustan las películas de acción. Y tú, ¿qué piensas del cine?

Luis: No me gusta ir al cine. Prefiero ver las películas en casa. Me encantan las comedias pero odio las películas románticas porque me parecen aburridas. ¿Qué piensas, Elena?

Elena: Sí, estoy de acuerdo. A veces son ridículas.

e.g. Why does Elena like going to the cinema? **Because it's fun.**

1. Does Luis prefer going to the cinema or watching films at home? [1]
2. Does Luis like romantic films? Why / Why not? [2]
3. What does Elena think of romantic films? [1]

Putting it All Together

Now you know all the ingredients that go into giving and justifying opinions, you need to be able to put them all together. This is really useful — you'll have something to say about any of the GCSE topics.

Putting your opinions together

este equipo	this team
esta revista	this magazine
esta música	this music
este grupo	this band
esta novela	this novel
este actor	this actor
esta actriz	this actress
esta película	this film
este periódico	this newspaper
esta canción	this song
esta tienda	this shop

Grammar — 'este' and 'esta'

'Este' means 'this', but it has to agree with the noun it comes before — see p.63 for more information.

	masculine	feminine
singular	este	esta
plural	estos	estas

¿Qué te parece este grupo? — *What do you think of this band?*

Esta música es fenomenal. — *This music is great.*

¿Qué piensas de estos actores? — *What do you think of these actors?*

Question
¿Cuál es tu opinión de esta revista?
What's your opinion of this magazine?

Simple Answer
Me gusta mucho esta revista.
I really like this magazine.

Extended Answer
Me gusta mucho esta revista porque es muy interesante.
I really like this magazine because it's very interesting.

Remember to always back up your opinions

¿Qué piensas de este grupo? — *What do you think of this band?*

Me encanta este grupo porque me gusta la música rock. — *I love this band because I like rock music.*

¿Estás de acuerdo? — *Do you agree?*

No, odio la música rock — prefiero la música pop. — *No, I hate rock music — I prefer pop music.*

this team — este equipo

their music is brilliant — su música es genial

And you, what do you think? — Y tú, ¿qué piensas?

I find rock music awful — encuentro la música rock horrible

Don't keep your opinions to yourself — share 'em.

TRACK LISTENING 02

Oyes una conversación entre Antonio y Carolina. Rellena el espacio de cada frase con una palabra del recuadro. Hay más palabras que espacios.

1(i) a. A Antonio no le gusta .... [1]
b. Dice que ir de compras es .... [1]
c. Cree que los periódicos son .... [1]

(ii) a. Carolina lee cuando quiere .... [1]
b. En su opinión, la música pop es .... [1]

interesantes	ver la tele
relajarse	ir de compras
ir a la piscina	divertido
guay	escuchar música
fenomenal	aburrida

About Yourself

Being able to talk about yourself is really important — you just can't get by without it.

Preséntate — *Introduce yourself*

el nombre	*name*	el cumpleaños	*birthday*	
el apellido	*surname*	cumplir años	*to have a birthday*	
llamarse	*to be called*	la edad	*age*	
nacer	*to be born*	tener ... años	*to be ... years old*	
el nacimiento	*birth*	la nacionalidad	*nationality*	

Grammar — saying your age

In Spanish, you 'have' an age, so you need the verb 'tener' to say how old you are. 'Tener' is a radical-changing verb — see p.77.

Tengo 16 años. *I'm 16 years old.*

¡Hola! Me llamo Juan.	Hello! I'm called Juan.
Tengo quince años.	I'm 15 years old.
Mi cumpleaños es el dos de abril.	My birthday is the 2nd of April.
Nací en (el año) dos mil dos.	I was born in (the year) 2002.
Soy británico/a. Nací en Surrey.	I'm British. I was born in Surrey.
Vivo en Málaga, en el sur de España.	I live in Málaga, in the south of Spain.

My name is Juan. — Mi nombre es Juan.
I'm Juan. — Soy Juan.

Check p.3 for a reminder of how to say dates.

English — inglés / inglesa
Scottish — escocés / escocesa
Welsh — galés / galesa
Irish — irlandés / irlandesa

the north — el norte
the east — el este
the west — el oeste

See p.37 for more countries.

¿Cómo se escribe? — *How do you spell it?*

You might have to spell something out, so learn how to pronounce the letters of the Spanish alphabet.

A — ah	F — effay	K — ka	O — oh	U — ooh
B — bay	G — hay	L — elay	P — pay	V — oohbay
C — thay	H — atchay	M — emay	Q — coo	W — oohbay doblay
D — day	I — ee	N — enay	R — eray	X — ekis
E — ay	J — hota	Ñ — enyay	S — essay	Y — yay
			T — tay	Z — thayta

'h' like 'lo*ch*'   Double 'l' makes a '*y*' sound.

Some Spanish words like 'adiós' have an accent to show which vowel you need to emphasise. Remember to write the accent too.

SPEAKING

It's all about me, me, me...

Read the question and then look at how Estefanía has answered it.
Háblame un poco de ti.

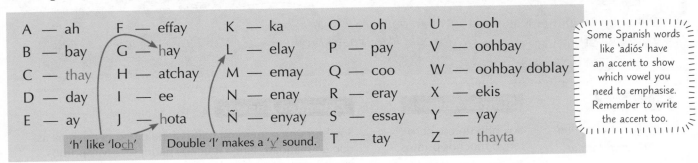

Mi **nombre de pila**[1] es Estefanía y soy de Venezuela. Vivo en el norte del país, cerca de la ciudad de Caracas. Mi cumpleaños es el veinticuatro de diciembre. Es un día muy especial, porque celebramos mi cumpleaños y la Navidad al mismo tiempo. Nací en el año dos mil.

Grade 6-7

[1]first name

Tick list:
✓ tenses: present, preterite
✓ correctly formed dates and years
✓ justifying opinions with 'porque'

To improve:
+ include an opinion about where you live and justify it

Now try to answer the same question.
Try to speak for about two minutes. [10 marks]

You could mention things like your name, where you're from and your birthday.

Your Family

Learning to talk about who's in your family is an absolute must — examiners seem to love asking about it.

Mi familia — *My family*

los parientes	*relatives*	los hijos	*children*	el abuelo	*grandfather*
el padre	*father*	el marido	*husband*	la abuela	*grandmother*
la madre	*mother*	la mujer	*wife*	los nietos	*grandchildren*
los padres	*parents*	el hermanastro	*stepbrother*	el/la tío/a	*uncle / aunt*
el padrastro	*stepfather*	la hermanastra	*stepsister*	el/la primo/a	*cousin*
la madrastra	*stepmother*	el/la gemelo/a	*twin*	el/la sobrino/a	*nephew/niece*

Háblame de tu familia — *Tell me about your family*

Grammar — saying 'my' and 'your'

Possessive adjectives like '<u>my</u>' and '<u>your</u>' have to <u>agree</u> with the noun they come before (see p.63). Remember — '<u>su(s)</u>' could also mean '<u>your</u>' if you're being <u>formal</u> — see p.63.

mi **padre**	*my **father***	tu **hermana**	*your **sister***	su **tía**	*his / her / their **aunt***
mis **padres**	*my **parents***	tus **hermanas**	*your **sisters***	sus **tías**	*his / her / their **aunts***

"And don't go asking your father either... The answer is no!"

Tengo una hermana mayor. Ella se llama Ramona.

I have an older sister. She is called Ramona.

an older brother — un hermano mayor
a younger sister — una hermana menor
a younger brother — un hermano menor

Hay cinco personas en mi familia — mi madre, mi padrastro, mis dos hermanastros menores y yo. Mis hermanastros se llaman David y Gabriel.

There are five people in my family — my mother, my stepfather, my two younger stepbrothers and me. My stepbrothers are called David and Gabriel.

only child (female) — hija única

Soy hijo único, pero me gustaría tener hermanos.

I'm an only child (male), but I would like to have brothers and sisters.

I like not having brothers and sisters — me gusta no tener hermanos

Question

¿Cómo es tu familia?

What's your family like?

Simple Answer

Soy hijo único, pero tengo muchos primos.

I'm an only child, but I have a lot of cousins.

Extended Answer

Soy hijo único, pero mi padre tiene cinco hermanos, así que en realidad, tengo muchos parientes. Mis primos viven cerca de aquí y siempre lo pasamos bien juntos.

I'm an only child, but my father has five brothers and sisters, so really, I have lots of relatives. My cousins live near here and we always have a good time together.

Examiners are fans of families — don't forget to revise them...

Translate this text **into English**. *[7 marks]*

Vivo con mi madre, mi hermana mayor y mis dos hermanas menores. Son gemelas. Para mí, es importante tener hermanos porque siempre tienes alguien con quien puedes salir. Los fines de semana, visito a mi padre, su mujer y mi hermanastro. Nació el año pasado y solo tiene seis meses. Me gustaría pasar más tiempo allí con ellos porque es muy divertido.

Describing People

You'll probably have to describe what people look like at some point in your exam — so carry on reading.

¿Cómo eres? — *What are you like?*

> You'll need the verbs 'tener' (*to have*) and 'ser' (*to be*) for this page. They're irregular, so check p.77-78 to see how they work.

alto/a	*tall*	joven	*young*	negro	*black*
bajo/a	*short*	viejo/a	*old*	castaño	*chestnut-brown*
de altura mediana	*medium height*	marrón	*brown*	largo	*long*
gordo/a	*fat*	azul	*blue*	corto	*short (hair)*
delgado/a	*slim*	verde	*green*	liso	*straight*
guapo/a	*good-looking*	rubio/a	*blonde*	rizado	*curly*

> 'Marrón' loses its accent in the plural form.

El aspecto físico — *Physical appearance*

Question	Simple Answer	Extended Answer
¿Cómo eres? *What are you like?*	Soy alta. Tengo los ojos azules y tengo el pelo castaño. *I'm tall. I have blue eyes and I have brown hair.*	Soy bastante alta. No soy ni gorda ni delgada. Tengo los ojos azules y llevo gafas. Tengo el pelo corto y rizado, y no tengo pecas. *I'm quite tall. I'm neither fat nor slim. I have blue eyes and I wear glasses. I have short, curly hair, and I don't have freckles.*

Grammar — adjectives agree

Adjectives must agree with the noun they describe.

'Los ojos' are masculine plural, so adjectives like 'blue' must be in the masculine plural form — azules.

'El pelo' is masculine singular, so adjectives like 'curly' need to be in the masculine singular form — rizado — even if you're a girl.

Soy muy bajo como mis padres. Sin embargo, mi hermano es mucho más alto que yo. Tengo el pelo rubio y tengo los ojos verdes. Tengo un piercing también.
I'm very short like my parents. However, my brother is much taller than me. I have blonde hair and I have green eyes. I have a piercing as well.

Soy bajo y delgado. Tengo el pelo negro y tengo los ojos marrones. Tengo una barba también.

I'm short and slim. I have black hair and I have brown eyes. I also have a beard.

- dark — moreno
- a moustache — un bigote
- a tattoo — un tatuaje

Es altísima. Lleva gafas y tiene los ojos azules. Tiene el pelo castaño y liso.

She's really tall. She wears glasses and she has blue eyes. She has straight, chestnut-brown hair.

- make-up — maquillaje
- curly — rizado

Es de altura mediana y bastante gordo. Es pelirrojo y tiene los ojos verdes.

He's medium height and quite fat. He's red-haired and he has green eyes.

- He's bald — Es calvo

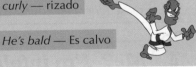

Describe people well and you'll look like a first-rate student...

TRACK LISTENING 03

María y Jaime describen estas cuatro personas. Empareja cada foto con la descripción de la persona.

 a)  b)  c)  d)

Descripción 1 = foto .....
Descripción 2 = foto .....
Descripción 3 = foto .....
Descripción 4 = foto .....

[4 marks]

Personalities

Just saying everyone's nice gets pretty dull pretty quickly, so use these adjectives to spice up your writing.

Mi personalidad — *My personality*

animado/a	*lively*	hablador/a	*chatty / talkative*	egoísta	*selfish*
alegre	*happy*	atrevido/a	*daring / cheeky*	maleducado/a	*rude*
cariñoso/a	*affectionate*	serio/a	*serious*	perezoso/a	*lazy*
comprensivo/a	*understanding*	sensible	*sensitive*	travieso/a	*naughty*
cortés	*polite*	callado/a	*quiet*	torpe	*clumsy*
gracioso/a	*funny*	valiente	*brave*	celoso/a	*jealous*

¿Cómo es...? — *What's... like?*

Mi mejor amigo es gracioso y siempre alegre. Es sensible también. Sin embargo, a veces es un poco maleducado porque dice cosas sin pensar.

My best friend is funny and always happy. He's sensitive too. However, sometimes he's a bit rude because he says things without thinking.

> My best friend (girl) — Mi mejor amiga

> he always arrives late when we go to the cinema — siempre llega tarde cuando vamos al cine

Mis padres son comprensivos y amables. Les gusta hacer buenas acciones. Mi madre es habladora pero mi padre es más callado.

My parents are understanding and kind. They like to do good deeds. My mother is chatty but my father is quieter.

> serious — serios

Mis profesoras son amables pero estrictas al mismo tiempo.

My teachers are friendly but strict at the same time.

> kind — simpáticas

Grammar — making adjectives agree

Adjectives have to agree with the nouns they describe.
See the normal rules for adjective agreement on p.61.
But some adjectives work differently, like those ending in '-or' or '-ísta/-ista'.

1) 'Hablador' — add an 'a' on the end for the feminine form and then 'es' and 'as' for the masculine and feminine plurals.

2) 'Egoísta' stays the same in the singular and becomes 'egoístas' for both the masculine and feminine plurals.

Mis amigos son habladores.
My friends are chatty.

Mi primo es un poco egoísta.
My cousin is a bit selfish.

Me? I'm intelligent, good-looking, wonderful, humble...

Óscar has written you an email telling you about himself, and his family and friends.

A **decir verdad**[1], mis padres son muy cariñosos, **aunque**[2] pueden ser estrictos, sobre todo **si no arreglo mi dormitorio**[3]. En mi opinión, mis amigos son alegres y atrevidos, pero **según**[4] mis padres, son maleducados. **Cuando era pequeño**[5], era bastante travieso, pero ahora creo que soy comprensivo y gracioso. Me gustaría ser más valiente. Y tú, ¿cómo eres?

Grade 6-7

[1]To tell the truth

[2]although

[3]if I don't tidy my bedroom

[4]according to

[5]When I was little

Tick list:
✓ tenses: present, imperfect, conditional
✓ varied adjectives that agree correctly
✓ conjunctions e.g. aunque, pero

To improve:
+ complex structures, e.g. subjunctive
+ use a wider range of tenses, e.g. future

*Contesta a Óscar y describe a tu familia. Escribe aproximadamente **80-90** palabras **en español**. [20 marks]*

Pets

Now's the perfect chance to make sure you don't make a dog's dinner out of your Spanish exams...

¿Tienes mascotas en casa? — *Do you have pets at home?*

el animal doméstico /	
la mascota	*pet*
el hámster	*hamster*
el conejo	*rabbit*
el cobayo /	
el conejillo de Indias	*guinea pig*
el pez tropical	*tropical fish*
el pez de colores	*goldfish*
la tortuga	*tortoise*

Sí, tengo un perro. Lo mejor de las mascotas es que no te juzgan.

Yes, I have a dog. The best thing about pets is that they don't judge you.

No tenemos ningún animal doméstico porque no podríamos pasar mucho tiempo con él, lo que sería cruel.

We don't have a pet because we wouldn't be able to spend much time with it, which would be cruel.

¿Cómo es tu mascota? — *What's your pet like?*

Me gustan los peces tropicales porque es relajante verlos nadar.

I like tropical fish because it's relaxing to watch them swim.

← but they don't live very long — pero no viven mucho tiempo

Tengo un gato. Es muy encantador, sobre todo cuando tiene hambre.

I have a cat. He's very charming, especially when he's hungry.

← adventurous and intelligent — atrevido e inteligente

Odio el olor de los perros.

I hate the smell of dogs.

← snakes because they scare me — las serpientes porque me dan miedo

Grammar — comparing things

Use 'más ... que' to say that something's 'more ... than' something else.
Use 'menos ... que' to say that something's 'less ... than' something else.

Pienso que los gatos son <u>más independientes que</u> los perros.
I think that cats are <u>more independent than</u> dogs.

Los hámsters parecen <u>menos atrevidos que</u> los cobayos.
Hamsters seem <u>less adventurous than</u> guinea pigs.

Jake knew their relationship was coming to an end — after all, they'd been going round in circles for years...

Question	**Simple Answer**	**Extended Answer**
¿Te gustaría tener algún animal doméstico en el futuro?	Sí, quiero un gato porque son muy inteligentes.	Cuando sea mayor, me gustaría tener un perro. Creo que los perros son más fieles que los gatos.
Would you like to have any pets in the future?	*Yes, I want a cat because they're very intelligent.*	*When I'm older, I'd like to have a dog. I think dogs are more loyal than cats.*

My pet mouse just sits on my desk and clicks at things...

*Translate this text **into English**.* [7 marks]

Tengo un pájaro como mascota. Siempre ha sido muy hablador — repite lo que dices y es muy divertido cuando dice cosas ofensivas. Lo bueno de los pájaros es que comen frutas, verduras y cereales, así que su comida no cuesta mucho. Sin embargo, el fin de semana que viene, tengo que llevarlo al veterinario y creo que costará mucho dinero.

Style and Fashion

Time to kit yourself out with some handy phrases you can use to talk about style and fashion.

La moda — *Fashion*

estar de moda	*to be in fashion*
pasado de moda	*out of fashion*
de estilo retro	*vintage style*
la marca	*brand*
de rayas / rayado	*striped*
de lunares	*spotty*
el tatuaje	*tattoo*
el maquillaje	*make-up*
el/la famoso/a	*celebrity*

Finally Elena had found a way of taking her tree-hugging passion to the next level...

Grammar — it suits me

To say that something <u>suits you</u>, use the verb '<u>quedar</u>', followed by '<u>bien</u>'. To say something <u>doesn't suit you</u>, use '<u>quedar</u>' followed by '<u>mal</u>'. '<u>Quedar</u>' works like '<u>gustar</u>', so you need to add an <u>indirect object pronoun</u> too (see p.70).

Esta blusa <u>me queda bien</u>. *This blouse <u>suits me</u>.*
Estas botas <u>me quedan mal</u>. *These boots <u>don't suit me</u>.*

Question

¿Cómo te vistes normalmente?
How do you dress normally?

Simple Answer

Normalmente llevo vaqueros y una camiseta. Prefiero la ropa cómoda.
I normally wear jeans and a t-shirt. I prefer comfortable clothes.

Extended Answer

Normalmente me visto de negro. No me importa ir vestido/a a la moda. Me gustan los tatuajes, así que cuando tenga dieciocho años, me tatuaré.
I normally dress in black. I'm not bothered about dressing fashionably. I like tattoos, so when I'm 18, I'll get a tattoo.

Gasto mucho dinero en las joyas — tengo cientos de pendientes, anillos y collares.

I spend a lot of money on jewellery — I've got hundreds of earrings, rings and necklaces.

trainers, because it's important to wear certain brands — las zapatillas de deporte, porque es importante llevar ciertas marcas

No me importa estar en la onda. Prefiero vestirme de estilo retro. El fin de semana pasado compré un vestido de lunares de los años cincuenta. Creo que me queda bien.

Being fashionable doesn't matter to me. I prefer to dress in a vintage style. Last weekend I bought a spotty dress from the fifties. I think it suits me.

a velvet jacket — una chaqueta de terciopelo
a straw hat — un sombrero de paja

A mí me gusta vestirme como los famosos que admiro. Su manera de vestirse me inspira mucho.

I like to dress like the celebrities I admire. The way they dress inspires me a lot.

I don't care what celebrities wear. I think many of them are conceited. — Me da igual cómo se visten los famosos. Creo que muchos de ellos son engreídos.

 ## I'm so retro I come to work in a toga sometimes...

Read Akemi's blog post about fashion and then use the text to complete the sentences.

Después de mucha investigación, creo que en los años ochenta había un estilo muy parecido a lo que se puede ver actualmente. Sin embargo, lo que ha cambiado desde entonces es la abundancia de tiendas. En el pasado existía una verdadera falta de tiendas.

Pienso que el Internet ha transformado todo. Puedes elegir algo y si te queda mal, no pasa nada, y lo puedes devolver fácilmente. Otro cambio es que hay más oportunidades para los **diseñadores**[1] jóvenes porque pueden usar la red como una tienda sin pagar los gastos altos de una tienda verdadera.

[1]designers

1. In the 1980s...
   A. fashion was similar to now.
   B. fashion was different to now.
   C. fashion was more important. [1]

2. The Internet has...
   A. made things harder for people in the fashion industry.
   B. made people spend more.
   C. made things easier for people in the fashion industry. [1]

Relationships

Saying whether you get on with people is a good way of showing you can use some more complex verbs.

Las relaciones — *Relationships*

You need the personal 'a' with 'conocer' and 'aguantar'. Have a look at p.75 for more information.

aguantar	*to put up with*	conocer	*to know (a person)*
confiar	*to trust*	hacer amigos	*to make friends*
fastidiar	*to annoy*	la amistad	*friendship*
pelearse	*to fight*	llevarse bien / mal (con)	*to get on well / badly (with)*
enamorarse	*to fall in love*	relacionarse (con)	*to be in contact (with)*
la discusión	*argument*	el modelo de conducta	*role model*

Grammar — 'confiar'

'Confiar' is an <u>irregular verb</u>. In the <u>present tense</u>, the '<u>i</u>' has an <u>accent</u> on it in every form <u>except</u> the '<u>we</u>' and '<u>you inf., plural</u>' forms.

<u>Confío</u> en él. *<u>I trust</u> him.*

To say you trust someone, you need to use 'en'.

Grammar — reflexive verbs

'<u>Llevarse</u>', '<u>relacionarse</u>' and '<u>pelearse</u>' are <u>reflexive verbs</u>. <u>Take off</u> the '<u>se</u>' and add the correct <u>ending</u> to the <u>stem</u> like a <u>normal verb</u> (see p.76). Then choose the right <u>pronoun</u> (see p.85) and put it <u>in front</u> of the verb.

<u>Me llevo bien</u> con mi hermana.   *<u>I get on well</u> with my sister.*
¿<u>Te relacionas</u> con ella?   *<u>Are you in contact</u> with her?*
<u>Nos peleamos</u> mucho.   *<u>We fight</u> a lot.*

Mis padres tienen una buena relación pero yo no me llevo bien con ellos debido a la barrera generacional entre nosotros.

My parents get on very well, but I don't get on well with them due to the generation gap between us.

> I get on badly with them — me llevo mal con ellos

Me llevo mejor con mi hermano porque me ayuda mucho. Tiene un buen sentido del humor.

I get on better with my brother because he helps me a lot. He has a good sense of humour.

> He's a good role model. — Es un buen modelo de conducta.

Mi hermana y yo nos peleamos mucho porque me fastidia.

My sister and I fight a lot because she annoys me.

> I can't stand my sister — No aguanto a mi hermana

Conozco muy bien a mi novio y confío en él. Nos enamoramos hace dos años y no discutimos nunca.

I know my boyfriend really well and I trust him. We fell in love two years ago and we never argue.

> 'Conozco' (I know) is the <u>only irregular bit</u> of the verb '<u>conocer</u>'.

SPEAKING

Luckily, I get on really well with Spanish revision...

Read the questions and Víctor's responses below.

¿Qué hay en la foto? ¿Te llevas bien con tu familia?

En esta foto, hay dos chicos — **quizás**[1] son hermanos, pero se llevan bien porque no se pelean.

Grade 6-7

Generalmente, sí. Confío en mi madre, así que hablo con ella cuando tengo **dificultades**[2] con **amistades**[3], por ejemplo. Mi padre es muy simpático y me conoce bien. No aguanto a mi hermana porque es muy maleducada y estúpida a veces.

[1]perhaps
[2]difficulties
[3]friendships

Tick list:
✓ range of adjectives which agree
✓ complex verbs e.g. 'confiar en'
✓ extended reasons given

To improve:
+ a few more complex structures
+ try to use another tense

*Now answer these questions **in Spanish**. Try to speak for about two minutes. ¿Te llevas bien con tus padres? ¿Tienes una buena relación con tus hermanos / tus primos? ¿Confías en tus amigos? [12 marks]*

Socialising with Friends and Family

Cast your mind back into the past and remember those glorious pre-revision days when you had a social life...

¿Eres un(a) buen(a) amigo/a? — *Are you a good friend?*

pasarlo bien	*to have a good time*	el/la conocido/a	*acquaintance*	optimista	*optimistic*
de buen humor	*in a good mood*	el/la compañero/a	*friend, colleague*	mimado	*spoilt*

Question

Para ti, ¿cómo es un(a) buen(a) amigo/a?
In your opinion, what's a good friend like?

Simple Answer

Un buen amigo es generoso y te escucha.
A good friend is generous and listens to you.

Extended Answer

Para mi la cualidad más importante en un amigo es que te hace reír. Soy una persona optimista y necesito que mis amigos sean alegres también.
For me, the most important quality in a friend is that they make you laugh. I'm an optimistic person and I need my friends to be cheerful too.

En mi tiempo libre... — *In my free time...*

Cuando no estoy en el colegio, me gusta socializar con mis amigos. Para mí es importante mantener las amistades.

When I'm not in school, I like to socialise with my friends. For me it's important to keep up my friendships.

Los domingos comemos en casa de mis abuelos. A veces preferiría estar con mis amigos, pero no quiero causar problemas.

On Sundays we have lunch at my grandparents' house. Sometimes I'd prefer to be with my friends, but I don't want to cause problems.

Cuando era pequeño, me gustaba jugar con mis primos menores, pero ahora me fastidian mucho. Creo que están un poco mimados.

When I was little, I liked playing with my younger cousins, but now they annoy me a lot. I think they're a bit spoilt.

Grammar — When I was little...

Use the imperfect tense (p.80) to say what you used to do when you were little.

Cuando era pequeño/a, <u>me gustaba</u> jugar con mi hermano.

When I was little, <u>I liked</u> playing with my brother.

Remember you'll need to use 'pequeño' if you're male and 'pequeña' if you're female.

Ahh yes, the time I "lost" my brother in the pumpkin patch...

WRITING — *Friendship tip #23: <u>Never</u> forget the doughnuts.*

Guillermo ha escrito un blog sobre lo que hace con sus amigos.

Cuando tengo tiempo libre, salgo con mis amigos **en pandilla**[1]. Normalmente somos un grupo de doce o trece jóvenes. Algunos son **mis amigos verdaderos**[2] porque son alegres y comprensivos. Sin embargo, otros son simplemente conocidos. Nos gusta ir al parque o al club de jóvenes en nuestro barrio. Cuando era pequeño, mis padres no me dejaban salir mucho por la tarde, pero ahora me dan más **libertad**[3].

Grade 6-7

[1]in a gang
[2]my true friends
[3]freedom

Tick list:
- ✓ tenses: present and imperfect.
- ✓ varied sentence structures

To improve:
+ add a future tense
+ give a few more opinions

Escribe tu propio blog sobre tu familia y tus amigos. Debes incluir los puntos siguientes:
- *si te gusta pasar tiempo con tu familia*
- *lo que te gustaba hacer con tu familia en el pasado*
- *si eres un(a) buen(a) amigo/a y por qué (no)*
- *lo que vas a hacer el fin de semana que viene.*

*Escribe aproximadamente **80-90** palabras **en español**.* [20 marks]

Partnership

Thinking about getting married is just round the corner — it might come up in your Spanish GCSE, in fact.

En el futuro... — *In the future...*

estar enamorado/a de	*to be in love with*
comprometerse	*to get engaged*
el casamiento / la boda	*wedding*
el/la novio/a	*boy/girlfriend, fiancé(e)*
el esposo / el marido	*husband*
la esposa / la mujer	*wife*
ser soltero/a	*to be single*
separarse	*to separate*
divorciarse	*to get divorced*

en mi opinión	*in my opinion*
a mi modo de ver	*the way I see it*
desde mi punto de vista	*from my point of view*
debo admitir que...	*I must admit that...*

Grammar — When I'm X years old...

To say 'when I'm 30' (or to say 'when' with a future event), use the subjunctive. See p.90.

Cuando tenga 60 años... *When I'm 60 years old...*

Question	**Simple Answer**	**Extended Answer**
¿Te gustaría casarte y tener hijos en el futuro? *Would you like to get married and have children in the future?*	No sé si quiero casarme, pero me gustaría tener hijos. *I don't know if I want to get married, but I'd like to have children.*	No sé si me casaré porque no me importa mucho. Me gustaría tener hijos cuando tenga treinta años, pero no sé cuántos hijos quiero tener. *I don't know if I'll get married because it's not very important to me. I'd like to have children when I'm 30, but I don't know how many I want to have.*

¿El matrimonio es importante? — *Is marriage important?*

Quiero casarme porque estoy enamorado de mi novia, y desde mi punto de vista, las bodas son muy románticas.

I want to get married because I'm in love with my girlfriend, and from my point of view, weddings are very romantic.

> *I want to celebrate with my family* — quiero celebrar con mi familia

Debo admitir que preferiría no casarme, porque una boda es bastante cara.

I must admit that I would prefer not to get married, because a wedding is quite expensive.

> *I never want to get married* — no quiero casarme nunca
>
> *I'd prefer to buy myself a house* — preferiría comprarme una casa

A mi modo de ver, no es necesario casarse antes de tener hijos, pero me gustaría hacerlo de todos modos.

The way I see it, it's not necessary to get married before having children, but I'd like to do it anyway.

> *marriage is important because it gives you stability* — el matrimonio es importante porque te da estabilidad

---

READING

Turkey and stuffing — a marriage made in heaven...

Read this extract from 'Las inquietudes de Shanti Andía' by Pío Baroja, and answer the questions.

Dolorcitas parecía **decidirse por**[1] mí; pero, al mismo tiempo, todo el mundo decía que iba a casarse con el hijo del **marqués**[2] de Vernay, un señor de Jerez, no muy rico, pero de familia aristocrática. Le escribí a Dolorcitas y le hablé varias veces **por la reja**[3].

[1]decide on
[2]marquis
[3]through the window bars

1. *Decide whether these statements are true or false.*

  a) Nobody thought Dolorcitas was going to get married.

  b) The Marquis of Vernay's son didn't have much money.

  c) The narrator never spoke to Dolorcitas.

2. *Use the information in the text to fill in the gap.*

  The Marquis of Vernay's son came from ....

[4 marks]

Everyday Life

Doing chores might be a bit of a drag, but at least talking about them in Spanish is more fun... probably.

Un día típico — *A typical day*

despertarse	*to wake up*
levantarse	*to get up*
ducharse	*to have a shower*
lavarse la cara	*to wash your face*
vestirse	*to get dressed*
acostarse	*to go to bed*
dormirse	*to go to sleep*

Grammar — reflexive verbs

All of these verbs are reflexive — they help you say what you do to yourself. To use them, remove the reflexive pronoun, conjugate the verb as normal, and put the reflexive pronoun back in front of the verb in its correct form (see p.85).

Me despierto a las siete. *I wake up at seven o'clock.*

¿A qué hora te levantas? *What time do you get up?*

Se acuestan temprano. *They go to bed early.*

Some of these verbs are radical-changing too. See p.77.

Question	**Simple Answer**	**Extended Answer**
¿Qué haces por la mañana?	Me despierto a las siete y luego me ducho.	Me despierto a las siete, pero no me levanto hasta las siete y media. Luego me ducho y me visto rápidamente.
What do you do in the morning?	*I wake up at seven o'clock and then I have a shower.*	*I wake up at seven o'clock, but I don't get up until half past seven. Then I have a shower and get dressed quickly.*

Las tareas domésticas — *Chores*

arreglar	*to tidy*	hacer la cama	*to make the bed*	pasar la aspiradora	*to do the vacuuming*
ayudar	*to help*	pasear al perro	*to walk the dog*	hacer las compras	*to do the shopping*
limpiar	*to clean*	cortar el césped	*to mow the lawn*	sacar la basura	*to take out the rubbish*

Hago mi cama y arreglo mi dormitorio antes de salir de casa. Es importante que todos ayuden en casa.

I make my bed and I tidy my bedroom before leaving the house. It's important that everyone helps at home.

'Es importante que' needs to be followed by the subjunctive form of 'ayudar' — 'ayuden'. See p.89-90.

Después de la cena, pongo todo en el lavaplatos y paseo al perro.

After dinner, I put everything in the dishwasher and I walk the dog.

I clear the table — quito la mesa
I take out the rubbish — saco la basura

En verano, corto el césped, pero mis padres no me dejan hacer las compras porque siempre compro cosas que no les gustan.

In the summer, I mow the lawn, but my parents don't let me do the shopping because I always buy things they don't like.

lay the table because I break the glasses — poner la mesa porque rompo los vasos

Si hago de canguro, mis padres me dan dinero de bolsillo.

If I babysit, my parents give me pocket money.

I wash the dishes — friego los platos

Hopefully your Spanish is now squeaky clean...

Translate this text **into English**. *[7 marks]*

Creo que es importante ayudar en casa, pero no pienso que sea justo si yo hago mucho y mi hermano menor hace muy poco. Me encanta pasear al perro. Mi padre me da dinero si corto el césped, así que lo haré el domingo que viene. La semana pasada tuve que limpiar el cuarto de baño. ¡Qué asco!

Food and Drink

This page is guaranteed to get your taste buds tingling — and it'll come in handy for your exam, too.

Los alimentos — *Foods*

la manzana	apple	las legumbres	vegetables, pulses	la zanahoria	carrot
el melocotón	peach	las verduras	vegetables	la col	cabbage
la fresa	strawberry	las judías verdes	green beans	la patata	potato
la naranja	orange	los champiñones	mushrooms	la cebolla	onion
el plátano	banana	los guisantes	peas	la lechuga	lettuce
la pera	pear				
las uvas	grapes				
la piña	pineapple				

		el aceite	oil	el arroz	rice
		el ajo	garlic	una barra de pan	a loaf of bread
		el huevo	egg	la tostada	toast
la carne	meat	la pimienta	ground pepper		
la carne de vaca	beef	la sal	salt	el café	coffee
la carne de cordero	lamb	el azúcar	sugar	el té	tea
la carne de cerdo	pork	la nata	cream	el zumo	juice
la carne de ternera	veal	el queso	cheese	la leche	milk
el filete	steak	la mantequilla	butter	el vino	wine
el jamón	ham			la cerveza	beer
el pollo	chicken	los calamares	squid		
la salchicha	sausage	el chorizo	Spanish sausage	el caramelo	boiled sweet
el pescado	fish	el gazpacho	cold soup	la mermelada	jam
el atún	tuna	la tortilla	omelette	la galleta	biscuit
las gambas	prawns	las tapas	nibbles, bar snacks	el pastel	cake, pie
los mariscos	seafood	los churros	long doughnuts	el helado	ice cream

¿Qué te gusta comer? — *What do you like to eat?*

Grammar — meal times

These are the nouns for Spanish meals:

el desayuno	*breakfast*
el almuerzo	*lunch* — You can also say 'la comida'.
la merienda	*afternoon snack*
la cena	*dinner*

These nouns can be made into verbs:

desayunar	**to have breakfast**
almorzar	**to have lunch** — You can say 'comer' too.
merendar	**to have an afternoon snack**
cenar	**to have dinner**

Almuerzo a la una. Suelo comer un bocadillo.
I have lunch at one o'clock. I usually eat a sandwich.

'Almorzar' (to have lunch) is a radical-changing verb ('o' to 'ue'). See p.77.

Mis padres trabajan mucho, así que comemos mucha comida basura. Mi plato preferido es pollo al curry.
My parents work a lot, so we eat a lot of junk food. My favourite meal is chicken curry.

I love Chinese / Mediterranean food. — Me encanta la comida china / mediterránea.

Whenever I seafood, I eat it...

TRACK LISTENING 04

Listen to three people's opinions about food. Tick the statements that are true. [3 marks]

e.g. When he was younger, Joaquín ate lots of sweets. ✓

1 a. Joaquín likes eating junk food.

b. Alejandra doesn't think she eats enough fruit.

c. Raquel thinks it's difficult to find things she can eat in restaurants.

Shopping

Time to indulge in some retail therapy and pick some marks up along the way.

¡Vamos al centro comercial! — *Let's go to the shopping centre!*

los grandes almacenes	*department store*
el/la dependiente/a	*sales assistant*
la talla / el número	*clothes size / shoe size*
el descuento	*discount*
las rebajas	*the sales*
el recibo	*receipt*
cambiar	*to change*
pagar	*to pay*
devolver	*to return (an item)*
reembolsar	*to refund*
quejarse	*to complain*
en efectivo	*(in) cash*
la tarjeta de crédito	*credit card*

Question

¿Te gusta ir de compras?
Do you like going shopping?

Simple Answer

Sí, me gusta ir de compras, sobre todo cuando hay rebajas.
Yes, I like going shopping, especially when there are sales.

Extended Answer

Sí, me gusta ir de compras pero a veces es estresante si no tienen la talla correcta o si tienes que cambiar algo.
Yes, I like going shopping but sometimes it's stressful if they don't have the right size or if you have to change something.

¿Me puede ayudar? — *Can you help me?*

You might have to pretend you're in a <u>shop</u> in the <u>role play</u>. Make sure you know how to ask a shop assistant for different <u>items</u>.

Grammar — I would like...

To say what you'd like, you can use '<u>quisiera</u>' as well as '<u>me gustaría</u>'. '<u>Quisiera</u>' is the <u>imperfect subjunctive</u> form of the verb '<u>querer</u>'. See p.90.

   <u>**Quisiera**</u> **un descuento, por favor.**   *<u>I'd like</u> a discount, please.*

If you're telling <u>someone</u> what you'd like <u>them</u> to do, you need the <u>present subjunctive</u> form of the verb. See p.89.

   Quisiera que <u>me reembolse</u>, por favor.   *I'd like <u>you (form., sing.) to give me a refund</u>, please.*

Me encanta esta rebeca pero me queda grande. ¿Hay otra talla?

I love this cardigan, but it's too big for me. Is there another size?

Use '<u>quedar</u>' with '<u>grande</u>' or '<u>pequeño</u>' to say that something is <u>too big</u> or <u>small</u> for you.

Estoy buscando un bolso de cuero que no sea muy caro.

I'm looking for a leather bag which is not too expensive.

When you're <u>imagining something</u> that may or may not exist, you need the <u>present subjunctive</u>. '<u>Sea</u>' is the present subjunctive form of '<u>ser</u>'. See p.89.

Quisiera un collar pero no quiero gastar demasiado.

I'd like a necklace, but I don't want to spend too much.

some earrings — unos pendientes
a tie — una corbata
a dress — un vestido

Quiero quejarme porque la falda tiene un agujero. Quisiera un reembolso, por favor.

I want to complain because the skirt has a hole. I'd like a refund, please.

has a stain — tiene una mancha
is ripped — está rasgada
is broken — está rota

Hoy hay muchas rebajas. Compré este chándal a mitad de precio.

There are a lot of sales today. I bought this tracksuit half-price.

I had to queue for ages. — Tuve que hacer cola durante mucho tiempo. '<u>Tener</u>' is <u>irregular</u> in the <u>preterite tense</u>. See p.79.

The queue for the fancy hats stretched right down the road...

Shopping

Going hungry in Spain wouldn't be fun — make sure you can ask for a box of biscuits or a slice of cake.

En la tienda de comestibles — *In the grocery shop*

la cantidad	*quantity*	una ración	*a portion*
una caja	*a box*	una bolsa	*a bag*
un cartón	*a carton*	lleno/a	*full*
una lata	*a tin*	vacío/a	*empty*
un pedazo	*a piece*	pesar	*to weigh*
un trozo	*a slice, piece*	un kilo	*a kilogram*
un tarro	*a jar*	un gramo	*a gram*
un paquete	*a packet*	varios/as	*several*

> ### Grammar — agreement with weights
> When you're talking in <u>hundreds</u> in Spanish, the <u>number</u> has to <u>agree</u> with the <u>weight</u>.
>
> **Doscien<u>tos</u> gram<u>os</u> de uvas, por favor.**
> ***Two hundred grams of grapes, please.***
>
> In Spanish, when you say '<u>half a kilo</u>', you <u>don't need</u> the '<u>a</u>' like in English.
>
> **Medio kilo de fresas, por favor.**
> ***Half <u>a</u> kilo of strawberries, please.***

Quisiera un trozo de tarta, por favor. ¿Cuánto cuesta?

I would like a slice of cake, please. How much does it cost?

Deme dos kilos de naranjas, por favor.

Give me two kilos of oranges, please.

¿Puede usted pesar estas peras, por favor?

Could you weigh these pears, please?

Necesitamos unos tomates.

We need some tomatoes.

> a portion of Manchego cheese — una ración de queso manchego

> Although this sounds a bit rude, it's <u>normal</u> to use the <u>imperative</u> 'give me' in Spanish when you're at a market. See p.91 for more imperatives.

> *We need* — Nos hacen falta
> Use '<u>hace</u>' instead of '<u>hacen</u>' to say you need a <u>singular</u> item.

Hacer las compras en la red — *Shopping online*

Question

¿Te gusta hacer las compras en la red?
Do you like shopping online?

Simple Answer

Sí, me gusta hacer las compras en la red porque es fácil.
Yes, I like shopping online because it's easy.

> ### Grammar — before / after doing something
> To say '<u>before doing something</u>', use '<u>antes de</u>' and the <u>infinitive</u>. To say '<u>after doing something</u>', use '<u>después de</u>' followed by the <u>infinitive</u>.
>
> <u>**Después de hacer**</u> **las compras, tomo un café.**
> ***After doing** the shopping, I have a coffee.*

Extended Answer

Sí, me gusta hacer las compras en la red porque resulta más barato. Además, no tienes que salir de casa porque hay un servicio de reparto a domicilio.
Yes, I like shopping online because it turns out cheaper. Besides, you don't have to leave the house because there's a home delivery service.

Prefiero ir de compras en un centro comercial porque para mí, es mejor ver las cosas antes de comprarlas.
I prefer to go shopping in a shopping centre because, for me, it's better to see things before buying them.

TRACK LISTENING 05

Don't shop 'til you drop — have a rest and do some practice...

*Montse is in a grocery shop. Listen to the dialogue and answer the questions **in English**.*

e.g. What is Montse making a tortilla for?　**a birthday party**

1 a. What quantity of onions does she need?　[1]

b. Which ingredient doesn't she need to buy?　[1]

c. Why doesn't the shopkeeper have any olive oil?　[1]

d. How much does the shopping cost in total?　[1]

All that onion-chopping resulted in a lot of tor-tears...

Section 3 — Daily Life

Technology

Technology changes really quickly — make sure you keep up to speed by looking carefully at these pages.

La tecnología en la vida diaria — *Technology in everyday life*

el ordenador	*computer*
el portátil	*laptop*
el móvil	*mobile phone*
el mensaje (de texto)	*(text) message*
mandar / enviar	*to send*
recibir	*to receive*
usar / utilizar	*to use*

Grammar — I could / couldn't ...

To imagine what you 'could do' or 'couldn't do', use the <u>conditional</u> tense of '<u>poder</u>' (see p.84) followed by the <u>infinitive</u>.

Sin mi móvil, <u>no podría hablar</u> con mis amigos.
Without my mobile phone, <u>I couldn't talk</u> to my friends.

<u>No podría hacer</u> mis deberes sin un portátil.
<u>I couldn't do</u> my homework without a laptop.

Question

¿Para qué usas tu móvil?
What do you use your mobile phone for?

Simple Answer

Uso mi móvil para mandar mensajes.
I use my mobile phone to send messages.

Extended Answer

Tener un móvil es muy importante para mí. Sin mi móvil, no podría ni mandar ni recibir mensajes.
Having a mobile phone is very important for me. Without my mobile phone, I couldn't send or receive messages.

Navegando por la red — *Surfing the Internet*

la red	*the Internet*	el usuario	*user*	el videojuego	*video game*
el internauta	*Internet user*	el correo electrónico	*email*	el buscador	*search engine*
el navegador	*browser*	descargar	*to download*	la herramienta	*tool*

Me encanta descargar canciones.

I love downloading songs.

Me gustan los videojuegos porque puedes comunicarte con otros usuarios.

I like video games because you can communicate with other users.

La red es una herramienta muy útil porque puedes usar un buscador para encontrar información.

The Internet is a very useful tool because you can use a search engine to find information.

crucial for modern life — crucial para la vida moderna

Mis padres usan la red para sus cuentas bancarias porque es más fácil que ir al banco.

My parents use the web for their bank accounts because it's easier than going to the bank.

Many Internet users — Muchos internautas

Gracias a la red, es más cómodo hacer las compras. Hace unos días, compré unos regalos por Internet y ya están aquí.

Thanks to the Internet, it's more convenient to do your shopping. A few days ago, I bought some presents online and they're already here.

However, it's difficult to know if you like the product or not because you buy it without seeing it in reality. — Sin embargo, es difícil saber si te gusta el producto o no porque lo compras sin verlo en realidad.

Technology

Singing technology's praises isn't enough — you also need to be able to talk about its disadvantages.

Lo malo de la tecnología... — *The bad thing about technology...*

Grammar — the ... thing is that...

In Spanish, you can say 'the good thing' or 'the bad thing' by using 'lo' followed by 'bueno' or 'malo'.

Lo bueno / malo es que... *The good / bad thing is that...*

You can do this with any adjective:

Lo mejor / peor es que... *The best / worst thing is that...*

Lo peligroso es que... *The dangerous thing is that...*

To say 'the most... thing', just add 'más' before the adjective:

Lo más útil es que... *The most useful thing is that...*

acceder	*to access*
el archivoˢ	*file*
borrar	*to erase / delete*
el buzón	*inbox, mailbox*
adjuntar	*to attach*
el correo basura	*spam*
la contraseña	*password*
el servidor de seguridad	*firewall*
el disco duro	*hard disk/drive*

Lo peor de los móviles **es que** la gente puede grabar videos sin informarte.

*The worst thing **about mobiles** **is that people can** record videos without telling you.*

> share your photos with other people you don't know — compartir tus fotos con otra gente a la que no conoces

Es importante tener una contraseña para proteger tu identidad. Si alguien averigua tu contraseña, puede acceder a tus archivos. Por eso no se debe utilizar nunca la red sin un buen servidor de seguridad.

It's important to have a password to protect your identity. If someone finds out your password, they can access your files. Therefore you should never use the Internet without a good firewall.

> ruin your hard disk — estropear tu disco duro

Me molesta cuando recibo correo basura porque tengo que borrar todos los mensajes de mi buzón para encontrar los que me importan.

It annoys me when I receive spam because I have to delete all the messages from my inbox to find the ones that matter to me.

> sometimes you receive a virus that damages your computer — a veces recibes un virus que daña tu ordenador

Question

Dame una desventaja de la tecnología.
Give me one disadvantage of technology.

Simple Answer

Una desventaja es que no puedes escapar de la tecnología.
One disadvantage is that you can't escape from technology.

Extended Answer

Una desventaja es que siempre tienes que estar conectado. Lo más irritante es cuando mis amigos se enfadan cuando no contesto a sus mensajes enseguida.
One disadvantage is that you always have to be connected. The most irritating thing is when my friends get angry when I don't reply to their messages straightaway.

Technically speaking, this page is really, really useful...

*Traduce el texto siguiente **al español**.* [12 marks]

I couldn't live without technology because it is very useful. I like playing video games online with my brother. We speak to Internet users in other countries. Yesterday, I played with a boy in Chile, but in order to protect my identity, I never use my name. The best thing about mobile phones is that you don't have to be at home to use the Internet. In the future, I think children will have mobile phones when they are 2 or 3 years old.

Social Media

Social media — love it or hate it, it's everywhere. And what's more, it might just come up in your exams.

Las redes sociales — *Social networks*

la red social	*social network*
el sitio web	*website*
el chat	*chat room*
el blog	*blog*
la cuenta	*account*
desactivar	*to deactivate / block*
charlar	*to chat*
subir	*to upload*
colgar	*to post (online)*

Grammar — colgar (*to post*)

'Colgar' (*to post*) is a radical-changing verb (see p.77) that changes in the present tense:

Mis amigos cuelgan fotos en mi muro.
My friends post photos on my wall.

Question

¿Usas las redes sociales?
Do you use social networks?

Simple Answer

Sí, me gusta charlar con mis amigos en las redes sociales.
Yes, I like chatting with my friends on social networks.

Extended Answer

Sí, comparto fotos con mis amigos. Mis padres tienen miedo de las redes sociales porque no las entienden.
Yes, I share photos with my friends. My parents are scared of social networks because they don't understand them.

After much posing, Gertrudis was finally happy with her profile picture...

Uso los medios sociales para... — *I use social media to...*

Me encanta usar las redes sociales para hablar con mis amigos que viven lejos de mí.

I love using social networks to talk to my friends who live far away from me.

my cousins who live in Canada — mis primos que viven en Canadá

Diría que los jóvenes pasan demasiado tiempo en las redes sociales.

I would say that young people spend too much time on social networks.

should spend more time outside — deberían pasar más tiempo al aire libre

Uso las redes sociales todos los días para chatear con la gente que comparte mis intereses. Me gusta cocinar, así que cuelgo recetas y fotos de la comida en unos sitios web.

I use social networks every day to chat online to people who share my interests. I like cooking, so I post recipes and photos of food on some websites.

I watch videos to learn more about cooking — veo vídeos para aprender más sobre la cocina

Time to make friends with social media...

Lee lo que dice Belén sobre las redes sociales y decide si las frases son verdaderas (V) o falsas (F).

Uso las redes sociales después del colegio. Es relajante charlar sobre cosas estúpidas. Sin embargo, a veces, mis amigos se pelean si alguien ha colgado una foto sin permiso. No podría vivir sin las redes sociales, pero me molesta cuando salgo con mi novio y pasa todo el tiempo viendo cosas ridículas en su móvil en lugar de charlar conmigo.

e.g. Belén sólo usa las redes sociales los sábados. **F**

1. Belén charla sobre cosas no muy serias. [1]

2. Las redes sociales causan problemas entre sus amigos. [1]

3. Según ella, la vida sería mejor sin las redes sociales. [1]

4. El novio de Belén cree que la red es estúpida. [1]

The Problems with Social Media

Being able to talk about the pros and cons of social media is really important for your GCSE.

Las ventajas y desventajas — *Advantages and disadvantages*

la ventaja	*advantage*	por una parte	*on one hand*	debido a	*due to*
la desventaja	*disadvantage*	por otra parte	*on the other hand*	gracias a	*thanks to*

Me encanta que siempre haya alguien con quien puedo charlar en las redes sociales.

I love that there's always someone I can chat to on social networks.

Por una parte, es muy fácil mantenerte en contacto con los amigos, pero por otra parte, creo que es muy importante salir con los amigos y estar juntos en la vida real.

On the one hand, it's very easy to keep in contact with your friends, but on the other hand, I believe it's very important to go out with your friends and be together in real life.

Debido a las redes sociales, sé lo que está pasando en el mundo.

Due to social networks, I know what's happening in the world.

Chat rooms are useful but they can be dangerous. — Los chats son útiles, pero pueden ser peligrosos.

often, the friends you have on social media aren't real friends — muchas veces, los amigos que tienes en las redes sociales no son amigos de verdad

I waste time looking at useless things — pierdo tiempo mirando cosas inútiles. '<u>Pierdo</u>' comes from '<u>perder</u>', which is a <u>radical-changing verb</u>. See p.77.

Looking at pug videos? Me?

Question

¿Cuál es tu opinión de las redes sociales?
What's your opinion of social networks?

Simple Answer

Es divertido usar las redes sociales pero el acoso cibernético es un gran problema.
It's fun to use social networks but cyber bullying is a big problem.

Extended Answer

Una ventaja es que no te aburres nunca. Sin embargo, no me gustan los chats porque la gente te puede mentir. Pienso que voy a desactivar mi cuenta.
An advantage is that you never get bored. However, I don't like chat rooms because people can lie to you. I think I'm going to deactivate my account.

SPEAKING

Update your status to 'revising' and try these questions...

Have a look at Manuel's answer to this question.

¿Crees que los jóvenes deberían pasar menos tiempo en las redes sociales?

A mi modo de ver, las redes sociales tienen más ventajas que desventajas. Mucha gente dice que pasamos demasiado tiempo charlando con los amigos en el mundo virtual, pero yo no estoy de acuerdo. No puedo salir con mis amigos después del colegio, así que es conveniente usar las redes sociales para comunicarme con ellos. Además, las redes sociales te pueden **enseñar**[1] mucho sobre el mundo y lo que pasa en tu **barrio**[2]. Puede ser más barato navegar por Internet para aprender estas cosas que comprar un periódico.

Grade 8-9

[1]teach
[2]neighbourhood

Tick list:
✓ tenses: present
✓ comparatives
✓ connectives e.g. además
✓ opinions

To improve:
+ use more tenses, e.g. future, conditional
+ use intensifiers e.g. muy, bastante

Now answer the following questions. Try to speak for about two minutes.

- *¿Te gusta usar las redes sociales?*
- *¿Cuáles son las desventajas de las redes sociales?*
- *¿Crees que los jóvenes deberían pasar menos tiempo en las redes sociales?*   [12 marks]

Celebrations and Festivals

Spanish-speaking countries have lots of different festivals that they celebrate throughout the year.
Over the next two pages, you'll find out about some of the most famous ones — life could be worse...

¡Celebremos! — *Let's celebrate!*

la fiesta	*festival, party*	¡Feliz cumpleaños!	*Happy Birthday!*
festejar	*to celebrate*	¡Felicitaciones!	*Congratulations!*
tener suerte	*to be lucky*	Nochevieja	*New Year's Eve*
el santo	*saint's day*	el Año Nuevo	*New Year*

Grammar — Let's...

To say 'let's...', use the 'we' form of the present subjunctive (see p.89).

Hablemos de las fiestas.
Let's talk about festivals.

'La Tomatina' es una fiesta en la que los participantes se lanzan tomates los unos a los otros.

'La Tomatina' is a festival in which participants throw tomatoes at each other.

Durante la fiesta de San Fermín, muchas personas corren por las calles estrechas con los toros hasta la plaza de toros.

During the festival of San Fermín, many people run through the narrow streets with the bulls to the bullring.

El Día de los Muertos, muchas familias mexicanas celebran las vidas de los muertos con calaveras de azúcar, flores y música.

On the Day of the Dead, many Mexican families celebrate the lives of the dead with sugar skulls, flowers and music.

¡Feliz Navidad! — *Merry Christmas!*

Nochebuena	*Christmas Eve*	el Día de Reyes	*Epiphany, 6th January*	Papá Noel	*Father Christmas*
Navidad	*Christmas*	el villancico	*Christmas carol*	el turrón	*Spanish nougat*

Muchas comunidades participan en la lotería el 22 de diciembre.

Many communities participate in the lottery draw on 22nd December.

because they want to win 'El Gordo', the big prize — porque quieren ganar 'El Gordo', el gran premio

Muchos españoles celebran el Día de Reyes. Los Reyes Magos traen regalos a los niños o, si no se han comportado bien, un trozo de carbón.

Many Spaniards celebrate Epiphany. The Three Kings bring the children presents or, if they haven't behaved well, a piece of coal.

I love to sing Christmas carols — me encanta cantar villancicos
we usually eat turkey — solemos comer pavo

En Navidad, me gusta comer turrón.

At Christmas, I like to eat nougat.

READING Fest-iv-al, a reading question...

What does the text on the right tell us?
Put a cross in each of the **two** correct boxes.

A	The festival started because of an argument between a local man and a tourist.	
B	The argument was settled calmly.	
C	The streets are full of people.	
D	Only people from Buñol can attend.	
E	They grow the tomatoes in Extremadura.	

[1]Tonnes

[2 marks]

La fiesta que se llama 'La Tomatina' comenzó en 1945 a causa de una disputa entre los habitantes. La disputa se convirtió en una pelea con verduras. Hoy en día, mucha gente viaja a Buñol para participar en la fiesta. **Toneladas**[1] de tomates vuelan por el aire y las calles están llenas de gente. La fiesta tiene lugar en Valencia, pero los tomates se cultivan en Extremadura.

Celebrations and Festivals

Last year, I asked Father Christmas for a second page of festival-based fun — and he didn't disappoint.

Semana Santa — *Easter week*

The Catholic festival <u>Semana Santa</u> is the biggest religious celebration in Spanish-speaking countries. It's a really big deal, so make sure you know all about it.

la Cuaresma	*Lent*
el Viernes Santo	*Good Friday*
la Pascua	*Easter*
el Lunes de Pascua	*Easter Monday*
el día festivo	*public holiday*
la costumbre	*custom / way*
el paso	*statue paraded at Easter*

Grammar — impersonal verbs

To say that something is done <u>without</u> saying <u>who</u> does it, use '<u>se</u>' and the <u>3rd person</u> part of the verb (p.88).
Se ven las procesiones.
***The processions** <u>are watched</u>.*

A traditional Easter procession in Spain.

Durante la Cuaresma, muchos cristianos dejan de comer ciertas cosas.

During Lent, many Christians stop eating certain things.

go to church — van a la iglesia

Mi madre compra panecillos de Pascua y los cenamos el Viernes Santo.

My mother buys hot cross buns and we eat them for dinner on Good Friday.

chocolate eggs for everyone — huevos de chocolate para todo el mundo

La Pascua es un evento sombrío en España. Hay muchas procesiones por las calles y los participantes llevan ropa que esconde sus identidades.

Easter is a sombre event in Spain. There are lots of processions through the streets and the participants wear clothes that hide their identities.

carry enormous statues — llevan pasos enormes

many Spanish people eat a traditional cake — muchos españoles comen un pastel tradicional.

El Lunes de Pascua mis padres no trabajan porque es un día festivo.

On Easter Monday my parents don't work because it's a public holiday.

Otras fiestas religiosas — *Other religious festivals*

El Eid al-Fitr es una fiesta musulmana que marca el fin del mes de Ramadán.

Eid al-Fitr is a Muslim festival that marks the end of the month of Ramadan.

Muchos judíos celebran Hanukkah. Se encienden velas y se comen alimentos fritos.

Many Jews celebrate Hanukkah. Candles are lit and fried food is eaten.

SPEAKING *My hot cross bun was angry, but at least it had its raisins...*

Laura has answered the following questions.

1. **¿Qué hiciste el año pasado para festejar tu cumpleaños?**
2. **¿Cuál es tu opinión de las fiestas en los países donde se habla español?**
3. **¿Cómo celebrarás la Nochevieja?**

Tick list:
✓ tenses: preterite, present, future
✓ good use of reflexive verbs

1. El año pasado fui a patinar sobre hielo para celebrar mi cumpleaños. Me lo pasé bien pero el único problema fue que me hice daño en el hielo. *Grade 6-7*

2. Me fascinan las fiestas del mundo hispanohablante. Por ejemplo, las tradiciones y las costumbres del Día de los Muertos me interesan mucho.

3. No estoy segura, ¡pero quizás comeré uvas como se hace en España!

To improve:
+ more detailed answers
+ more adjectives

Now answer the same questions. Speak for about two minutes. [12 marks]

Books and Reading

Time to think about your favourite book, whether it's a thriller, a fantasy or your Spanish Revision Guide...

¿Lees mucho? — *Do you read a lot?*

la lectura	*reading*	la revista	*magazine*
leer	*to read*	el periódico	*newspaper*
el libro	*book*	la prensa	*the press*
la novela	*novel*	el libro electrónico	*e-book*
el tebeo	*comic strip*	el lector de libros electrónicos	*e-reader*

Greg soon realised that economic policy wasn't the most entertaining reading material on earth...

Grammar — 'leer' in the preterite tense

The verb 'leer' (*to read*) is irregular in the preterite tense (see p.79). In both of the 'you' forms and the 'we' form, there's an accent on the first 'i'. The 'he/she/it' and 'they' forms have a 'y' in them.

Leíste un buen libro ayer. *You (inf., sing.) read a good book yesterday.*
Ana leyó tres libros. *Ana read three books.*

A mí me encanta leer las novelas de suspense porque las tramas suelen ser emocionantes.
I love reading thrillers because the plots are usually exciting.

detective novels — las novelas policíacas

Desafortunadamente, no tengo mucho tiempo para leer novelas largas.
Unfortunately, I don't have much time to read long novels.

the newspaper every day — el periódico todos los días

Los libros no me interesan mucho. Prefiero ver películas porque no tengo que concentrarme tanto.
Books don't interest me much. I prefer to watch films because I don't have to concentrate as much.

to read comic strips — leer los tebeos

Question	Simple Answer	Extended Answer
¿Cuál es tu opinión de los lectores de libros electrónicos? *What's your opinion of e-readers?*	Son una buena idea porque puedes llevar varios libros contigo. *They are a good idea because you can take several books with you.*	Prefiero los libros en papel, pero debo admitir que los libros electrónicos son prácticos, sobre todo cuando vas de vacaciones. *I prefer paper books, but I must admit that e-books are practical, especially when you go on holiday.*

SPEAKING — Make sure you stay in the examiner's good books...

Have a look at this example role play. Javier is talking to a librarian.

Librarian: ¿Le gusta leer?
Javier: No leo mucho, pero me gustaría leer más.
Librarian: Hábleme de un libro que le ha gustado.
Javier: El año pasado leí una novela policíaca que se llama 'La noche oscura'. Me gustó mucho. ¿Tiene usted alguna recomendación?
Librarian: Sí, recomendaría 'El jardín misterioso'. ¿Le gustan los libros electrónicos?
Javier: Prefiero los libros electrónicos porque son más ligeros que los libros de papel. ¿Usted tiene un lector de libros electrónicos?
Librarian: Sí, pero no lo utilizo mucho.

Grade 6-7

To improve:
+ Use different opinion phrases to avoid repeating 'gustar'.

Tick list:
✓ tenses: present, preterite, conditional
✓ correct use of 'usted'

Now prepare your own role play. Use 'usted' and speak for about two minutes. [10 marks]

Usted está en una biblioteca. Habla con el/la empleado/a.
- leer — frecuencia
- !
- ? género preferido
- los periódicos — opinión
- ? lector de libros electrónicos — precio

Music

Music often comes up in GCSE exams, so learn your stuff and dazzle the examiners.

La música — *Music*

la batería	*drums*
la canción	*song*
el / la cantante	*singer*
cantar	*to sing*
la letra	*song lyrics*
el grupo	*band*
el / la músico/a	*musician*
tocar	*to play (an instrument)*
la orquesta	*orchestra*
en directo	*live*

Grammar — 'tocar' + instrument

Use the verb 'tocar' to say you play an instrument.

When you're using the 'yo' form of 'tocar' in the preterite tense (see p.79), the 'c' changes to 'qu'.

Toco el violín.	*I play the violin.*
Toqué el violín ayer.	*I played the violin yesterday.*
Tocaba el violín.	*I used to play the violin.*

Use the imperfect tense (p.80) to say what you used to do.

Question

¿Tocas algún instrumento?
Do you play an instrument?

Simple Answer

Sí, toco la guitarra y el clarinete.
Yes, I play the guitar and the clarinet.

Extended Answer

Sí, toco la batería en un grupo. Cuando era pequeño, tocaba el piano. Me gustaría aprender a tocar la trompeta, pero mis padres no me dejarán hacerlo.
Yes, I play the drums in a band. When I was little, I used to play the piano. I would like to learn to play the trumpet, but my parents won't let me do it.

¿Te gusta escuchar música? — *Do you like listening to music?*

Me encanta escuchar música porque me hace sentir relajado/a. No me gusta la música pop. Diría que mi género de música preferido es el hip-hop.

I love listening to music because it makes me feel relaxed. I don't like pop music. I'd say that my favourite genre of music is hip-hop.

Puedo descargar muchos tipos de música instantáneamente, lo que me parece fenomenal.

I can download many types of music instantly, which seems great to me.

Adoro a DiskoBeetz e intento ir a todos sus conciertos. Sus videos musicales son siempre entretenidos y originales.

I adore DiskoBeetz and I try to go to all their concerts. Their music videos are always entertaining and original.

rap music — la música rap
rock music — la música rock
classical music — la música clásica
folk music — la música folklórica

take my music with me and listen to it while I'm jogging or on the train — llevar la música conmigo y escucharla cuando salgo a correr o cuando estoy en el tren

Their song lyrics are interesting. — La letra de sus canciones es interesante. I love live music. — Me encanta la música en directo.

It's time to face the music and try this exam style question...

Marisol is a Spanish singer. Listen to what she says and then answer the questions in English.

e.g. What kind of music is most important to Marisol's sister? **pop music**

1 a. Which instrument would Marisol like to learn to play? [1]

b. What two advantages of listening to music on the Internet does Marisol mention? [2]

c. Why does Marisol like going to concerts? [1]

Film and TV

Thinking about your favourite film or TV programme definitely doesn't count as work... or does it?

En el cine — *At the cinema*

la película	*film*
el actor	*actor*
la actriz	*actress*
el papel	*role*
el reparto	*cast*
la banda sonora	*soundtrack*
la entrada	*ticket*
los subtítulos	*subtitles*

Grammar — 'se trata de'

Use '<u>se trata de</u>' to say what a film is about:

Se trata de unos jóvenes muy ricos.
It's about some very rich young people.

And you can use it in the <u>imperfect</u> to say what a film <u>was</u> about:

Se trataba del amor. *It was about love.*

↖ Remember — 'de' + 'el' = 'del' (p.74).

Me encantan las películas policíacas porque son muy emocionantes.

I love detective films because they're very exciting.

science fiction — de ciencia ficción

Prefiero las películas de aventura porque me dan menos miedo que las películas de terror.

I prefer adventure films because they scare me less than horror films.

often the special effects are great — muchas veces los efectos especiales son fenomenales

No me gustan las películas de ciencia ficción porque es difícil seguir la trama.

I don't like science fiction films because it's difficult to follow the plot.

Romantic films annoy me — Las películas románticas me fastidian

you always know what's going to happen — siempre sabes lo que va a pasar

¿Qué hay en la tele? — *What's on TV?*

el programa	*programme*	el documental	*documentary*	el programa concurso	*quiz show*
la cadena	*channel*	las noticias	*the news*	los dibujos animados	*cartoons*
el anuncio	*advert*	la telenovela	*soap opera*	la comedia de situación	*sitcom*

Question	**Simple Answer**	**Extended Answer**
¿Te gusta ver la tele? *Do you like watching TV?*	Sí, me gusta ver la tele los fines de semana. *Yes, I like watching TV at the weekend.*	Sí, me encanta ver la tele. Mi cadena preferida es BBC1 porque hay pocos anuncios y mucha diversidad. *Yes, I love watching TV. My favourite channel is BBC1 because there are few adverts and a lot of diversity.*
¿Te gustan las telenovelas? *Do you like soap operas?*	Sí, a mí me gustan porque me ayudan a relajarme. *Yes, I like them because they help me relax.*	No, creo que son aburridas y ridículas. Pienso que hay mucha basura en la televisión hoy en día. *No, I think they're boring and ridiculous. I think there's a lot of rubbish on TV nowadays.*

WRITING

Don't let your Spanish GCSE become a horror film...

Traduce el texto siguiente al español. [12 marks]

I love films. In my opinion, detective films are the best. They are the most entertaining films because you have to think about the plot. Last week, I saw a really funny film. I like seeing films with my friends at the weekend. In the future, I would love to be an actress.

Make sure you're always using the right tense.

Sport

It doesn't matter if you're not the sportiest person on earth — you still need to learn the vocab on this page so you can recognise the names of sports and say which ones you like or don't like doing.

¿Practicas algún deporte? — *Do you play any sports?*

el fútbol	*football*	el baloncesto	*basketball*	la pesca	*fishing*
el rugby	*rugby*	la equitación	*horse riding*	el atletismo	*athletics*
el tenis	*tennis*	la natación	*swimming*	el alpinismo	*mountaineering*
el hockey	*hockey*	la vela	*sailing*	el patinaje	*skating*
el bádminton	*badminton*	el piragüismo	*canoeing*	los deportes extremos	*extreme sports*

Question

¿Te gusta practicar deporte?
Do you like doing sport?

Simple Answer

Me gusta montar en bici porque es divertido.
I like riding my bike because it's fun.

Extended Answer

Me gusta montar en bici después del colegio porque es divertido estar con mis amigos al aire libre.
I like riding my bike after school because it's fun to be with my friends in the fresh air.

montar a caballo	*to ride a horse*
montar en bici	*to ride a bike*
ser aficionado/a a...	*to be fond / a fan of...*

Grammar — 'jugar' + 'a' + sport

Use 'jugar a' to say what sports you play. In Spanish, you can't say 'Juego a el fútbol'. So if the sport is a masculine noun (like 'el fútbol'), the 'a' and the article 'el' combine to form 'al' (see p.74).

Juego al hockey. *I play hockey.*
Juegas al tenis. *You play tennis.*

'Jugar' is a radical-changing verb — its stem changes from 'u' to 'ue' in the present tense. See p.77.

Me encanta montar a caballo varias veces por semana.
Para mí, es crucial hacer deporte.

En el futuro, me gustaría probar el tiro con arco.

I love going horse riding a few times per week. For me, it's crucial to do sport.

In the future, I would like to try archery.

going rowing on the river — practicar el remo en el río

fencing — la esgrima
table tennis — el tenis de mesa
martial arts — artes marciales
paragliding — el parapente

WRITING
Be a good sport and try out this practice writing question...

Julia has written a blog about the sporting opportunities her school provides.

Mi colegio se llama Westwater College. Quisiera compartir unos **datos**[1] con vosotros **para que sepáis**[2] por qué es un colegio excepcional. **En cuanto a**[3] la educación física, se puede elegir entre varios deportes, entre ellos el tenis, el baloncesto y el hockey. **Tenemos mucha suerte**[4] porque nuestro profesor de hockey participó en los Juegos Olímpicos. Además, tenemos una piscina enorme. Después del colegio, se puede practicar deportes extremos, **incluso**[5] el parapente.

Grade 8-9

[1] information, facts
[2] so that you know
[3] With regard to
[4] We're very lucky
[5] even

To improve:
+ use another tense
  e.g. future

Usted ha probado un deporte nuevo. Escriba un artículo sobre sus experiencias. Debe incluir los puntos siguientes:

- *el deporte que hizo*
- *sus opiniones de este deporte*
- *cómo son las instalaciones de deporte en su barrio*
- *los deportes que le gustaría hacer en el futuro.*

Justifique sus ideas y sus opiniones.
Escriba aproximadamente **130-150** palabras **en español**. *[28 marks]*

Tick list:
✓ tenses: present, preterite, present and imperfect subjunctives
✓ connectives e.g. 'además'
✓ idiomatic phrases e.g. 'tenemos mucha suerte'
✓ complex sentences including opinions

Talking About Where You Live

For your Spanish GCSE, you'll need to be able to describe where you live, even if it's not remotely exciting...

En mi barrio... — *In my neighbourhood...*

el pueblo	*town*	el mercado	*market*	Correos	*Post Office*		
el centro	*centre*	el parque	*park*	la peluquería	*hairdresser's*		
las afueras	*outskirts*	la mezquita	*mosque*	la carnicería	*butcher's*		
el edificio	*building*	la biblioteca	*library*	el estanco	*tobacconist's*		
el ayuntamiento	*town hall*	el museo	*museum*	la farmacia	*chemist's*		
el aparcamiento	*parking*	la fábrica	*factory*	el puerto	*port / harbour*		

'Correos' doesn't have an article.

Question

¿Dónde vives?
Where do you live?

Simple Answer

Vivo en un pueblo en Cumbria.
I live in a town in Cumbria.

Grammar — adding 'ito'

In Spanish, you can <u>add bits</u> onto the ends of <u>nouns</u> and <u>adjectives</u> to <u>change</u> their <u>meanings</u>. Adding '<u>ito/a/os/as</u>' makes the word <u>smaller</u> or <u>cuter</u>. Find out more on p.68.

Extended Answer

Vivo en un pueblo pequeñito en el campo. Preferiría vivir más cerca de Londres porque hay más que hacer. Aquí no hay ni una tienda de ropa, lo que me fastidia mucho.
I live in a really small town in the countryside. I'd prefer to live closer to London because there's more to do. Here there's not a single clothes shop, which annoys me a lot.

Háblame de tu pueblo — *Talk to me about your town*

En mi barrio, hay mucho que hacer. Por ejemplo, el viernes fui al teatro. Sería casi perfecto si tuviera una bolera.

In my neighbourhood, there's a lot to do. For example, on Friday I went to the theatre. It would be almost perfect if it had a bowling alley.

> if it had a pedestrian zone — si tuviera una zona peatonal
> '<u>Tuviera</u>' is the <u>imperfect subjunctive</u> of '<u>tener</u>' — see p.90.

Mi ciudad tiene varios edificios impresionantes. También hay una carnicería y una librería.

My city has various impressive buildings. There's also a butcher's and a bookshop.

> pretty — bonitos
> modern — modernos

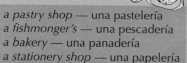

> a pastry shop — una pastelería
> a fishmonger's — una pescadería
> a bakery — una panadería
> a stationery shop — una papelería

Creo que es mejor vivir en el campo que en la ciudad. En un mundo ideal, viviría más lejos de las fábricas porque hacen mucho ruido.

I think it's better to live in the countryside than in the city. In an ideal world, I'd live further away from the factories because they make a lot of noise.

> from the shopping centre because there are so many people — del centro comercial porque hay tanta gente

Go to town on your Spanish revision...

WRITING

Tu amigo español te ha escrito para describir su pueblo.

¡Hola George! Voy a contarte todo sobre el pueblo que visitarás el mes que viene. En el centro, hay varios edificios oficiales. Además, se puede visitar un museo y hay **un montón de**[1] tiendas. Según mi padre, van a construir un polideportivo, lo que sería fenomenal, porque ahora hay poco que hacer por la tarde después del colegio y los jóvenes **acaban**[2] en la calle, molestando a la gente.

Grade 8-9

[1]loads of
[2]end up

To improve:
+ use a past tense
+ use a comparative

Escriba un informe para turistas que quieren visitar su pueblo. Debe incluir los puntos siguientes:

- *qué hay en su barrio*
- *una visita que usted ha hecho a algún sitio en su barrio*
- *unas recomendaciones para los turistas*
- *cómo usted cambiaría su barrio.*

*Justifique sus ideas y sus opiniones. Escriba aproximadamente **130-150** palabras **en español**.* [28 marks]

Tick list:
✓ tenses: present, future, conditional
✓ connectives
✓ use of 'se puede'

The Home

Home is where the heart is — and where the marks are — so you need to be able to describe it.

Mi casa — *My house*

mudarse (de casa)	*to move house*	el salón	*lounge*
la casa (adosada)	*(semi-detached) house*	la cocina	*kitchen*
el piso	*flat*	el comedor	*dining room*
la planta baja	*ground floor*	la escalera	*stairs*
la segunda planta	*second floor*	el dormitorio	*bedroom*
la habitación	*room*	los muebles	*furniture*
el cuarto de baño	*bathroom*	la estantería	*shelves*
el aseo	*toilet*	la pared	*wall*
la ducha	*shower*	el sótano	*basement*

Grammar — there is / are

To say what there is in your house, use 'hay'. It stays the same regardless of whether the thing you're talking about is singular or plural.

En mi casa, hay un salón.
In my house, there is a lounge.

Hay siete habitaciones.
There are seven rooms.

Vivo en una casa adosada.
En mi dormitorio, hay una cama, un armario, una alfombra en el suelo, una mesita, y un espejo.

I live in a semi-detached house.
In my bedroom, there's a bed, a wardrobe, a carpet on the floor, a little table, and a mirror.

In the kitchen, there's a sink, a fridge and an oven. —
En la cocina, hay un fregadero, una nevera y un horno.

Vivimos en un piso pequeño.
La habitación que más me gusta es el salón porque es cómodo.

We live in a small flat. The room I like best is the lounge because it's comfortable.

there are armchairs — hay sillones

Me gustaría mudarme a una casa más grande.

I'd like to move to a bigger house.

to have more electrical appliances — tener más electrodomésticos

---

Question

¿Cómo sería tu casa ideal?
What would your ideal house be like?

Simple Answer

Mi casa ideal tendría muchas habitaciones y un jardín grande.
My ideal house would have a lot of rooms and a big garden.

Extended Answer

La casa de mis sueños tendría un jardín enorme y una piscina de lujo. Además, sería mejor si no tuviera que compartir mi habitación.
The house of my dreams would have an enormous garden and a luxury pool. It would also be better if I didn't have to share my room.

Make yourself at home and try this question for size...

READING

Read this passage from 'Pepita Jiménez' by Juan Valera.

Tiene la casa limpísima y todo en un orden perfecto. Los muebles no son artísticos ni elegantes; pero tampoco **se advierte**[1] en ellos nada pretencioso y de mal gusto. **Para poetizar su estancia**[2], tanto en el patio como en las salas y galerías, hay multitud de flores y plantas. No tiene, en verdad, ninguna planta rara ni ninguna flor exótica; pero sus plantas y sus flores, de lo más común que hay por aquí, están cuidadas con extraordinario **mimo**[3].

[1]is observed   [2]To make her surroundings more poetic   [3]care

Which of the following statements are true?
Put a cross in the two correct boxes.

A	The furniture is elegant.	
B	The flowers are only in the kitchen.	
C	There are many flowers and plants.	
D	The flowers are mostly exotic.	
E	The flowers are well looked after.	

[2 marks]

Weather

Come rain or shine, moaning about the weather is a favourite British pastime — enjoy.

Hace buen / mal tiempo — *It's good / bad weather*

Está...	It's...		
nublado	*cloudy*	soleado	*sunny*
lloviendo	*raining*	caluroso	*hot*
nevando	*snowing*	fresco	*fresh*
granizando	*hailing*	tormentoso	*stormy*
		seco	*dry*

Hace...	It's...
sol	*sunny*
viento	*windy*
calor	*hot*
frío	*cold*

Hay...	There is / there are...
niebla	*fog*
hielo	*ice*
tormenta	*a storm*
chubascos	*showers*

el clima *climate*   el pronóstico del tiempo *weather forecast*   el cielo *sky*

Question

¿Qué tiempo hace?
What's the weather like?

Simple Answer

Hace buen tiempo hoy.
It's good weather today.

The British summer was going swimmingly...

Extended Answer

Hoy hace mucho sol en el sur, pero mañana cambiará: habrá truenos y relámpagos.
Today it's really sunny in the south, but tomorrow it will change: there will be thunder and lightning.

Grammar — weather verbs

To describe the weather in English, you often use 'to be', e.g. 'it's rainy'. You can do this in Spanish with some types of weather:

Está nublado / nevando / lloviendo / seco.
It's cloudy / snowing / raining / dry.

But sometimes, you have to use the verb 'hacer' instead:

Hace sol / viento / frío.   ***It's sunny / windy / cold.***

And sometimes, you need the verb 'haber':

Hay niebla / hielo.   ***There's fog / ice.***

It sounds complicated, but just learn which types of weather go with which verb. Remember you can put the verbs into different tenses too.

¿Qué tiempo habrá? — *What will the weather be like?*

Estará tormentoso por todas partes.	*It will be stormy everywhere.*	dry — seco
Nevará en Inglaterra este invierno.	*It will snow in England this winter.*	It will rain — Lloverá
Hará mucho calor en el sur de Europa este verano. Sería mejor si no hiciera tanto calor porque prefiero las temperaturas más bajas.	*It will be very hot in the south of Europe this summer. It would be better if it weren't so hot because I prefer lower temperatures.*	See p.3 for the seasons.

It would be perfect if it were just as hot all the time. — Sería perfecto si hiciera tanto calor todo el tiempo.

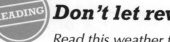

Don't let revision rain on your parade...

Read this weather forecast, and then answer the questions **in English.**

Hoy en el norte de España, habrá niebla, mientras que en el sur, estará soleado. En el oeste, cerca de Portugal, hará frío, con la posibilidad de lluvia. Para el fin de semana, hará buen tiempo por toda España, pero para la semana que viene, podemos esperar que las temperaturas bajen, con un riesgo de tormentas.

e.g. What will the weather be like in the north of Spain today? **It will be foggy.**

1. Where will people be able to enjoy the sunshine? *[1]*
2. Where will it be cold? *[1]*
3. What will it be like at the weekend? *[1]*
4. What'll happen to the temperatures next week? *[1]*
5. What else might happen next week? *[1]*

Where to Go

Grab some sun cream and pack your suitcase because you're off on holiday...

¿Adónde vas? — *Where are you going to?*

Gran Bretaña	*Great Britain*
Inglaterra	*England*
País de Gales	*Wales*
Alemania	*Germany*
los Países Bajos	*the Netherlands*
Grecia	*Greece*
Europa	*Europe*
los Estados Unidos	*United States*
Canadá	*Canada*
América Latina	*Latin America*
México	*Mexico*
Perú	*Peru*
Brasil	*Brazil*
la India	*India*

Andalucía	*Andalusia*
Cataluña	*Catalonia*
Galicia	*Galicia*
el País Vasco	*the Basque Country*

el mar Mediterráneo	*Mediterranean Sea*
los Pirineos	*the Pyrenees*

These regions are all 'comunidades autónomas'. This means that they have some power to govern themselves.

Grammar — adónde

Normally you use '<u>dónde</u>' when you want to ask a '<u>where</u>' question. But when you're asking someone 'where ... <u>to</u>' you need to use '<u>adónde</u>' instead.

¿Dónde vives?	*Where do you live?*
¿<u>A</u>dónde fuiste?	*Where did you go <u>to</u>?*

Voy de vacaciones a... — *I'm going on holiday to...*

Mi padre es medio irlandés, así que vamos de vacaciones a Irlanda a menudo.

My father is half Irish, so we often go on holiday to Ireland.

Mi padre es griego y me encanta ir a Grecia para quedarme con mi familia.

My father is Greek and I love going to Greece to stay with my family.

Luisa fue a Londres el año pasado y le gustó mucho la comida británica. Va a volver este año.

Luisa went to London last year and she really liked British food. She's going to return this year.

Question	**Simple Answer**	**Extended Answer**
¿Adónde quisiera ir de vacaciones?	Quisiera ir al norte de España.	Me gustaría ir a un centro turístico costero en el norte de España. Mi tía nació en Asturias y quisiera visitar su pueblo también.
Where would you like to go on holiday?	*I would like to go to the north of Spain.*	*I would like to go to a seaside resort in the north of Spain. My aunt was born in Asturias and I would like to visit her town too.*

This page about countries will have you going places...

Arturo has written a leaflet to help promote his region.

¡Ven a visitar la región bellísima de Galicia! Está situada en la costa del Océano Atlántico en el norte de España. Aquí se puede conocer las ciudades famosas de Vigo, Pontevedra, Ourense, o Santiago de Compostela, que es más conocida por su catedral y sus **peregrinaciones**[1] todos los años. ¡Hay tantas cosas que hacer! Por ejemplo, se puede **alquilar**[2] un barco en Pontevedra, explorar las calles antiguas de Vigo, o nadar en uno de los **ríos**[3] en Ourense!

Lee este texto, y luego contesta a las preguntas **en español**.

e.g. ¿Qué región se menciona?   Galicia.

1. ¿Dónde está Galicia? Da dos detalles. [2]

2. ¿Por qué es la ciudad de Santiago de Compostela famosa? Da dos razones. [2]

3. ¿Qué se puede hacer en Ourense? [1]

[1]pilgrimages   [2]to rent, hire   [3]rivers

Accommodation

So you've chosen which country you're going to visit — now all you need is somewhere to stay...

Busco alojamiento... — *I'm looking for accommodation...*

alojarse / quedarse	*to stay*	media pensión	*half board*
el albergue juvenil	*youth hostel*	pensión completa	*full board*
la pensión	*boarding house (B&B)*	la habitación doble	*double room*
(irse de) camping	*(to go) camping*	la habitación individual	*single room*
la tienda	*tent*	la cama de matrimonio	*double bed*
las instalaciones	*facilities*	el aire acondicionado	*air-conditioning*

Juliet was desperate for a room with a balcony...

Quisiera quedarme aquí cuatro noches.

I would like to stay here for four nights.

> a room with a balcony — una habitación con balcón

Es esencial encontrar una habitación que tenga aire acondicionado.

It's essential to find a room that has air-conditioning.

> that has a bathroom — que tenga cuarto de baño

Question	**Simple Answer**	**Extended Answer**
¿Qué tipo de habitación quisiera usted?	Quisiera una habitación con vista al mar.	Somos una familia de tres, así que quisiéramos dos habitaciones — una individual y una doble.
What type of room would you like?	*I would like a room with a sea view.*	*We are a family of three, so we would like two rooms — a single and a double.*

Me gusta alojarme en... — *I like staying in...*

Nos gusta quedarnos en un albergue juvenil para conocer a gente nueva.

We like to stay in a youth hostel in order to meet new people.

> to go on package holidays because the hotels are good quality — hacer viajes organizados porque los hoteles son de buena calidad

El año pasado nos quedamos en una pensión pequeñita cerca de la playa. ¡Me encantó!

Last year we stayed in a tiny B&B close to the beach. I loved it!

Me fui de camping con mis amigos en junio. Lo mejor es que puedes seguir tu propio horario. Por ejemplo, no tienes que desayunar entre las siete y las diez.

I went camping with my friends in June. The best thing is that you can follow your own timetable. For example, you don't have to have breakfast between seven and ten.

> it doesn't cost much money — no cuesta mucho dinero

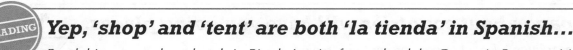

READING — *Yep, 'shop' and 'tent' are both 'la tienda' in Spanish...*

Read this extract about hotels in Rio de Janeiro from a book by Gorgonio Petano y Mazariegos.

Es una gran casa, de moderna y elegante construcción, sólida, con anchas y magníficas habitaciones: un gran jardín al pie del mar, vistas admirables, comodidades muchas. El hotel todo está **alumbrado**[1] por el gas: tiene baños, billares y grande capacidad: en el Hotel de los Extranjeros, viven la mayor parte de los individuos del Cuerpo Diplomático extranjero.

[1]lit

Fill in the gaps using the words in the box. You won't need to use all the words.

The *Hotel de los Extranjeros* is .... and .... Most people from the *Cuerpo Diplomático extranjero* .... at the hotel.

small	modern	eat dinner	live
strange	have meetings	elegant	

[3 marks]

Section 6 — Travel and Tourism

Getting Ready to Go

That holiday won't book itself. Thankfully, there's plenty of vocab here to help you get something sorted.

Reservando unas vacaciones — *Booking a holiday*

la agencia de viajes	*travel agent's*	el folleto	*leaflet*
libre / disponible	*available*	el regreso	*return*
el pasaporte	*passport*	el guía	*guide*
el permiso de conducir	*driving licence*	la guía	*guidebook*
la maleta	*suitcase*	buscar	*to look for*
el equipaje	*luggage*	informarse	*to find out*
la ficha / el formulario	*registration form*	el lugar / sitio	*place*

Grammar — I need...

When talking about the features of something you <u>require</u>, use the <u>subjunctive</u> (p.90).

Busco un hotel grande que <u>tenga</u> una piscina.

I'm looking for a big hotel that <u>has</u> a pool.

Question

¿Estás listo/a para tus vacaciones?
Are you ready for your holidays?

Simple Answer

Sí, he hecho mi maleta.
Yes, I have packed my suitcase.

Extended Answer

Sí, he hecho mi maleta, pero todavía no he comprado una guía. Necesito una guía que incluya información sobre España e Italia.
Yes, I've packed my suitcase, but I haven't bought a guidebook yet. I need a guidebook that includes information about Spain and Italy.

¿En qué puedo servirle? — *How can I help you?*

Por favor, ¿puedo reservar la mejor habitación disponible?

Please can I reserve the best room available?

a room on the ground floor — una habitación en la planta baja

Quisiera ir a un lugar donde pueda nadar.

I would like to go to a place where I can swim.

canoe — hacer piragüismo

¿Puede usted darnos unos folletos? Queremos informarnos sobre lo que hay en esta región.

Can you give us some leaflets? We want to find out about what there is in this region.

tell us if there are rooms available — decirnos si hay habitaciones libres

to know what time the museum opens — saber cuándo abre el museo

---

You shouldn't have reservations when it comes to booking...

Read the following scene from a Spanish TV show script. A travel agent is speaking to Bea.

Agente de Viajes (AV): Dígame, Señora.

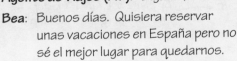
Grade 6-7

Bea: Buenos días. Quisiera reservar unas vacaciones en España pero no sé el mejor lugar para quedarnos. Quiero ir con cuatro amigos.

AV: Bueno. Pues, ¿cuándo quisiera usted venir?

Bea: Preferiríamos ir durante las vacaciones de verano, desde el 3 de agosto hasta el 11 de agosto. Nos gustan las montañas.

AV: Hace buen tiempo durante agosto. Le recomendaría ir a Gijón, en el norte de España, porque se puede visitar la costa y los Picos de Europa, que son estupendos.

Tick list:
✓ tenses: present, imperfect subjunctive, conditional
✓ superlative

To improve:
+ use subjunctive to say what you require
+ include more adjectives
+ use more conjunctions

Vas de vacaciones mañana. Escribes un email a tu amigo sobre tus planes. Debes incluir los puntos siguientes:

* adónde vas y por cuánto tiempo
* qué hiciste el verano pasado
* qué vas a hacer cuando estás de vacaciones
* si estás listo/a para tus vacaciones.

Escribe aproximadamente **80-90** palabras **en español**. [20 marks]

How to Get There

Boats, buses, cars, coaches, trains and trams — this page will get you from A to B.

Cómo llegar a tu destino — *How to get to your destination*

el avión	*aeroplane*	el pasajero / viajero	*passenger / traveller*
el aeropuerto	*airport*	hacer transbordo	*to change, transfer*
el vuelo	*flight*	el billete (de ida / de ida y vuelta)	*(single / return) ticket*
el barco	*boat*	la estación (de autobuses / de trenes)	*(bus / train) station*
conducir	*to drive*	el andén	*platform*
la autopista	*motorway*	la red de ferrocarril	*railway network*
el tranvía	*tram*	la estación de servicio	*service station*
el viaje	*journey*	la gasolina (sin plomo)	*(unleaded) petrol*

Preferiría ir a España en avión porque me encuentro mal cuando voy en barco.

I would prefer to go to Spain by plane because I feel ill when I go by boat.

by car because it's cheaper — en coche porque es más barato

Fuimos a la playa a pie ya que está cerca de nuestro hotel.

We went to the beach on foot since it's near our hotel.

by taxi because our feet were hurting — en taxi porque nos dolían los pies

Viajaremos en autobús porque siempre nos perdemos cuando vamos en coche.

We will travel by bus because we always get lost when we go by car.

the airport workers are on strike — los empleados del aeropuerto están en huelga

Is it a boat?
Is it a car? It would appear to be both...

El tren está retrasado — *The train is delayed*

¿A qué hora sale el tranvía?

At what time does the tram leave?

does the train arrive — llega el tren

Necesito reservar un coche. ¿Tengo que rellenar una ficha?

I need to reserve a car. Do I have to fill in a registration form?

have my driving licence with me — tener mi permiso de conducir conmigo

Coge el metro porque hay un atasco en la autopista.

Take the underground because there's a traffic jam on the motorway.

the train has been cancelled — el tren ha sido cancelado

No me importa viajar en autocar, pero prefiero ir en tren porque es más cómodo.

I don't mind travelling by coach, but I prefer to go by train because it's more comfortable.

by plane because it's faster — en avión porque es más rápido

 READING

This transport stuff is driving me crazy...

Translate this text **into English**. *[7 marks]*

Mi ciudad tiene varios tipos de transporte. El metro, que abrió en 1924, es muy limpio y rápido. Además, existe una red de tranvías en la que se puede visitar la mayoría de los barrios de la ciudad. Desde el aeropuerto, es posible volar a todas las ciudades importantes de Europa y no está muy lejos del centro. Pronto, van a mejorar la red de autobuses, lo que será fenomenal.

What to Do

Accommodation? Check. Transport? Check. Now the fun can begin...

Hay varias actividades... — *There are various activities...*

la excursión	*trip, excursion*	caminar	*to walk*
el mar	*the sea*	esquiar	*to ski*
bañarse	*to swim*	sacar / hacer fotos	*to take photos*
tomar el sol	*to sunbathe*	el parque de atracciones	*fairground*
broncearse	*to get a tan*	el parque temático	*theme park*
los deportes acuáticos	*water sports*	el recuerdo	*souvenir*

Question

¿Qué actividades hiciste durante tus vacaciones?
What activities did you do during your holiday?

Simple Answer

Fuimos a la playa — fue muy relajante.
We went to the beach — it was very relaxing.

Extended Answer

Pasamos mucho tiempo en la playa porque hacía sol. Me bañé y tomé el sol con mis primos.
We spent a lot of time on the beach because it was sunny. I swam and sunbathed with my cousins.

Grammar — la foto

Watch out for nouns that don't fit the masculine / feminine rule of ending with an '-o' or '-a' (p.59):

la foto	*the photo*
el agua	*the water*

('Water' is actually a feminine noun, but it takes 'el' as its article because 'la agua' is too awkward to pronounce.)

Estamos de vacaciones — *We're on holiday*

Para mí, lo importante es encontrar un parque de atracciones.

For me, the important thing is to find a fairground.

to buy souvenirs — comprar recuerdos
to go to a museum — visitar un museo

Nos gusta nada más que dar un paseo por las calles.

We like nothing more than to go for a stroll around the streets.

to try the region's typical food — probar la comida típica de la región

Cuando estoy de vacaciones, suelo sacar muchas fotos.

When I'm on holiday, I usually take lots of photos.

go on various excursions — hacer varias excursiones

SPEAKING *So much to do, so little time...*

Tom and his teacher are discussing holiday activities. Look at Tom's response to this question:
¿Te gusta ir de vacaciones a lugares donde se puede practicar deportes acuáticos?

Depende del lugar. Cuando voy a un país donde hace calor, como España, tengo ganas de hacer deportes acuáticos. Voy a ir a **Noruega**[1] el año que viene. Practicaremos el piragüismo, pero pienso que el agua estará muy fría.

Grade 6-7

[1]Norway

Tick list:
✓ tenses: present, immediate future, proper future

To improve:
+ be more descriptive
+ more tenses

Mira la foto y prepara las respuestas a los puntos siguientes:
- la descripción de la foto
- tu opinión de este tipo de vacaciones
- el lugar más interesante que has visitado
- tus vacaciones ideales
- !

[24 marks]

Eating Out

Restaurants often come up in the role play section of the exam — so get learning your stuff.

¡Vamos al restaurante! — *Let's go to the restaurant!*

pedir	*to order, ask for*	el plato (combinado)	*(set) dish*		
traer	*to bring*	la entrada	*starter*		
el camarero	*waiter*	el plato principal	*main course*		
la camarera	*waitress*	el postre	*dessert*		
la carta	*the menu*	la bebida	*drink*		
el tenedor	*fork*	la cuenta	*bill*		
el cuchillo	*knife*	la propina	*tip*		
la cuchara	*spoon*	a la plancha	*grilled*		
el vaso	*glass*	tener hambre	*to be hungry*		
incluido	*included*	tener sed	*to be thirsty*		

Grammar — ordering politely

Use 'quisiera' to order what you'd like politely. 'Quisiera' comes from the imperfect subjunctive of 'querer' (*to want*). See p.84 and 90.

Quisiera un filete.
I'd like a steak.

You can also say 'me apetece', which means 'I fancy'.

Me apetece un café.
I fancy a coffee.

Question	**Simple Answer**	**Extended Answer**
¿Qué le gustaría tomar?	Quiero la sopa, por favor.	Para empezar, quisiera la sopa, y de plato principal, el atún.
What would you like?	*I want the soup, please.*	*To begin with, I'd like the soup, and for main course, the tuna.*

Me encanta ir a restaurantes pero normalmente no puedo comer mucho. Sin embargo, siempre pido un postre porque me gustan las cosas dulces.

I love going to restaurants but normally I can't eat much. However, I always order a dessert because I like sweet things.

but sometimes it's hard to choose what you want to eat — pero a veces es difícil elegir lo que quieres comer

Comemos en restaurantes a menudo, especialmente cuando tenemos hambre y no tenemos tiempo para cocinar.

We often eat in restaurants, especially when we're hungry and we don't have time to cook.

To say you're hungry or thirsty, you need to use the verb 'tener' (*to have*). I'm thirsty — tengo sed

Una vez probé unas gambas a la plancha — estaban muy saladas.

Once I tried some grilled prawns — they were very salty.

fried — fritas

spicy — picantes

Hopefully this page has given you some food for thought...

Here's an example of a role play — Pedro is eating in a restaurant.

Pedro está hablando con un camarero en un restaurante. *Grade 8-9*

Camarero: Buenas tardes. **¿En qué puedo servirle?**[1]

Pedro: Quisiera gambas a la plancha con verduras y arroz.

Camarero: De acuerdo.

Pedro: ¿Usted tiene algo para mi amigo? No le gustan los mariscos.

Camarero: Sí, le recomendaría una pizza margarita con ensalada.

Pedro: ¡Muy bien! Y, de postre, me apetece un helado grande con dos cucharas.

Camarero: Sí, muy bien.

[1]How can I help you?

Tick list:
✓ tenses: present, imperfect subjunctive, conditional
✓ correct use of 'usted'

To improve:
+ use more varied conjunctions

Usted habla con un camarero.
- comer — qué quiere
- este restaurante — opinión
- !
- ? comida vegetariana
- ? postre — recomendación

Prepare the role play on the right. Address the waiter as 'usted', and try to speak for about two minutes. [10 marks]

Practical Stuff

Picture this: you're on a motorway in Spain and suddenly your car breaks down — very inconvenient. But help is at hand... after reading this page, you'll be able to sort it out in Spanish.

¡He perdido mi billete! — *I've lost my ticket!*

la comisaría	*police station*
el monedero	*purse*
la cartera	*wallet*
robar	*to steal / rob*
el garaje	*garage*
la gasolina	*petrol*
la avería	*breakdown*
el desvío	*diversion*
el cajero automático	*ATM / cashpoint*
confirmar	*to validate (ticket)*

Question

¿Usted ha perdido su billete?
Have you lost your ticket?

Simple Answer

Sí, lo perdí en el andén.
Yes, I lost it on the platform.

Extended Answer

No sé dónde está. Lo he buscado por todas partes pero no lo he encontrado.
I don't know where it is. I've looked for it everywhere but I haven't found it.

When you use public transport in Spain, you often have to validate your ticket in a machine before you travel.

Grammar — the perfect tense

Say what you 'have done' using the perfect tense. To make the perfect tense, you need the right form of the verb 'haber' in the present tense for the 'have' bit and the past participle of the verb for the 'done' bit.

He confirmado mi billete. — *I have validated my ticket.*
El coche ha chocado contra un árbol. — *The car has crashed into a tree.*

For more information, have a look at p.82.

Tengo un problema — *I have a problem*

El coche de mi madre tiene una avería. ¿Hay un garaje por aquí? — *My mother's car has broken down. Is there a garage around here?*

a service station — una estación de servicio

Tengo que ir a la comisaría porque alguien me ha robado la cartera. — *I have to go to the police station because someone has stolen my wallet.*

I left my keys on the bus — dejé mis llaves en el autobús

Cuando estaba de vacaciones en Francia tuve un accidente y me llevaron al hospital. — *When I was on holiday in France I had an accident and they took me to hospital.*

I broke my arm — me rompí el brazo

WRITING: Time to confirm your one-way ticket to exam success...

Gael has written about a problem that occurred last weekend.

El fin de semana pasado estaba viajando a Liverpool en tren cuando **me di cuenta de que**[1] había dejado mi cartera en el andén. Cuando vino **el revisor**[2], le expliqué que no tenía mi billete porque lo había perdido. Yo estaba muy preocupado porque pensé que él no me creería, pero **sonrió**[3] y me dio mi cartera. Alguien lo había encontrado en la estación y **se lo había entregado**[4] al revisor. ¡Qué suerte!

Grade 8-9

[1] I noticed that
[2] the ticket inspector
[3] he smiled
[4] he/she had handed it in

Tick list:
✓ tenses: preterite, imperfect, pluperfect, conditional
✓ good subject-specific vocab
✓ good use of pronouns

To improve:
+ use more varied conjunctions e.g. ya que, por eso

Escriba usted un artículo sobre los problemas que tuvo cuando estaba de vacaciones el año pasado:

Debe incluir los puntos siguientes:
- dónde estaba usted y con quién
- qué le pasó
- cómo usted solucionó el problema
- sus planes de vacaciones para el año que viene.

Escriba aproximadamente **130-150** palabras **en español**. [28 marks]

Giving and Asking for Directions

If you're feeling a bit lost, this is the page for you — you'll be on the straight and narrow in no time.

¿Dónde está? — *Where is it?*

cruzar	*to cross*
tomar	*to take (a road)*
seguir	*to continue*
a la izquierda	*on the left*
a la derecha	*on the right*
al lado de	*next to*
detrás de	*behind*
delante de	*in front of*
entre	*between*
enfrente de	*opposite*
en la esquina	*on the corner*
al final de	*at the end of*

≡ For more prepositions, see p.74. ≡

Question

¿Dónde está la peluquería?
Where's the hairdresser's?

Simple Answer

La peluquería está al final de la calle mayor.
The hairdresser's is at the end of the main street.

Extended Answer

La peluquería está justo al lado de la piscina, enfrente del cine. Es muy fácil encontrarla.
The hairdresser's is right next to the swimming pool, opposite the cinema. It's very easy to find it.

Wilbur was feeling really very lost...

Grammar — 'estar' for locations

In Spanish, there are two verbs for 'to be' — 'ser' and 'estar'. To describe where things are, you need to use 'estar' — see p.78. You can also use 'estar situado' to say where something is situated.

La estación está enfrente de Correos, en el norte de la ciudad.	*The station is opposite the post office, in the north of the city.*	See p.11 for the other compass points.
El banco está situado detrás de la iglesia.	*The bank is situated behind the church.*	*is on the right of —* está a la derecha de
Los servicios están en la esquina.	*The toilets are on the corner.*	*on the left —* a la izquierda

¿Cómo se llega a...? — *How do you get to...?*

Siga todo recto y el museo está entre la catedral y la biblioteca.

Continue straight on and the museum is between the cathedral and the library.

behind — detrás de

El parque está detrás del colegio. Tome esa calle y verá un semáforo. Luego gire a la izquierda.

The park is behind the school. Take that road and you'll see some traffic lights. Then turn left.

the police station — la comisaría

Grammar — giving instructions

To give instructions, use the imperative. See how to form it on p.91.
You probably won't know the person who's asked for directions, so you should use the 'usted' form.

Siga todo recto y cruce la calle.
Continue straight on and cross the street.

Tome la segunda calle a la derecha.
Take the second street on the right.

Stay on the right track with your Spanish revision...

TRACK LISTENING 07

Escucha a Iker describir su barrio. Rellena el espacio de cada frase con una palabra del recuadro. Hay más palabras que espacios.

1 a. Los restaurantes están en el .... del barrio. [1]

b. Ahora hay .... supermercados que en el pasado. [1]

c. Hay un supermercado .... de la comisaría. [1]

d. Para llegar a la iglesia, hay que tomar una calle a la .... [1]

lejos	detrás	
derecha	menos	
este	más	norte
izquierda	enfrente	

School Subjects

School subjects — as if you don't get enough of that at school. However, it's important to learn them and to be able to say what you think about them.

Las asignaturas — *School subjects*

el español	*Spanish*		el dibujo	*art*
el alemán	*German*		el arte dramático	*drama*
el francés	*French*		la música	*music*
el inglés	*English*		las matemáticas	*maths*
las ciencias	*science*		la economía	*economics*
la biología	*biology*		las empresariales / el comercio	*business studies*
la química	*chemistry*		la informática	*IT*
la física	*physics*		la cocina	*food technology*
la geografía	*geography*		los trabajos manuales	*handicrafts*
la historia	*history*		la gimnasia	*gymnastics*
la religión	*RE*		la educación física	*PE*

The thought of so many different subjects gave David a real fright.

Mi asignatura preferida es... — *My favourite subject is...*

Question	Simple Answer	Extended Answer
¿Cuál es tu asignatura preferida? *What's your favourite subject?*	Mi asignatura preferida es la música. Me encanta tocar la guitarra. *My favourite subject is music. I love to play the guitar.*	El español es mi asignatura preferida ya que es muy interesante. Es útil también porque espero ir a España el verano que viene. *Spanish is my favourite subject as it's very interesting. It's useful too because I hope to go to Spain next summer.*

Me encanta la historia. Es interesante aprender sobre el pasado.

I love history. It's interesting to learn about the past.

I hate — Odio

boring — aburrido

Nos gustan mucho las matemáticas. Es fascinante trabajar con números.

We really like maths. It's fascinating to work with numbers.

useful — útil

Miguel odia la química porque es tan difícil.

Miguel hates chemistry because it's so difficult.

José finds art awful — José encuentra el dibujo horrible

WRITING *I'm subjected to school every day...*

Gabriela has written about her school subjects in a chat room.

Tick list
✓ range of vocabulary
✓ adjectives agree

To improve...
+ use different tenses
+ extend opinions

Generalmente, me gustan mis asignaturas. Me encantan las lenguas porque son divertidas, así que **opté por estudiar**[1] el francés y el inglés este **curso**[2]. Sin embargo, lo malo es que son difíciles. Por otro lado, me fastidia la profesora de ciencias porque es demasiado estricta. Pero a decir verdad, mi asignatura preferida es la educación física porque me gusta jugar al baloncesto.

Grade 6–7

Escriba usted un artículo sobre las asignaturas. Debe incluir los puntos siguientes:

- *las asignaturas más útiles en su opinión*
- *las asignaturas que menos le gustaron el año pasado*
- *si es justo que algunas asignaturas sean obligatorias*
- *alguna asignatura que le gustaría estudiar.*

*Escriba aproximadamente **130-150** palabras **en español**.*

[28 marks]

[1] I chose to study [2] school year

School Routine

Same old routine, day in, day out. At least routines are quite easy to talk about in the exam...

Mi rutina escolar — *My school routine*

el trimestre	*(school) term*
la agenda	*diary*
el horario	*timetable*
la clase	*lesson*
el recreo	*break*

Grammar — telling the time

If you're saying what time something is at, remember to put '<u>a</u>' first.
La hora de comer es <u>a la una</u>. *Lunchtime is <u>at one o'clock</u>*.
For more about time, see p.2.

Mi colegio empieza a las nueve, y a las nueve y cinco, el profesor pasa la lista.

My school starts at nine o'clock, and at five past nine, the teacher calls the register.

at twenty to nine — a las nueve menos veinte

we go to the assembly room — vamos al salón de actos

Tengo cinco clases por día, y cada clase dura cuarenta minutos. El día escolar termina a las tres y media.

I have five lessons a day, and each lesson lasts forty minutes. The school day finishes at half past three.

I return home at quarter past three. — Vuelvo a casa a las tres y cuarto.

¿Qué haces durante el recreo? — *What do you do during break?*

Durante el recreo, juego al fútbol con mis amigos, y a la hora de comer, vamos a la cantina para almorzar.

During break, I play football with my friends, and at lunchtime, we go to the canteen to eat lunch.

I chat — charlo

we sit outside and eat lunch — nos sentamos afuera y almorzamos

Prefiero pasar el recreo en la biblioteca porque mis amigos van al club de tenis, que a mí no me gusta.

I prefer to spend my break in the library because my friends go to tennis club, which I don't like.

go to gymnastics club — van al club de gimnasia

En mi mochila, pongo... — *In my rucksack, I put...*

el bolígrafo	*pen*	la regla	*ruler*	el cuaderno	*exercise book*
el lápiz	*pencil*	las tijeras	*scissors*	el libro	*book*
el rotulador	*felt tip*	la goma	*rubber*	los auriculares	*earphones*

Eduardo was ready for whatever maths could throw at him.

En mi mochila, hay un estuche.

In my rucksack, there's a pencil case.

Se me ha olvidado mi lápiz.
¿Me puedes prestar un boli por favor?

I have forgotten my pencil.
Can you lend me a pen please?

In Spanish, '<u>bolígrafo</u>' (*pen*) is often shortened to '<u>boli</u>'.

Una clase — *let that be a lesson to you...*

TRACK LISTENING 08

Listen to Juan and Marta. Choose the correct answer to complete each statement.

1 a. On Mondays, English is... **A.** before break **B.** before Maths **C.** after business studies [1]

   b. Marta thinks Tuesdays are... **A.** better than Mondays **B.** the best days **C.** the worst days [1]

   c. Juan likes Wednesdays because he can be... **A.** active **B.** theatrical **C.** creative [1]

Section 7 — Current and Future Study and Employment

School Life

Now's your chance to talk about what your school's like and what it has and hasn't got.

¿A qué tipo de colegio asistes? — *What type of school do you attend?*

el instituto	*secondary school*	mixto	*mixed*	privado	*private*
la escuela primaria	*primary school*	religioso	*religious*	público	*state*

Mi instituto es un colegio mixto. Está a unos cinco kilómetros de mi casa.

My school is a mixed school. It's about five kilometres from my house.

boarding school — un internado

about 400 — unos cuatrocientos
950 — novecientos cincuenta

Hay quinientos alumnos en mi instituto y llevamos uniforme.

There are 500 students at my school and we wear a uniform.

we don't have to wear a uniform — no tenemos que llevar uniforme

Soy alumno/a aquí desde hace tres años. Me gusta este colegio y me llevo bien con los profesores.

I've been a student here for 3 years. I like this school and I get on well with the teachers.

the teachers are very nice — los profesores son muy simpáticos

¿Cómo es tu instituto? — *What's your school like?*

Grammar — el aula

'Aula' is <u>feminine</u>, but it uses '<u>el</u>' when it's <u>singular</u>. Any <u>adjectives</u> must be in the <u>feminine</u> form.
El aula es <u>estupenda</u>.
*<u>The</u> **classroom is <u>fantastic</u>.***

el aula (f)	*classroom*	el taller	*workshop*
la pizarra interactiva	*smart board*	el campo de deportes	*sports field*
el proyector	*projector*	el gimnasio	*gymnasium*
la sala de profesores	*staffroom*	los vestuarios	*changing rooms*

Mi colegio tiene un campo de deportes grande donde podemos jugar al hockey.

My school has a big sports field where we can play hockey.

a small gym where we can keep fit — un gimnasio pequeño donde podemos mantenernos en forma

En general, mi instituto es muy moderno. Encuentro las aulas maravillosas porque tienen pizarras interactivas.

In general, my school is very modern. I find the classrooms marvellous because they have smart boards.

quite old — bastante antiguo

horrible because the heating doesn't work well — horribles porque la calefacción no funciona bien

My school just had lots of fish...

Read what Sofía has written about her school below. Then in the table, indicate the three sentences that are true by putting a cross in the three correct boxes. [3 marks]

¡Hola! Soy Sofía. Te escribo para hablarte de mi colegio. Está situado en Madrid a unos siete kilómetros de mi casa y hay ochocientos alumnos. Normalmente, mi padre me lleva en coche al colegio. Tengo suerte porque puedo coger el metro también — es muy eficaz si hay atascos en las carreteras. El día empieza a las ocho menos diez. Las clases duran unos cuarenta minutos y tengo un recreo de quince minutos. El descanso para comer empieza a la una y media y dura una hora y media. Generalmente **las instalaciones**[1] en mi colegio son modernas, pero lo malo es el gimnasio. Es muy sucio. ¡Qué horror! ¿Cómo es tu colegio? ¡Adiós!

A	Sofía usually takes the underground to school.	
B	Sofía is positive about the underground.	
C	Sofía is negative about the underground.	
D	The facilities are old.	
E	The facilities are modern.	
F	Sofía dislikes the gym.	

[1] the facilities

School Pressures

A chance to vent your frustrations now — should be refreshing after all this stressful revision...

Las reglas — *The rules*

(no) hay que...	*you (don't) have to...*
(no) tienes que...	*you (don't) have to...*
(no) se debe...	*you must (not)...*
(no) es obligatorio...	*it's (not) compulsory...*
(no) deberías...	*you shouldn't...*

No deberías **comer chicle ni beber bebidas gaseosas.** *You shouldn't eat chewing gum nor drink fizzy drinks.*

Hay que **levantar la mano antes de hablar.** *You have to raise your hand before speaking.*

La presión escolar — *Pressure at school*

la presión	*pressure*	el éxito	*success*	suspender	*to fail*	el apoyo	*support*
estresante	*stressful*	aprobar	*to pass*	repasar	*to revise*	apoyar	*to support*

La vida escolar es estresante. Hay mucha presión y tengo muchos deberes. Afortunadamente, los profesores apoyan a los alumnos estresados.

School life is stressful. There's a lot of pressure and I have a lot of homework. Luckily, the teachers support stressed students.

Si no saco sobresalientes, no podré ir a la universidad.

If I don't get outstanding marks, I won't be able to go to university.

I'm afraid of failing my exams — tengo miedo de suspender mis exámenes

get good marks — saco buenas notas

pass this exam — apruebo este examen

El acoso (escolar) — *(School) bullying*

El acoso es un problema muy grave en mi colegio.

Bullying is a serious problem in my school.

Bullying doesn't happen much — La intimidación no ocurre mucho

El mal comportamiento arruina las clases.

Bad behaviour ruins lessons.

is a distraction — es una distracción

SPEAKING — It's compulsory to answer these questions carefully...

Have a look at this photo question. Use the example to give you some inspiration.

¿Hay mucha violencia en los institutos hoy en día?

En mi instituto, la violencia no es un problema. Si la conducta de un alumno es peligrosa, el director **castigará**[1] a ese alumno. Pero a mi modo de ver, muchos institutos tienen problemas con peleas y **falta de respeto**[2]. Sería difícil estudiar en esos colegios.

Grade 6-7

[1]will punish [2]lack of respect

Tick list:
✓ tenses: present, future, conditional
✓ varied vocab

To improve:
+ more opinion phrases with explanations
+ use past tenses, e.g. preterite and imperfect

Mira la foto y prepara las respuestas a los puntos siguientes:

• *la descripción de la foto*
• *la vida escolar en tu escuela primaria*
• *la violencia en los institutos*
• *una regla que cambiarías*
• !

[24 marks]

School Events

Every year, schools up and down the country hold exciting events, like trips and... err... parents' evenings.

¿Qué pasa en tu colegio? — *What's happening at your school?*

participar en	to participate in	la vuelta al colegio	first day back at school
la excursión (del colegio)	(school) trip	el autobús escolar	school bus
el intercambio	exchange	el grupo escolar	school group
(al) extranjero	abroad	la reunión de padres	parents' evening

Question

¿Qué pasa en tu colegio esta semana?
What's happening at your school this week?

Simple Answer

Esta semana hay una excursión del colegio al campo.
This week there's a school trip to the countryside.

Extended Answer

Esta semana hay reunión de padres. Mis padres hablarán con mis profesores sobre mi rendimiento escolar.
This week it's parents' evening. My parents will talk to my teachers about my academic achievement.

Grammar — saying what's happening

In Spanish, you can use the normal present tense to say things like 'I am doing' as well as 'I do'.

You only have to use the present continuous form (see p.86) when you really want to emphasise that something's happening right now.

Participo en un intercambio.
I'm participating in an exchange (soon).

Estoy participando en un intercambio.
I'm participating in an exchange (right now).

El año pasado hice un intercambio al extranjero. Me quedé con Miguel durante una semana y ahora somos amigos por correspondencia.

Last year I did an exchange trip abroad. I stayed with Miguel for a week and now we're penfriends.

I participated in — participé en

Pronto haremos una excursión a un museo. Ya que somos un grupo escolar, nos darán una visita guiada.

Soon we will go on a trip to a museum. As we're a school group, they'll give us a guided tour.

a discount — un descuento

A veces hay ventas de pasteles durante el recreo. Damos todo el dinero a organizaciones caritativas.

Sometimes there are cake sales during break time. We give all the money to charities.

there is a fancy dress day — hay un día de disfraces

Todos los años el instituto realiza una entrega de premios. Los profesores dan premios a los alumnos que han sacado las mejores notas.

Every year the school holds a prize-giving ceremony. The teachers give prizes to the students who have got the best marks.

who have tried the hardest — que se han esforzado más

WRITING — *Prepare for any event-uality with this question...*

Yann ha escrito una carta sobre un evento en su colegio.

[1] will be seventy years old

El 3 de septiembre, mi instituto **cumplirá setenta años**[1] y habrá una gran fiesta para toda la comunidad. Cualquier persona que asistía al instituto podrá venir para celebrar con nosotros. Mis amigos van a hacer un pastel, y yo voy a ayudar con las visitas guiadas. Lo mejor es que han cancelado las clases ese día. ¡Qué suerte!

Grade 6-7

Tick list
✓ tenses: present, imperfect, perfect and future
✓ 'lo' + adjective
✓ good use of exclamation

To improve...
+ use more varied conjunctions
+ add more opinions

Ahora escribe una carta sobre una excursión del colegio reciente. Debes incluir los puntos siguientes:

* lo que hiciste
* lo bueno de las excursiones
* alguna desventaja de las excursiones
* una excursión del colegio que te gustaría hacer

Escribe aproximadamente **80-90** palabras **en español**. [20 marks]

Section 7 — Current and Future Study and Employment

Education Post-16

It might not be something you've thought a lot about, but your future plans could come up in the exam.
Learn this page and it might even give you some ideas...

Cuando tenga 16 años... — *When I'm 16...*

el/la aprendiz/a	*apprentice*	la academia	*academy, school post-16 (for certain careers)*
la experiencia laboral	*work experience*		
la práctica	*work placement*	las perspectivas	*employment*
hacer el bachillerato	*to do A-levels*	laborales	*prospects*

Apparently, this wasn't what Mrs Adams meant when she told me to look for work experience...

Quiero seguir mis estudios y hacer el bachillerato porque espero estudiar Derecho en la universidad.

I want to continue my studies and do my A-levels because I hope to study law at university.

Para mejorar nuestras perspectivas laborales, el profesor recomienda que busquemos experiencia laboral.

In order to improve our employment prospects, the teacher recommends that we look for work experience.

to do a work placement — hacer una práctica

to become a plumber's apprentice — hacerme aprendiz/a de fontanero
to get a degree — obtener una licenciatura

You often need to use the subjunctive when someone wants someone else to do something. See p.90.

Después del bachillerato... — *After A-levels...*

el año libre / sabático	*gap year*	la carrera	*career*	el título	*qualification*
la formación (profesional)	*vocational training*	calificado	*competent*	la universidad	*university*

Question
¿Qué quieres hacer después de terminar el bachillerato?
What do you want to do after you finish your A-levels?

Simple Answer
Después de terminar el bachillerato, quiero empezar a trabajar.
After finishing my A-levels, I want to start working.

Extended Answer
Voy a dedicarme a mis estudios porque quiero ser traductor/a. Si quiero ser traductor/a calificado/a, tendré que estudiar mucho.
I'm going to focus on my studies because I want to be a translator. If I want to be a competent translator, I'll have to study a lot.

Quisiera tomarme un año sabático, luego me gustaría ir a la universidad porque quiero hacer carrera en medicina.

I would like to take a gap year, then I would like to go to university because I want to have a career in medicine.

Me gustaría ser electricista, pero primero, necesito formación profesional.

I would like to be an electrician, but first, I need vocational training.

Grammar — conditional

To talk about something that could, should or would happen, use the conditional tense (p.84).

Me gustaría estudiar música.
I would like to study music.

Remember that 'quisiera' can be used to say 'I would like' too (p.84).

After school I want to have my tea and watch Hollyoaks...

Traduce el texto siguiente al español. [12 marks]

When I was young, I thought I would like to be a teacher. My parents are teachers and although they find the work interesting, my father says that it is quite stressful. Now I have decided that I'm going to go to an academy to study photography. I would love to take photos of weddings!

Career Choices and Ambitions

All this revising is hard work and now you've got another job to do — learn about careers.

Los empleos — *Jobs*

el/la empleado/a	*employee*	el/la fontanero/a	*plumber*	
el/la abogado/a	*lawyer*	el/la ingeniero/a	*engineer*	
el/la arquitecto/a	*architect*	el/la mecánico/a	*mechanic*	
el/la bombero/a	*firefighter*	el/la médico/a	*doctor*	
el/la cocinero/a	*chef*	el/la oficial de policía	*police officer*	
el/la constructor/a	*builder*	el/la periodista	*journalist*	
el/la contable	*accountant*	el/la veterinario/a	*vet*	
el/la enfermero/a	*nurse*	estar en paro	*to be unemployed*	

Grammar — I'm a...

When talking about jobs, <u>usually</u> you <u>don't</u> need the article 'un(a)' (p.60).

<u>Quiero ser</u> funcionario/a
I want to be a civil servant.

You <u>do</u> though if you use an <u>adjective</u>.

Soy <u>un(a) buen(a)</u> **técnico/a.**
I'm <u>a good</u> technician.

a tiempo completo	*full-time*	ganar	*to earn*
a tiempo parcial	*part-time*	el sueldo	*salary*

For more jobs, have a look at the vocab list starting on p.109.

Mi empleo ideal sería periodista. Trabajaría en una oficina y escribiría artículos interesantes.

My ideal job would be a journalist. I would work in an office and I would write interesting articles.

full time — a tiempo completo

Para mí, es importante tener un empleo desafiante.

For me, it's important to have a challenging job.

stimulating — estimulante
rewarding — gratificante
varied — variado

Mi madre es enfermera. Es un trabajo difícil porque tiene mucha responsabilidad, pero a ella le encanta ayudar a la gente.

My mother is a nurse. It's a difficult job because she has a lot of responsibility, but she loves helping people.

there's a lot of pressure — hay mucha presión

Tengo un empleo a tiempo parcial — *I have a part-time job*

Soy dependiente en una tienda de ropa. Lo mejor es charlar con los clientes.

I'm a shop assistant in a clothes shop. The best thing is chatting with customers.

waiter/waitress in a restaurant — camarero/a en un restaurante

that there are discounts for employees — que hay descuentos para los empleados

No tengo empleo a tiempo parcial, pero a veces cuido a mi hermana y recibo paga.

I don't have a part-time job, but sometimes I look after my sister and I receive pocket money.

Trabajo en una peluquería los sábados. Me gusta el empleo pero no gano mucho.

I work in a hairdresser's on Saturdays. I like the job, but I don't earn a lot.

I hope to find another job and earn more money — espero conseguir otro empleo y ganar más dinero

---

Before you go careering onto the next page...

... translate this text **into English**. *[7 marks]*

— Cuando yo tenía quince años, era difícil conseguir un trabajo — dijo mi madre.

— Sí, pero mucho ha cambiado en los últimos años — le respondí. — Quiero ser abogada. Ganan un buen sueldo y me gustaría ayudar a la gente. ¡El trabajo sería tan variado!

Languages for the Future

There's life beyond GCSE — your Spanish might help you make friends, or even land you a job. Bullseye.

¿Hablas otro idioma? — *Do you speak another language?*

la lengua / el idioma	*language*
conocer a alguien	*to get to know someone*
viajar por el mundo	*to travel the world*
expresarse	*to express yourself*
comunicarse	*to communicate*
traducir	*to translate*
pronunciar	*to pronounce*
el/la auxiliar de lengua	*foreign language assistant*
el laboratorio de idiomas	*language lab*

Grammar — articles + languages

When a language is the subject of the sentence, you need to use the definite article with it.

El español es fácil. *Spanish is easy.*

However, when you use a language as the object of the verbs 'saber', 'aprender' or 'hablar', you don't need to use the article.

Aprendo árabe. *I'm learning Arabic.*

Have a look at p.69-70 for a reminder about subjects and objects.

Quiero trabajar por una empresa internacional, así que los idiomas son importantes para mí.

I want to work for an international company, so languages are important to me.

En mi instituto tenemos auxiliares de lenguas. Me parece un trabajo muy divertido. Me gustaría hacer algo parecido en el futuro.

In my school we have foreign language assistants. It seems like a very fun job. I'd like to do something similar in the future.

Voy a viajar por Asia después del bachillerato, así que he aprendido algunas frases útiles para poder comprar cosas y pedir comida.

I'm going to travel around Asia after my A-Levels, so I have learnt some useful phrases so I can buy things and order food.

Aprender una lengua extranjera — *To learn a foreign language*

Question

¿Es importante aprender otro idioma?
Is it important to learn another language?

Simple Answer

Sí, porque no todo el mundo habla inglés.
Yes, because not everyone speaks English.

Extended Answer

Sí, es importante que aprendamos idiomas extranjeros porque vivimos en una sociedad multicultural.
Yes, it's important that we learn foreign languages because we live in a multicultural society.

En mi opinión es una pérdida de tiempo aprender una lengua extranjera. Si necesitas comunicarte en el extranjero, hay aplicaciones que te pueden ayudar.
In my opinion it's a waste of time to learn a foreign language. If you need to communicate abroad, there are apps that can help you.

Whilst in Athens, this guy offered to paint me a vase. At least, I think that's what he said — it was all Greek to me...

READING — I'm always Russian around learning other languages...

*Read what David says about the languages he speaks and then answer the questions **in English**.*

Me llamo David y soy **azafato**[1]. Para nosotros es esencial saber por lo menos tres lenguas para poder comunicarnos con los clientes. Aprendí inglés y francés en el instituto, y pronto asistiré a **clases nocturnas**[2] de alemán en una escuela donde hay laboratorios de idiomas. Creo que la parte más difícil para mí será la pronunciación.

[1]flight attendant [2]evening classes

1. Give one requirement of David's job. [1]
2. What will he do in the near future? [1]
3. What will the venue be like? [1]
4. What does he think will be challenging? [1]

Applying for Jobs

Trawling through job adverts isn't exactly entertaining — but actually getting a job's a pretty good reward.

Solicitar un puesto de trabajo — *To apply for a job*

el anuncio de trabajo	*job advertisement*	las condiciones de empleo	*terms of employment*
la vacante	*vacancy*	las posibilidades de promoción	*promotion prospects*
la carta de solicitud	*application letter*	el sueldo	*salary*
la solicitud	*application form*	bien pagado	*well-paid*
adjuntar	*to attach*	por hora	*per hour*
la entrevista	*interview*	el/la jefe	*boss*

Question

¿Por qué decidió usted solicitar este puesto de trabajo?
Why did you decide to apply for this job?

Simple Answer

Cuando leí el anuncio de trabajo, me interesó mucho.
When I read the job advertisement, it really interested me.

Extended Answer

Es un trabajo bien pagado y las condiciones de empleo me parecen justas. Además, hay buenas posibilidades de promoción.
It's a well-paid job and the terms of employment seem fair to me. Moreover, there are good promotion prospects.

Mi amigo me dijo que había vacantes en su empresa, así que decidí rellenar el formulario y mandarles mi currículum.

My friend told me that there were vacancies in his company, so I decided to fill in the form and send them my CV.

to write an application letter — escribir una carta de solicitud

La semana que viene tengo una entrevista de trabajo. Tendré que prepararme bien, porque conoceré al director.

Next week I have a job interview. I'll have to prepare myself well because I'll meet the manager.

it's a very well-paid job — es un trabajo muy bien pagado

Cuando buscas un trabajo, es una buena idea pensar en las condiciones de empleo y el sueldo.

When you're looking for a job, it's a good idea to think about the terms of employment and the salary.

the skills you have — las habilidades que tienes

SPEAKING — *I applied to be an astronaut, but they said there was no space...*

Read this role play. Blanca is having an interview with Carlos, a careers adviser.

[1]computer skills

Carlos:	¿Qué tipo de trabajo le gustaría hacer?
Blanca:	No sé exactamente. Ese es el problema que tengo.
Carlos:	¿Qué habilidades tiene usted?
Blanca:	Aprendo rápidamente y me gusta trabajar con los ordenadores.
Carlos:	¿Tiene usted alguna experiencia laboral?
Blanca:	Sí, hice una práctica en una oficina hace un año.
Carlos:	¿Ha visto este anuncio? Lo acabamos de recibir. Buscan individuos que tengan buenas **habilidades informáticas**[1] y que sepan trabajar en grupo. ¿Le interesa?
Blanca:	Sí. A lo mejor les mandaré un correo. Gracias.

Grade 8-9

Tick list:
✓ good variety of tenses
✓ correct use of 'usted'

To improve:
+ try to use more subject-specific vocab

Usted está hablando con el director de su instituto.
- trabajo ideal — opinión
- experiencia laboral
- !
- ? ser profesor — opinión
- ? consejos para encontrar un trabajo

Now prepare the role-play on the right. You must address the head teacher as 'usted', and try to speak for about two minutes. [10 marks]

Environmental Problems

Time to think green and start talking about the things that affect the environment.

El medio ambiente — *The environment*

la Tierra	*Earth*	el carbón	*coal*	el hambre (f)	*famine*
el calentamiento global	*global warming*	el petróleo	*oil*	el huracán	*hurricane*
la polución	*pollution*	el gas	*gas*	la inundación	*flood*
la basura	*rubbish*	la energía	*energy*	el agua potable (f)	*drinking water*
los recursos naturales	*natural resources*	el desastre	*disaster*	una falta de	*a lack of*
la selva (tropical)	*(rain) forest*	la sequía	*drought*	preocuparse	*to worry*

Question	**Simple Answer**	**Extended Answer**
¿El medio ambiente es importante para ti? *Is the environment important to you?*	Sí, creo que es muy importante proteger el medio ambiente. *Yes, I think it's very important to protect the environment.*	Es importantísimo proteger el medio ambiente. Si no actuamos ahora, las selvas tropicales desaparecerán. *It's really important to protect the environment. If we don't act now, the rain forests will disappear.*

El cambio climático — *Climate change*

El cambio climático es un problema que me preocupa bastante. El uso de ciertos combustibles contamina el aire y causa el calentamiento global.

Climate change is a problem that worries me quite a lot. The use of certain fuels pollutes the air and causes global warming.

Debido al efecto invernadero, las temperaturas suben, lo que causa una escasez de agua en algunas regiones del mundo.

Due to the greenhouse effect, temperatures rise, which causes a shortage of water in some regions of the world.

La deforestación — *Deforestation*

Los bosques son importantes porque reducen la cantidad de dióxido de carbono en la atmósfera.

Forests are important because they reduce the amount of carbon dioxide in the atmosphere.

Hoy en día cortamos muchos árboles para producir combustibles. Esto contribuye a la destrucción de los bosques, y al cambio climático.

Nowadays we cut down lots of trees to produce fuel. This contributes to the destruction of forests, and to climate change.

La polución — *Pollution*

A veces el petróleo ensucia el mar y las playas. Luego, los peces y los pájaros sufren mucho.

Sometimes oil makes the sea and the beaches dirty. Then, the fish and birds suffer a lot.

Oil is harmful for many creatures. — El petróleo es nocivo para muchas criaturas.

Aquí, tenemos un problema con la cantidad de basura. Es muy fácil olvidarse de la basura cuando está en un vertedero y no en la calle.

Here, we have a problem with the amount of rubbish. It's very easy to forget about rubbish when it's in a tip and not in the street.

I don't understand it because it's easy to recycle things. — No lo entiendo, porque es fácil reciclar cosas.

Environmental Problems

Raise your nature-loving credentials and impress the examiners by spicing up your opinions.

Los desastres naturales — *Natural disasters*

El año pasado hubo un incendio. Fue causado parcialmente por la falta de lluvia.

Last year there was a fire. It was caused partly by the lack of rain.

A forest was destroyed. — Un bosque fue destruido.

He leído sobre un terremoto en Asia. Muchas personas fueron afectadas y varios pueblos están todavía en ruinas.

I have read about an earthquake in Asia. Many people were affected and several towns are still in ruins.

millions of homes were damaged — millones de casas fueron dañadas

El gobierno ayudará a las víctimas de la sequía.

The government will help the victims of the drought.

The public — El público

Algunos problemas graves — *Some serious problems*

Grammar — using the subjunctive

Use the subjunctive to give your opinion and say what you want to happen. Check how to form it on p.89-90.

You need it after 'no pienso que...' (*I don't think that...*).

No pienso que sea justo echar toda la culpa a las fábricas.
I don't think that it's fair to put all the blame on factories.

It can also be used to express an emotion about something.

Es terrible que haya tanta basura en la calle.
It's terrible that there is so much rubbish in the street.

And when you're saying what you want someone else to do, use 'quiero que' followed by the subjunctive.

Quiero que el gobierno haga más por la naturaleza.
I want the government to do more for nature.

Grammar — the future

To talk about what things might be like in the future, you can use the immediate future tense (ir + a + infinitive) or the proper future tense (iré — *I will go*, tendré — *I will have*, etc.) See p.83.

Es esencial que protejamos la naturaleza porque sin ella, no podremos vivir.

It's essential that we protect nature because we won't be able to live without it.

we combat the effects of climate change, because if not, we're going to suffer — combatamos los efectos del cambio climático porque si no, vamos a sufrir

Quiero que todos hagan más para reducir la cantidad de basura que producimos. Si no, los vertederos estarán llenos pronto.

I want everyone to do more to reduce the amount of rubbish that we produce. If not, the rubbish tips will be full soon.

think more about the environment and not waste so many things — piensen más en el medio ambiente y no gasten tantas cosas

Es terrible que no pensemos más en el futuro de la Tierra.

It's terrible that we don't think more about the Earth's future.

future generations — las generaciones del futuro

Learn Spanish and the world's your (polluted) oyster... nice.

Traduce el texto siguiente al español. [12 marks]

Climate change worries me a lot. Factories and cars contribute to the greenhouse effect. For me, the worst thing is that people in some poor countries suffer due to floods and droughts. It isn't fair. I think we should work together to reduce the effects of climate change, but it will be very difficult.

Caring for the Environment

So now you've battled through nature's woes, it's time to get creative and find some solutions.

¿Qué podemos hacer? — *What can we do?*

la basura	*rubbish*	renovable	*renewable*
los desechos / los residuos	*rubbish*	la energía solar	*solar power*
el reciclaje	*recycling*	el abono	*compost*
reciclar	*to recycle*	salvar el planeta	*to save the planet*

Siempre separamos nuestra basura antes de reciclarla.

We always separate our rubbish before recycling it.

Deberíamos usar menos electricidad.

We should use less electricity.

Acabo de participar en una protesta en contra del uso de los combustibles fósiles.

I have just participated in a protest against the use of fossil fuels.

Compro productos de comercio justo porque suelen ser más ecológicos.

I buy fair trade products because they're usually more environmentally friendly.

save energy — ahorrar energía

'Acabar de' + infinitive means 'to have just done something'. See p.86.

¿Cómo podemos ayudar? — *How can we help?*

Question

¿Qué haces para proteger el medio ambiente?
What do you do to protect the environment?

¿Qué más podrías hacer para salvar el planeta?
What else could you do to save the planet?

Simple Answer

Apago las luces para ahorrar energía.
I turn the lights off to save energy.

Podría ducharme en vez de bañarme.
I could have a shower instead of having a bath.

Extended Answer

Cuando voy de compras, siempre reutilizo las bolsas en vez de comprar nuevas.
When I go shopping, I always reuse the bags instead of buying new ones.

Podría generar un poco de energía solar en casa. Creo que es necesario usar más energía renovable.
I could generate a bit of solar power at home. I believe it's necessary to use more renewable energy.

SPEAKING — *I rode there and back... that's enough recycling, right?*

Look at this sample response, then it's time for a photo question. Talk for about three minutes.
¿Recicláis mucho en casa? ¿Qué haremos en el futuro para proteger el medio ambiente?

Sí, intentamos reciclar muchas cosas. Reciclamos envases de plástico, botellas y **cartón**[1]. Si no podemos reciclar algo, intentamos reutilizarlo **para que no acabe**[2] en un vertedero.

Creo que tendremos coches eléctricos. También reduciremos la cantidad de basura que producimos y reutilizaremos las cosas más antes de tirarlas.

Grade 8-9

To improve:
+ explain opinions more
+ more complex connectives e.g. sin embargo

Tick list:
✓ tenses: present, future, present subjunctive
✓ topical vocab, e.g. cartón, vertedero

Mira la foto y prepara las respuestas a los puntos siguientes:
* *la descripción de la foto*
* *lo que has hecho recientemente para salvar el planeta*
* *la importancia de reciclar*
* *si crees que usaremos más energía solar en el futuro*
* *!*   *[24 marks]*

[1]cardboard   [2]so that it doesn't end up

Problems in Society

Time for another cheerful topic to make your day happy and joyful — it's social problems.

Los problemas sociales — *Social problems*

el gobierno	*government*	la desigualdad	*inequality*
la libertad	*freedom*	la tienda benéfica	*charity shop*
el peligro	*danger*	la guerra	*war*
la pobreza	*poverty*	los "sin techo"	*homeless people*
la violencia	*violence*	el desempleo	*unemployment*
el prejuicio	*prejudice*	estar en paro	*to be unemployed*

Grammar — 'me parece'

Use '<u>me parece</u>' to say how something '<u>seems</u>' to you. You can use it to <u>vary</u> your language.

<u>Me parece</u> **inquietante que...**
*<u>It seems</u> **worrying** <u>to me</u> **that...***

<u>Me parece</u> **interesante que...**
*<u>It seems</u> **interesting** <u>to me</u> **that...***

La pobreza — *Poverty*

Question

¿Crees que hay mucha pobreza en este país?
Do you believe there is a lot of poverty in this country?

Extended Answer

Creo que hay demasiada pobreza en nuestra sociedad. Deberíamos ayudar a los más necesitados porque es fácil acabar en la pobreza si pierdes tu trabajo.
I think there's too much poverty in our society. We should help the most needy people because it's easy to end up in poverty if you lose your job.

Simple Answer

Sí, me parece que hay más pobreza que hace diez años.
It seems to me that there's more poverty than ten years ago.

Grammar — 'deber'

To say what someone should do, use '<u>deber</u>' followed by the <u>infinitive</u>.

<u>Deberíamos luchar</u> **contra la pobreza.**
*<u>We should fight</u> **against poverty.***

El desempleo — *Unemployment*

Hay mucha gente en paro en mi ciudad.

There are lots of unemployed people in my city.

Casi todos los estudiantes por aquí se preocupan por el desempleo. Si pudiera cambiar algo, crearía más trabajos.

Nearly all the students around here worry about unemployment. If I could change anything, I'd create more jobs.

Nobody has a problem finding work — Nadie tiene problemas para encontrar trabajo

'Pudiera' is a form of 'poder' in the imperfect subjunctive. You don't have to be able to use this tense — just know how to recognise it. See p.90.

Well, that was a bit bleak — and unfortunately, there's more...

TRACK LISTENING 09

*A charity is talking about homelessness in Spain. Listen, and then answer the questions **in English**.*

e.g. How many people are homeless in Spain?   **Thousands**

1 a. According to the report, what has caused people to lose their jobs?   [1]

   b. According to the report, what sort of life do homeless people have?   [1]

   c. What are homeless people often the victims of?   [1]

   d. According to the report, what do many people think of homeless people?   [1]

   e. According to the report, what should be done to change the situation?   [1]

Global Events

Covering everything from music festivals to hard-hitting campaigns, global events is a pretty wide topic. Use this page to make sure you're well prepared for anything that might come up in the exam.

Los eventos internacionales — *International events*

asistir a	*to attend*
el evento	*event*
la campaña	*campaign*
recaudar dinero	*to raise money*
a beneficio de	*in aid of*
la organización caritativa	*charitable organisation*
el festival (de música)	*(music) festival*
los Juegos Olímpicos	*Olympic Games*
el Mundial	*World Cup (football)*

Grammar — capital letters

Just as in English, there are some nouns which have capital letters in Spanish, wherever in the sentence they come, like the Olympic Games and the World Cup — 'los Juegos Olímpicos' and 'el Mundial'.

Sometimes you might see 'mundial' with a lower case 'm' — in this case, it's an adjective meaning 'worldwide' or 'global'.

Question

¿Has asistido a algún evento internacional?
Have you attended any international events?

Simple Answer

No, pero me gustaría asistir a los Juegos Olímpicos.
No, but I would like to attend the Olympic Games.

Sí, fui a un festival de música rock en Escocia.
Yes, I went to a rock music festival in Scotland.

Extended Answer

El año pasado fui a Benicàssim para un festival internacional de música. Atrae a gente de muchos países.
Last year I went to Benicàssim for an international music festival. It attracts people from all around the world.

No, pero planeamos ir al próximo Mundial. Habrá un ambiente fenomenal.
No, but we're planning to go to the next World Cup. There will be a great atmosphere.

Las campañas mundiales — *Global campaigns*

Las campañas mundiales nos enseñan sobre los problemas del mundo.

Global campaigns teach us about the world's problems.

→ the importance of working together — la importancia de trabajar juntos

Lo malo de las campañas es que cuando terminan, mucha gente se olvide de ellas rápidamente. Es difícil cambiar el mundo para siempre.

The bad thing about campaigns is that when they finish, many people forget about them quickly. It's difficult to change the world permanently.

→ people's behaviour — el comportamiento de la gente

Dedicar días especiales a las campañas mundiales es una buena manera de recaudar dinero y cambiar el mundo.

Dedicating special days to global campaigns is a good way of raising money and changing the world.

→ attracting people's attention — llamar la atención de la gente

 WRITING

What do we want? More revision! When do we want it? Now!

Traduce el texto siguiente **al español**. *[12 marks]*

This year, we have worked with a charity which helps disadvantaged children in Asia. We organised a concert and we wrote to some singers to ask them if they would support us. Three of them came and everyone had a good time. In the future, I would love to go to the World Cup. I think it would be really fun.

| **Words for People and Objects** | Nouns |

Nouns are like the building blocks of a language — it's really important to know how to use them.

Every Spanish noun is masculine or feminine

When you learn a new noun, learn its gender too.

1) Whether a word is masculine, feminine or plural affects lots of things.

2) All 'the' and 'a' words change depending on the word's gender, and so do any adjectives which describe the noun.

el árbol alto (m.) *the tall tree*
la casa alta (f.) *the tall house*

These rules help you guess what gender a word is

1) If you see a word with 'el' or 'un' before it, it's usually masculine.

2) 'La' or 'una' in front of a word means it's feminine.

3) If you don't have these clues, there are other tricks you can use to help you guess.

MASCULINE	Most nouns that end in: -o -l -n -r -s -ta -aje	AND	Male people, days, months, languages, seas, rivers, oceans and mountains.
FEMININE	Most nouns that end in: -a -ción -sión -tad -tud -dad -umbre	AND	Female people, letters of the alphabet.

4) You can't tell whether a noun ending in 'e' or 'ista' is masculine or feminine — you have to learn them.

| el coche *the car* | la gente *the people* | el turista *the tourist (male)* | la turista *the tourist (female)* |

These are some of the exceptions to the rules. You'll just need to learn these ones off by heart.

el día	*day*	la foto	*photo*
el problema	*problem*	la moto	*motorbike*
el mapa	*map*	la mano	*hand*

Making nouns plural

1) Some nouns in Spanish end in a vowel. To make them plural, just add 's' — 'una cama' (*one bed*) becomes 'dos camas' (*two beds*).

2) There are some exceptions to these rules though:

Type of noun	To make it plural...	Example
ends in a consonant except 'z'	add 'es'	una flor *one flower* → dos flores *two flowers*
ends in 'z'	drop the 'z' and add 'ces'	un lápiz *one pencil* → dos lápices *two pencils*
days ending in 's'	make the article plural but keep the noun the same	el viernes *Friday* → los viernes *Fridays*
family surnames		Los Simpson *The Simpsons*

Sometimes you need to add or remove an accent in the plural to avoid changing the pronunciation of the word. Here are a couple of common examples.

un inglés *one English person* → dos ingleses *two English people*
un joven *one young man* → dos jóvenes *two young men*

Ignore genders at your peril...

Write 'el' or 'la' for each of these words. Then write each one in the plural form with 'los' or 'las'.

1. sombrero
2. problema
3. tradición
4. viernes
5. porcentaje
6. francés
7. tensión
8. dificultad
9. ciudad
10. mapa

| Articles & Indefinite Adjectives | 'The', 'A', 'Some' and Other Little Words |

In Spanish, 'the' and 'a' change depending on the gender of the noun and whether it's singular or plural.

El, la, los, las — *the*

'El', 'la', 'los' and 'las' are definite articles.

	Masculine	Feminine
singular	el	la
plural	los	las

1) The word for 'the' changes depending on the gender of the noun, and whether it's singular or plural.

2) Use 'el' before feminine nouns which start with a stressed 'a'.

   El agua está fría. *The water is cold.*

3) Sometimes you need a definite article in Spanish where you wouldn't use one in English...

   a) with nouns used in a general sense: No me gusta el café. *I don't like coffee.*
   b) in front of the days of the week and times: los lunes a las seis *Mondays at six o'clock*
   c) in front of weights and measurements: dos euros el kilo *two euros a kilo*
   d) when you use a person's title: ¿Cómo está el señor Gómez? *How is Mr Gómez?*

4) There's a neuter article 'lo' for things that aren't masculine or feminine.

   lo mejor / peor / aburrido es que... *the best / worst / boring thing is that...*

   When you use 'lo' in front of an adjective, the adjective has to be in the masculine form — see p.61.

Un, una, unos, unas — *a and some*

'Un', 'una', 'unos' and 'unas' are indefinite articles.

1) 'Un' and 'una' mean 'a'.

   un gato   *a cat*
   una casa   *a house*

2) 'Un' is used for masculine words and 'una' is used for feminine words.

3) When you make 'un' or 'una' plural, they become 'unos' and 'unas' — they mean 'some' or 'a few'.

   unos gatos   *some cats*
   unas casas   *some houses*

4) Watch out, though — 'a' is left out...

   a) ...after the verb 'ser' when talking about someone's occupation or nationality: Soy estudiante. *I'm a student.*
   b) ...after a negative verb: No tengo perro. *I haven't got a dog.*

Any, another, each, all

These are known as indefinite adjectives. See p.61-63 for more adjectives.

1) There's no special word for 'any' in Spanish.   ¿Tienes manzanas? *Have you got any apples?*

2) Use 'otro' or 'otra' for 'another'.   Lo haré otro día. *I'll do it another day.*

   You don't need to write 'un' or 'una' before 'otro/a'.

3) 'Cada' means 'each'. It's the same for masculine and feminine nouns.   Cada otoño voy a Irlanda. *Each autumn I go to Ireland.*

4) 'Todo/a/os/as' means 'all'.   Compré todos los libros en la librería. *I bought all the books in the bookshop.*

Articles are most definitely important...

Translate these sentences into Spanish.

1. I like chocolate.
2. I don't have any water.
3. She is a teacher.
4. He wants some potatoes.
5. I want to speak to Mrs López.
6. Each person has two dogs.

Words to Describe Things

Jazz up your work with some flashy describing words — and collect more marks while you're at it.

Adjectives describe things — *learn these common ones*

grande	*big*	guapo/a	*good-looking*
pequeño/a	*small*	feliz	*happy*
alto/a	*tall / high*	triste	*sad*
bajo/a	*short / low*	fácil	*easy*
largo/a	*long*	difícil	*difficult*
gordo/a	*fat*	malo/a	*bad*
delgado/a	*slim*	nuevo/a	*new*
viejo/a	*old*	rápido/a	*fast*
joven	*young*	lento/a	*slow*

interesante	*interesting*
simpático	*kind*
aburrido	*boring*

When you look up an adjective in the dictionary, it'll be in the masculine singular form.

Adjectives need to agree with the noun

1) Adjectives have to <u>agree</u> with the <u>noun</u> they refer to, <u>even if they aren't right next to it</u>.

2) This means the <u>adjective changes</u> depending on the <u>gender</u> of the <u>noun</u> and whether it's <u>singular</u> or <u>plural</u>.

3) Adjectives that end in '<u>o</u>' in the <u>masculine singular</u> form change the '<u>o</u>' to '<u>a</u>' in the <u>feminine</u> form. When <u>plural</u>, the adjective ends in '<u>os</u>' (masculine) or '<u>as</u>' (feminine).

Masculine singular	Feminine singular	Masculine plural	Feminine plural
el chico pequeño	la chica pequeña	los chicos pequeños	las chicas pequeñas
the small boy	*the small girl*	*the small boys*	*the small girls*

4) Adjectives which <u>don't</u> end in '<u>o</u>' or '<u>a</u>' <u>don't change</u> in the singular.
If the noun is <u>plural</u>, add '<u>s</u>' if it ends in a vowel, or '<u>es</u>' if it ends in a consonant.

Masculine singular	Feminine singular	Masculine plural	Feminine plural
el hombre triste	la mujer triste	los hombres tristes	las mujeres tristes
the sad man	*the sad woman*	*the sad men*	*the sad women*

If the adjective ends in 'z', remove the 'z' and add 'ces'. See p.59 for nouns that work in a similar way.

Some adjectives don't change to agree

Some adjectives <u>don't change at all</u>.

Most adjectives that don't change are colours.

beis	*beige*	rosa	*pink*
lila	*lilac*	turquesa	*turquoise*
naranja	*orange*	violeta	*violet*

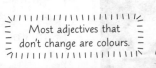
tres coches naranja   *three orange cars*
siete trenes rosa   *seven pink trains*

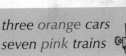

Adjectives agree (and I'm sure you do too) that this page is great...

Translate these phrases, making sure the adjectives agree with the nouns (where they need to).

1. the happy dog	**3.** the blue cars	**5.** five small cats	**7.** four beige books
2. seven red skirts	**4.** two short women	**6.** nine violet chairs	**8.** one sad person

Adjectives	# Words to Describe Things

Once you know loads of adjectives, you need to know where to put them.

Most adjectives go after the word they describe

1) In Spanish, <u>most adjectives go after the noun</u> (the word they describe).

2) But that's not always the case — some adjectives always go <u>in front of the noun</u> they're describing, like these ones:

Es un vestido horrible.
It's a horrible dress.

mucho/a	*a lot of*	tanto/a	*so much*	primero/a, segundo/a...	*first, second...*
muchos/as	*lots of*	tantos/as	*so many*	próximo/a	*next*
otro/a	*another*	poco/a	*little*	último/a	*last*
otros/as	*other*	pocos/as	*few*		
alguno/a	*some*	cada	*each*		

'Otro', 'cada', and 'alguno/a' are all indefinite adjectives. For more on indefinite adjectives, see p.60.

Some adjectives change before masculine nouns...

Some adjectives <u>lose</u> the final '<u>o</u>' when they go in front of a <u>masculine noun</u>.

bueno/a	*good*	tercero/a	*third*	ninguno/a	*none*
primero/a	*first*	alguno/a	*some*	malo/a	*bad*

un buen día	*a good day*	el tercer libro	*the third book*	algún día	*some day*

①	'<u>Alguno</u>' and '<u>ninguno</u>' <u>drop</u> the final '<u>o</u>' and <u>add an accent</u>.	No hay ningún taxi libre.	*There's no taxi free.*
②	'<u>Grande</u>' is the only adjective that <u>drops</u> '<u>de</u>' in front of both <u>masculine and feminine</u> words.	una gran señora	*a great lady*

...and some change their meaning depending on their position

Paloma couldn't wait to try out the power steering in her new car.

Adjective	Before the noun...	After the noun...
grande	un gran hombre *a great man*	un hombre grande *a big man*
mismo	el mismo día *the same day*	yo mismo *I myself*
nuevo	un nuevo coche *a new (to owner) car*	un coche nuevo *a brand new car*
viejo	un viejo amigo *a long-standing friend*	un amigo viejo *an old (elderly) friend*

Don't let those adjectives trip you up — learn where they go...

Translate these phrases and sentences into Spanish, making sure the adjectives go in the right place.

1. There are lots of cats.
2. the first day
3. the same dog
4. the other pupils
5. Some people think that...
6. He's a great teacher.

Words to Describe Things

Adjectives are also really useful for saying what's yours and for pointing things out.

Mi, tu, nuestro — *my, your, our*

'Mi', 'tu', 'nuestro' etc. are possessive adjectives.

Words like '<u>my</u>' and '<u>your</u>' in Spanish have to <u>agree</u> with the <u>noun</u> they're describing — <u>not the owner</u>.

Possessive	Masculine singular	Feminine singular	Masculine plural	Feminine plural
my	mi (mío)	mi (mía)	mis (míos)	mis (mías)
your (inf., sing.)	tu (tuyo)	tu (tuya)	tus (tuyos)	tus (tuyas)
his/her/its/your (form., sing.)	su (suyo)	su (suya)	sus (suyos)	sus (suyas)
our	nuestro	nuestra	nuestros	nuestras
your (inf., pl.)	vuestro	vuestra	vuestros	vuestras
their/your (form., pl.)	su (suyo)	su (suya)	sus (suyos)	sus (suyas)

'Su(s)' can mean 'his', 'her', 'its', 'their' and 'your' (formal). Use the rest of the information in the sentence to work out which of these it is.

mi libro
my book

su perro
his dog

The forms <u>in pink</u> (in brackets) are the <u>special long forms</u> — put them <u>after the noun</u>:

las casas tuyas   *your houses*

el gato nuestro   *our cat*

The '<u>our</u>' and '<u>your (inf., pl.)</u>' forms are the <u>same</u> in the <u>short</u> and <u>long</u> forms.

Este, ese, aquel — *this, that, that over there*

'Este, 'ese' and 'aquel' are demonstrative adjectives.

1) Use '<u>este</u>' to say '<u>this</u>'. It's an adjective, so it <u>changes to agree</u> with the noun. When the noun is <u>feminine</u>, use '<u>esta</u>', and when it's <u>plural</u>, use '<u>estos</u>' (masculine) or '<u>estas</u>' (feminine).

   este tigre   *this tiger*   esta leche   *this milk*   estos huevos   *these eggs*   estas caras   *these faces*

2) In Spanish, there are <u>two words</u> for '<u>that</u>', but their meanings are slightly different. '<u>Ese</u>' is used when you'd normally say '<u>that</u>' in English. Use '<u>esa</u>' for feminine nouns, and '<u>esos</u>' or '<u>esas</u>' for plural nouns.

   ese tigre   *that tiger*   esa leche   *that milk*   esos huevos   *those eggs*   esas caras   *those faces*

3) '<u>Aquel</u>' is used for things that are <u>even further away</u> — in English, you might say '<u>that over there</u>'. 'Aquel' changes to '<u>aquella</u>' in the <u>feminine</u> form and '<u>aquellos</u>' and '<u>aquellas</u>' for the <u>plural</u> forms.

   aquel tigre   *that tiger over there*   aquellos huevos   *those eggs over there*
   aquella leche   *that milk over there*   aquellas caras   *those faces over there*

Cuyo — *whose*

'Cuyo' is a relative adjective.

To say '<u>whose</u>' in Spanish, use '<u>cuyo/a/os/as</u>'. The <u>ending</u> agrees with the <u>noun following</u>, <u>not with its owner</u>.

	Masculine singular	Feminine singular	Masculine plural	Feminine plural
whose	cuyo	cuya	cuyos	cuyas

Eva es la chica cuyo gato está allí.
Eva is the girl whose cat is there.

It's your turn now — help yourself to these quick questions...

Translate these sentences into Spanish.

1. Their books are new.
2. I want that apple.
3. That lion over there is eating.
4. These pears are good.
5. That man, whose wife is Spanish, is tall.
6. Lucas is the boy whose parents are nice.

Adverbs — Words to Describe Actions

Adverbs describe verbs by adding more information about how an action is done. Using them makes your Spanish much more interesting and complex, which can only be a good thing...

Adverbs help you describe how actions are done

1) If you wanted to <u>describe how you run</u>, you could say 'I run <u>slowly</u>' — '<u>slowly</u>' is an <u>adverb</u>.

2) In English, you add '-<u>ly</u>' to the adjective '<u>slow</u>' to make '<u>slowly</u>'.

3) It's similar in Spanish — to form an adverb, you add '-<u>mente</u>' to the end of the <u>adjective</u>. <u>But</u>, you need to make sure the adjective is in the <u>feminine form</u> first.

> lento (*slow*) ⟶ lenta (*feminine form of 'slow'*) **+** -mente ⟶ lentamente (*slowly*)

4) With adjectives that <u>don't end</u> in '<u>o</u>', you can just add '-<u>mente</u>'.

> fácil (*easy*) **+** -mente ⟶ fácilmente (*easily*)

5) Unlike with adjectives (see p.61), adverbs don't need to <u>agree</u>. This is because they're <u>describing</u> an <u>action</u>, not the <u>person</u> doing the action.

> Hablamos sinceramente.   *We speak sincerely.*
> Habla alegremente.   *She speaks happily.*

6) Adverbs come <u>after</u> the <u>verb</u>.

> Estudio tranquilamente.   *I study quietly.*

Alexa spoke happily of the time she managed to take off her skis without falling over.

Some adverbs are formed differently

1) Just like in English, there are a couple of <u>exceptions</u>.

2) You don't say 'I sing <u>goodly</u>' in English, and you can't say '<u>buenamente</u>' in Spanish either.

> bueno/a   *good* ⟶ bien   *well*   Canto bien. ⟶ *I sing well.*
> malo/a   *bad* ⟶ mal   *badly*   Canto mal. ⟶ *I sing badly.*

3) Even though you can use '<u>rápidamente</u>' and '<u>lentamente</u>' for '<u>quickly</u>' and '<u>slowly</u>', you can also use the <u>irregular</u> forms — '<u>deprisa</u>' (*quickly*) and '<u>despacio</u>' (*slowly*). They <u>don't</u> add '-<u>mente</u>' or <u>change their ending</u>.

> Escribes deprisa.   *You write quickly.*

> Escribes despacio.   *You write slowly.*

Just like regular adverbs, these ones come after the verb.

Make sure you're speaking Spanish maravillosamente...

Try translating these sentences into Spanish.

1. They cry noisily.
2. He lives healthily.
3. She speaks clearly.
4. We speak intelligently.
5. The baby sleeps well.
6. I run quickly.
7. You dance badly.
8. I read slowly.

Words to Describe Actions

And here's another page on adverbs. This time, it's how to form adverbs using 'con', and some handy lists of adverbs that help you say where or when something is happening.

You can also form adverbs using 'con' + noun

1) In English, you can say someone did something 'with ease' instead of saying 'easily'.

2) You can do the same in Spanish by putting 'con' with a noun.

Lo hago con facilidad. *I do it with ease / easily.*	Hablaste con arrogancia. *You spoke with arrogance / arrogantly.*	¡Con cuidado! *With care! / Carefully!*

Adverbs can tell you where something is done...

You can put these handy words into sentences to say where things happen.

aquí	*here*
ahí	*(just) there*
allá / allí	*(over) there*
cerca	*near*
lejos	*far away*
en / por todas partes	*everywhere*

Mi tía trabaja aquí.   *My aunt works here.* ← *just there — ahí*
Hay gatos por todas partes.   *There are cats everywhere.*
Está muy cerca.   *It's very near.* ← *far away — lejos*

To say where something is, you need the verb 'estar' (p.78).

...or when it's happening

1) Use these adverbs to help you say when something is being done.

ahora	*now / nowadays*	antes (de)	*before*	
ya	*already*	después (de)	*after(wards)*	
al mismo tiempo	*at the same time*	en seguida	*straightaway*	
de momento	*at the moment*	mientras tanto	*meanwhile*	
de repente	*suddenly*	pronto	*soon*	
de nuevo	*again*	todavía	*still, yet*	

Ya tengo un reloj. *I already have a watch.*

Estaré allí pronto. *I'll be there soon.*

2) These ones are really useful for saying how often something is done.

a diario	*daily*
a menudo	*often*
a veces	*sometimes*
de vez en cuando	*from time to time*
pocas veces	*rarely, a few times*
siempre	*always*

Siempre juego al fútbol en el parque con mis amigos. *I always play football in the park with my friends.*

A veces voy a la tienda. *I sometimes go to the shop.*

Use loads of adverbs and start raking in the marks with ease...

Translate these sentences into Spanish using all your adverb knowledge.

1. My shoes are here.
2. I want to do it again.
3. I did it patiently. (Use 'con'.)
4. We live far away.
5. She did it straightaway.
6. He danced enthusiastically. (Use 'con'.)

Comparatives & Superlatives

Words to Compare Things

To make your Spanish even more brilliant, learn how to compare things.

Más, el más — *more, the most*

'More' is a comparative and 'the most' is a superlative.

1) In Spanish you can't say 'cheaper' or 'cheapest' — you have to say '<u>more cheap</u>' or '<u>the most cheap</u>'.

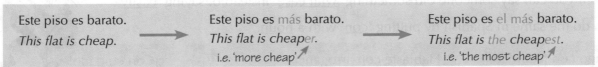

Este piso es barato.
This flat is cheap. → Este piso es más barato.
This flat is cheaper.
i.e. 'more cheap' → Este piso es el más barato.
This flat is the cheapest.
i.e. 'the most cheap'

2) To say '<u>less cheap</u>' or '<u>the least cheap</u>', use '<u>menos</u>'.

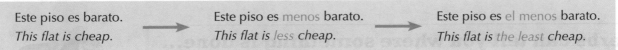

Este piso es barato.
This flat is cheap. → Este piso es menos barato.
This flat is less cheap. → Este piso es el menos barato.
This flat is the least cheap.

3) To say 'the most / least' if the word you're describing is <u>feminine</u>, use 'la más / menos'. For <u>plural</u> words, use 'los/las más / menos'.

Laura es la más baja.   *Laura is the shortest.*
Jo y Ed son los menos altos.   *Jo and Ed are the least tall.*

Más / menos ... que — *more / less ... than*

1) Use '<u>más</u> ... <u>que</u>' (*more ... than*) and '<u>menos</u> ... <u>que</u>' (*less ... than*) to <u>compare</u> two things <u>directly</u>.

Catalina es más inteligente que Jorge.   *Catalina is more intelligent than Jorge.*
Jorge es menos inteligente que Catalina.   *Jorge is less intelligent than Catalina.*

2) Or to say two things are <u>as</u> young or old or brilliant <u>as</u> each other, use '<u>tan</u> ... <u>como</u>' (*as ... as*).

Catalina es tan feliz como Jorge.   *Catalina is as happy as Jorge.*

There are some exceptions...

As usual, there are a few trickier ones — learn these exceptions.

If the noun is feminine or plural, you'll need to change the 'el' to 'la', 'los' or 'las'.

bueno	good	→	mejor	better	→	el mejor	the best
malo	bad	→	peor	worse	→	el peor	the worst
viejo	old (for people only)	→	mayor	older	→	el mayor	the oldest
joven	young (for people only)	→	menor	younger	→	el menor	the youngest

Manuela es la mayor de mis hermanas.   *Manuela is the oldest of my sisters.*

All the comparatives and superlatives stay the same for the masculine and feminine forms, but they add 'es' for the plural forms.

Blanca y Renata son las menores.   *Blanca and Renata are the youngest.*

El gorro azul es el mejor.   *The blue cap is the best.*

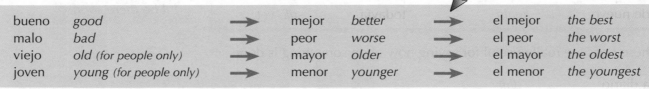

Making comparisons is the best thing ever...

Translate these sentences into Spanish — watch out for the irregular adjectives though.

1. My cat is the fattest.   **3.** Juan is older than Marta.   **5.** The film is better than the book.
2. I am as tall as my father.   **4.** It was the worst day of the week.   **6.** Our magazine is the most interesting.

Words to Compare Actions

Now you've got to grips with comparing things, you can use some of the same techniques to compare actions.

Using adverbs to say 'more ...ly' and 'less ...ly'

Adverbial phrases like this are called comparatives.

1) To say that something is done '<u>more ...ly</u>', use '<u>más ... que</u>'.

> Eva trabaja más alegremente que Inés.   *Eva works more happily than Inés.*

2) If you want to say that something is done '<u>less ...ly</u>', use '<u>menos ... que</u>'.

> Inés trabaja menos alegremente que Eva.   *Inés works less happily than Eva.*

3) To say that someone does something '<u>as ... as</u>' someone else, use '<u>tan ... como</u>'.

> Eva trabaja tan alegremente como Inés.   *Eva works as happily as Inés.*

Using adverbs to say the 'most ...ly'

This kind of construction is called a 'superlative'.

To say someone does something '<u>the most ...ly</u>', follow this pattern.
(Make sure you remember to change '<u>el</u>' to '<u>la</u>' if the subject is <u>feminine</u>, '<u>los</u>' if it's a <u>masculine plural</u> subject, and '<u>las</u>' for a <u>feminine plural</u> subject.)

> Daniela es la que trabaja más alegremente.   *Daniela works the most happily.*
> Juan es el que baila menos rápidamente.   *Juan dances the least quickly.*

Watch out for irregular comparatives and superlatives

Yes, you guessed it — there are some more <u>lovely irregular forms</u>.

| bien (*well*) | → | mejor (*better*) | → | el que mejor ... (*the one who ... the best*) |
| mal (*badly*) | → | peor (*worse*) | → | el que peor ... (*the one who ... the worst*) |

> Cocino mejor que mis amigos.   *I cook better than my friends.*
> Escribes peor que un niño.   *You write worse than a child.*
> Él es el que peor juega.   *He's the one who plays the worst.*
> Ellas son las que mejor bailan.   *They are the ones who dance the best.*

Use adverbs and you'll be speaking Spanish the most fluently...

Have a go at using what you know about adverbs to translate these sentences.

1. Carmen eats more quickly.
2. Luis sings as well as Adela.
3. Selina drives the best.
4. I study better than my friends.
5. We walk more slowly than Rob.
6. Ed is the one who runs the worst.

Words to Say How Much

You can use quantifiers and intensifiers with other words to give more detailed descriptions.

Use quantifiers to say how many or how much

1) Just saying 'I have apples' is boring. Use quantifiers to say you only have a few apples — or loads.

2) Quantifiers go before the noun, and most change their endings to agree with it, just like adjectives do.

mucho	a lot/lots of
poco	only a little/only a few
un poco de	a bit of
demasiado	too much/too many
tanto	so much/so many
bastante	enough

Tengo muchos deberes.	I have a lot of homework.
Tengo pocas cartas.	I only have a few letters.
Haces demasiado ruido.	You make too much noise.
Hay tanta gente.	There are so many people.
Tienes bastantes zapatos.	You have enough shoes.
Comí un poco de chocolate.	I ate a bit of chocolate.

'Un poco de' doesn't change its ending.

3) You don't just have to use these quantifiers with nouns — you can also use them with verbs. When you use them with verbs, they work like adverbs, so they go after the verb and don't change their endings.

Hablas demasiado.	You talk too much.
Come mucho.	She eats a lot.

Use intensifiers to strengthen what you're saying

1) You can use intensifiers like 'very' and 'quite' to add detail to what you're saying.

2) Intensifiers go before the word they're modifying, but their endings don't change at all.

muy	very
poco	not very
demasiado	too
bastante	quite

Simón está muy feliz.	Simón is very happy.
Es poco cortés.	He's not very polite.
Habla demasiado tranquilamente.	She speaks too quietly.
Comes bastante bien.	You eat quite well.

Add '-ito' or '-ísimo' to make adjectives smaller or stronger

1) You can add 'ito/a/os/as' to the end of most adjectives to make something seem smaller or cuter.

El bebé está enfermito.	The baby is poorly.

2) Add 'ísimo/a/os/as' to make the meaning of what you're saying stronger. It's as if you're adding 'really' to the adjective — so if 'bueno' is 'good', then 'buenísimo' would mean 'really good' or 'wonderful'.

La película es malísima.	The film is terrible.

That's enough of quantifiers and intensifiers for now...

Translate these sentences into Spanish.

1. There are too many cats here.
2. It's quite interesting.
3. I have lots of friends.
4. They speak too slowly.
5. There are so many beaches in Spain.
6. The book is really good.

I, You, We

Pronouns are really handy little words that save you from needing to repeat nouns all the time.

Subject and object

Before you get started on pronouns, you need to know how to find the subject and the object of a sentence.

The subject of a sentence is the noun doing the action. → Pau come la pera. *Pau eats the pear.* ← The object of a sentence is the noun having the action done to it.

Yo, tú, él, ella — *I, you, he, she*

1) Pronouns are words that replace nouns — like 'you' or 'them'. You use them to avoid repeating nouns.

Jessica went to the beach and she sat on the sand.

In English, the pronoun 'she' replaces Jessica's name. 'She' is a 'subject pronoun' because it replaces the subject of the sentence — Jessica.

2) You don't normally include subject pronouns in Spanish sentences — but you still need to know them.

I	yo	we	nosotros/as
you (inf., sing.)	tú	you (inf., pl.)	vosotros/as
he/it	él	they (masc.)	ellos
she/it	ella	they (fem.)	ellas
you (form., sing.)	usted	you (form., sing.)	ustedes

The masculine 'they' form is also used for groups made up of masculine and feminine nouns.

There's also 'se' which means 'one'. It's used in phrases like 'se puede' (one can / you can). It uses the third person singular form of the verb. See p.88 for more impersonal verbs.

Remember there are four ways to say 'you' in Spanish — see p.7 for more.

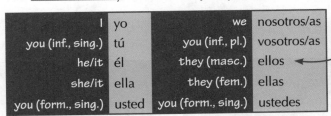

Here, you don't need the pronoun 'yo' because you can see from the first person verb forms 'fui' and 'comí' that the person speaking ('I') is doing the action.

Fui a la playa y comí un helado.   *I went to the beach and I ate an ice cream.*

You can use subject pronouns for emphasis

Although you don't usually need subject pronouns in Spanish, they help emphasise exactly who does what:

¿Qué queréis hacer el fin de semana que viene?   *What would you (inf., pl.) like to do next weekend?*

Pues, yo quiero ir de compras, pero él quiere ir al cine.
Well, I want to go shopping, but he wants to go to the cinema.

You include the pronouns here to emphasise who wants what. They're used in Spanish in cases when extra stress is put on pronouns in English.

¿Quieren visitar el museo?   *Do they / you (form., sing.) want to visit the museum?*

Pues, yo sí, pero ella no.   *Well, I do but she doesn't.*

Remember that if you're using 'ustedes', you need the 'they' form of the verb.

Pronouns make your writing sound smoother — use them...

Write down the Spanish subject pronoun you'd use to replace each of these subjects.
1. Juan y Jorge
2. Anabel
3. Pedro y yo
4. Alberto y tú
5. Ramón
6. el señor Pérez y usted
7. Miranda, Alicia y Lina
8. Alberto y Tania

Object Pronouns	**Me, You, Them**

Now you've got to grips with subject pronouns, it's time for object pronouns — bet you didn't see that coming.

Me, te, lo — *me, you, him*

'Me', 'you', 'him' and 'her' are direct object pronouns. They replace the object of a sentence — the thing having an action done to it.

Use <u>direct object pronouns</u> when you're talking about <u>who</u> or <u>what</u> an action is <u>done to</u>.

me	me	us	nos
you (inf., sing.)	te	you (inf., pl.)	os
him/it	lo	them (masc.)	los
her/it	la	them (fem.)	las
you (form., sing.)	lo/la	you (form., sing.)	los/las

The pronoun usually goes <u>before</u> the verb.

Ricardo lava el perro. → Ricardo lo lava.
Ricardo washes the dog. *Ricardo washes it.*

The action is done to <u>the dog</u> ('el perro' — <u>masculine</u>), so the pronoun '<u>it</u>' needs to be in the <u>masculine singular form</u>.

Me, te, les — *to me, to you, to them*

1) If you want to talk about doing something '<u>to</u>' or '<u>for</u>' <u>someone</u>, you need an <u>indirect object pronoun</u>.

El perro da el cepillo a Ricardo. → El perro le da el cepillo.
The dog gives the brush to Ricardo. *The dog gives the brush to him.*

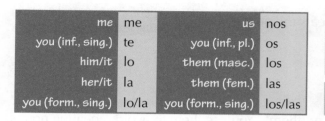

2) These pronouns are the same ones you use with the verb '<u>gustar</u>' when you say you <u>like something</u>. This is because 'me gusta el chocolate' literally means 'chocolate is pleasing <u>to me</u>'.

to me	me	to us	nos
to you (inf., sing.)	te	to you (inf., pl.)	os
to him / her / it / you (form., sing.)	le	to them / you (form., pl.)	les

3) If the thing you like is <u>singular</u>, you need 'gusta'. If it's <u>plural</u>, you need 'gustan'.

¿Te gusta el español? *Do you like Spanish?*
Le gustan los parques. *He likes the parks.*

Getting the order right

1) Object pronouns <u>normally</u> come <u>before the verb</u>, but they can go <u>before</u> or <u>after</u> the verb if it's an <u>infinitive</u> (p.76) or a <u>present participle</u> (p.86).

Often you need to <u>add an accent</u> to keep the pronunciation right.

Lo quiero ver. **OR** Quiero verlo.
I want to see it.

Le estamos hablando. **OR** Estamos hablándole.
We're talking to him.

2) With <u>commands</u>, the pronoun is <u>tacked on to the end</u>.

Escríbeme, por favor. *Write to me, please.*

3) When <u>two object pronouns</u> come together, the <u>indirect</u> one comes <u>first</u>.

4) And if the <u>indirect object pronoun</u> is '<u>le</u>' or '<u>les</u>', it becomes '<u>se</u>' when it's in front of '<u>lo</u>', '<u>la</u>', '<u>los</u>' or '<u>las</u>'.

direct object pronoun

Te la enviaré. *I'll send it to you.*

indirect object pronoun

direct object pronoun

Debo dárselo. *I must give it to him/her/them/you (form.).*

indirect object pronoun

Pronouns are tricky — but if you can use them, you'll be flying...

Translate these sentences into Spanish — try to use the correct pronouns and get the order right.
1. She breaks it (the window).   **3.** He bought a skirt for her.   **5.** I want to do it.
2. I drink it (the milk).   **4.** I send him an email.   **6.** He said it to us.

More Pronouns

Pronouns can be a bit confusing — but they're really useful for adding extra detail and asking questions.

Some pronouns change after certain prepositions

Watch out — 'mí' needs an accent, but 'ti' doesn't.

1) The words for '<u>me</u>' and '<u>you</u>' (inf., sing.) become '<u>mí</u>' and '<u>ti</u>' after <u>prepositions</u> like '<u>a</u>' (*to*), '<u>para</u>' (*for*), and '<u>sobre</u>' / '<u>de</u>' (*about*).

me	mí	us	nosotros/as
you (inf., sing.)	ti	you (inf., pl.)	vosotros/as
him	él/ella	them (masc.)	ellos/as
you (form., sing.)	usted	you (form., sing.)	ustedes

No es para mí, es para él.   *It isn't for me, it's for him.*

2) '<u>With me</u>' becomes '<u>conmigo</u>' and '<u>with you</u>' becomes '<u>contigo</u>':   Está conmigo.   *He's with me.*

Que — *that, which, who*

1) '<u>Que</u>' can mean '<u>that</u>', '<u>which</u>' or '<u>who</u>' — it's a <u>relative pronoun</u>.

2) You can use it to start a <u>relative clause</u>, which is a way of <u>adding detail</u> to a sentence.

Fui a Menorca, que es una isla preciosa.	*I went to Menorca, which is a beautiful island.*
¿Dónde está el pan que compraste ayer?	*Where's the bread that you bought yesterday?*
Allí está el hombre que vive en nuestra calle.	*There's the man who lives on our road.*

3) If you're talking about an <u>idea</u> instead of an object, you need '<u>lo que</u>'.

Van a venir, lo que es maravilloso.   *They're going to come, which is wonderful.*

4) <u>After prepositions</u>, like '<u>con</u>', '<u>a</u>' and '<u>de</u>', use '<u>quien</u>' for 'who' or '<u>el / la que</u>' or '<u>el / la cual</u>' for 'that / which.'

el hombre con quien estoy hablando
the man with whom I'm talking

el mercado del cual compro flores
the market from which I buy flowers

If you were talking about a plural noun, you'd need to use 'con quienes' or 'de los / las cuales' instead.

Using pronouns to ask questions

Pronouns for asking questions are called 'interrogative pronouns'.

1) Normally, you can use '<u>¿Qué...</u>' to ask a question that starts with '<u>What...</u>' in English.

¿Qué te gustaría hacer?   *What would you like to do?*

2) Use '<u>¿Cuál...</u>' when you'd use '<u>Which...</u>' or '<u>Which one...</u>' in English. But remember — sometimes you need '<u>¿Cuál...</u>' when you'd actually use 'What...' in English — see p.4.

¿Cuál es mejor?   *Which (one) is better?*   ¿Cuál es tu apellido?   *What is your surname?*

If 'cuál' is being used before a noun, it needs to agree with it. Use 'cuál' for all singular nouns and 'cuáles' for all plural nouns.

3) '<u>¿Quién...</u>' means '<u>Who...</u>'. You often use '<u>¿Quién...</u>' with <u>prepositions</u>.

¿Quién es?   *Who is it?*   ¿Con quién?   *With whom?*   ¿De quién son?   *Whose are they?*

This page, which is very useful, will help you greatly...

Pronouns are tricky — so the best way to tackle them is by practising. Translate these sentences into Spanish.
1. My sister, who is seven, is short.
2. I went to Madrid, which is the capital of Spain.
3. What's your address?
4. Who do you live with?
5. Whose is this dog?
6. Which do you prefer?

More Pronouns

It's well worth being able to use these pronouns, so make sure you get your head around them.

El mío, el tuyo... — *mine, yours...*

1) Use possessive pronouns to say '<u>mine</u>' or '<u>yours</u>'.

'el mío', 'el tuyo', 'el nuestro'
etc. are possessive pronouns.

2) Possessive pronouns <u>agree</u> in <u>gender</u> and <u>number</u> with the <u>noun</u> they're replacing.

Possessive pronoun	Masculine singular	Feminine singular	Masculine plural	Feminine plural
mine	el mío	la mía	los míos	las mías
yours (inf., sing.)	el tuyo	la tuya	los tuyos	las tuyas
his/hers/its/yours (form.)	el suyo	la suya	los suyos	las suyas
ours	el nuestro	la nuestra	los nuestros	las nuestras
yours (inf., pl.)	el vuestro	la vuestra	los vuestros	las vuestras
theirs/yours (form., pl.)	el suyo	la suya	los suyos	las suyas

¿Es tu casa?   *Is it your house?*
No, la mía es más alta.   *No, mine is taller.*

¿Es vuestro hotel?   *Is it your (inf., pl.) hotel?*
No, el nuestro está allí.   *No, ours is there.*

Algo, alguien — *something, someone*

'Algo' and 'alguien' are indefinite pronouns.

'<u>Algo</u>' means '<u>something</u>':   ¿Queréis algo?   *Do you (inf., pl.) want something?*

'<u>Alguien</u>' means '<u>someone</u>':   Vi a alguien.   *I saw someone.*

When you 'see someone' in Spanish, you have to add the <u>personal 'a'</u>. See p.75.

Este, ese, aquel — *this one, that one, that one over there*

Sometimes you might see these pronouns written with an accent on the first 'e' — e.g. 'éste'.

1) <u>Demonstrative pronouns</u> are <u>the same as</u> the <u>demonstrative adjectives</u> on p.63.

2) Remember to <u>change the ending</u> to <u>agree</u> with the noun it refers back to.

Demonstrative pronoun	Masculine singular	Feminine singular	Masculine plural	Feminine plural
this/these one(s)	este	esta	estos	estas
that/those one(s)	ese	esa	esos	esas
that/those one(s) over there	aquel	aquella	aquellos	aquellas

Me gustaría este.
I'd like this one.

Prefiere esas.
She prefers those.

3) Use the <u>neuter forms</u> '<u>esto</u>', '<u>eso</u>' and '<u>aquello</u>' if you <u>don't</u> know the <u>gender</u> of the noun.

¿Qué es eso?   *What's that?*

Ahh pronouns — these will get you good marks...

Translate these sentences into Spanish, using the correct pronouns.

1. They're mine. *(cats)*
2. What's that over there?
3. This bed is bigger than that one over there.
4. This book is more interesting than that one.
5. Is it yours (inf., pl.)? *(hat)*
6. Someone's talking quietly.

Conjunctions

Conjunctions help you link your ideas together to make longer, more complex sentences.

Y — and

1) '<u>Y</u>' means '<u>and</u>' — you use it just like you would in English.

| Me gusta jugar al fútbol. *I like playing football.* | AND | Me gusta jugar al rugby. *I like playing rugby.* | = | Me gusta jugar al fútbol y al rugby. *I like playing football and rugby.* |

2) '<u>Y</u>' changes to '<u>e</u>' <u>before</u> a word starting with '<u>i</u>' or '<u>hi</u>'.

Hablo español e inglés.   *I speak Spanish and English.*

O — or

1) '<u>O</u>' means '<u>or</u>'.

| Juego al fútbol los sábados. *I play football on Saturdays.* | OR | Juego al rugby los sábados. *I play rugby on Saturdays.* | = | Juego al fútbol o al rugby los sábados. *I play football or rugby on Saturdays.* |

2) When '<u>o</u>' comes just <u>before</u> a word starting with '<u>o</u>' or '<u>ho</u>', it changes to '<u>u</u>'.

Cuesta siete u ocho euros.   *It costs seven or eight euros.*

Pero — but

1) '<u>Pero</u>' means '<u>but</u>'.

| Me gusta el fútbol. *I like football.* | BUT | No me gusta el rugby. *I don't like rugby.* | = | Me gusta el fútbol, pero no me gusta el rugby. *I like football, but I don't like rugby.* |

2) When '<u>but</u>' means '<u>but rather</u>', it becomes '<u>sino</u>'.

No es español, sino francés.   *He isn't Spanish, but (rather) French.*

Porque — because

'<u>Porque</u>' helps you <u>give opinions</u>:   Me gusta porque es sabroso.   *I like it because it's tasty.*

There's more about 'porque' and opinions on p.9.

Other conjunctions you need to know

cuando	*when*	así que	*so, therefore*	como	*as, since*
si	*if*	de manera que	*such that*	pues	*well, then*
sin embargo	*however*	mientras	*while*	entonces	*then*

Tiene hambre, así que va a comer.

He's hungry, so he's going to eat.

You don't want to sound like a robot, so start using conjunctions...

Translate these sentences into Spanish, deciding which conjunctions you need to use.

1. Geography is fun, but it's difficult.
2. I like history because it's easy.
3. As I'm ill, I'm staying at home.
4. I go to the park when it's hot.
5. I speak French and Italian.
6. Do you prefer blue or yellow?

Prepositions

Prepositions are sneaky little words — but you've got to learn them if you want the highest marks.

Use these words to say where something is...

Don't forget to use 'estar' (see p.78) to say where something is.

al lado de	*next to*	bajo / debajo de	*below / under*	enfrente de	*opposite*
detrás de	*behind*	en / sobre	*on / upon*	en / dentro de	*in / into / inside*
delante de	*in front of*	encima de	*above / on top of*	al fondo de	*at the back of*
entre	*between*	contra	*against*	hacia	*towards*

A, hasta — *to*

To say '<u>to</u>' in Spanish, you <u>normally</u> say '<u>a</u>'. But when '<u>to</u>' means '<u>as far as</u>', use '<u>hasta</u>'.

Va a Liverpool. *She's going to Liverpool.*	Solo va hasta Manchester. *He's only going to Manchester.*

En, dentro de — *in, inside*

'<u>In</u>' is just '<u>en</u>' and '<u>inside</u>' is '<u>dentro de</u>'. The verb '<u>entrar</u>' (*to go in / enter*) is normally followed by '<u>en</u>'.

En Leeds... *In Leeds...*	dentro de la caja *inside the box*	Entro en la tienda. *I enter the shop.*

De — *of*

'<u>De</u>' is usually '<u>of</u>'. You can also use '<u>de</u>' to say what something's <u>made of</u>.

Es de oro. *It's made of gold.*	al final del pasillo *at the end of the corridor*

You <u>can't</u> say 'de el' or 'a el' in Spanish. Instead, you <u>combine</u> 'a' or 'de' with the <u>definite article</u> (p.60).

	el	la
a	al	a la
de	del	de la

En, a — *at*

You can <u>normally</u> use '<u>en</u>' when you want to say '<u>at</u>'. Sometimes you need '<u>a</u>' instead...

Está en el colegio. *He's at school.*	en casa *at home*	a las seis *at six o'clock*

Sobre, en — *on*

For '<u>on (top of)</u>', use '<u>sobre</u>' or '<u>en</u>'. When you mean '<u>on</u>' but not '<u>on top of</u>', use '<u>en</u>'.

You don't need 'on' for days of the week.

Está sobre la mesa. *It's on the table.*	Lo vi en la tele. *I saw it on TV.*	El lunes... *On Monday...*

De, desde, a partir de — *from*

'<u>From</u>' is normally '<u>de</u>'. Use '<u>desde</u>' when there's a <u>starting</u> and <u>ending</u> point and '<u>a partir de</u>' for dates.

Es de Kent. *He's from Kent.*	desde Fife hasta Ayr *from Fife to Ayr*	a partir de julio *from July*

Learn these prepositions inside out and back to front...

Use what you know about prepositions to translate these sentences into Spanish.
1. The house is opposite the bank.
2. The train goes as far as Italy.
3. I heard it on the radio.
4. I enter the supermarket.
5. I'm from Hull, but I live in Crewe.
6. From September, I will have a job.

'Por', 'Para' and the Personal 'a'

'Por', 'para' and the personal 'a' are also prepositions, but they don't always translate easily into English.

Use 'para' to...

1) ...say <u>who</u> something is <u>for</u>.

> Este dinero es para ti.   *This money is for you.*

2) ...talk about <u>destinations</u>.

> el tren para Bilbao   *the train to Bilbao*

3) ...say '<u>to</u>' or '<u>in order to</u>'.

> Veo la tele para descansar.   *I watch TV to relax.*

4) ...say '<u>by</u>' in <u>time phrases</u>.

> para mañana   *by tomorrow*

5) ...say '<u>for</u>' in phrases like '<u>for X days</u>' when you're talking about the <u>future</u>.

> Quiero el coche para un día.   *I want the car for one day.*

6) ...say '<u>in my / your opinion</u>'.

> Para mí, es muy bonito.   *In my opinion, it's very pretty.*

'Según' is another <u>preposition</u>. It means '<u>according to</u>'.

7) ...say '<u>about to</u>'.

> Según él, está para llover.   *According to him, it's about to rain.*

Use 'por' to...

In certain cases, for the future you need to use 'por': Estaré en Galicia por dos años.

1) ...say '<u>for</u>' in phrases like '<u>for X years / months</u>' in the <u>past</u>.

> Vivió allí por un año.   *He lived there for a year.*

2) ...talk about <u>parts of the day</u> when you want to say '<u>in</u>'.

> por la mañana   *in the morning*

3) ...say '<u>through</u>'.

> Entré por la puerta sin hablar.   *I came through the door without speaking.*

'Sin' is a <u>preposition</u> which means '<u>without</u>'.

4) ...say '<u>per</u>' or '<u>a</u>' in <u>number phrases</u>.

> tres veces por día   *three times a day*

5) ...talk about <u>exchanges</u>.

> Pagó dos euros por el té.   *He paid 2 euros for the tea.*

6) ...say '<u>on behalf of</u>'.

> Lo hice por ti.   *I did it for you.*

7) ...say '<u>thank you</u>'.

> Gracias por el pastel.   *Thanks for the cake.*

The personal 'a'

You don't usually use the personal 'a' after 'tener' or 'ser'.

You need an <u>extra</u> '<u>a</u>' <u>before</u> the word for any <u>human being</u> or <u>pet</u> after every single <u>verb</u>.

> Estoy buscando a Juan.   *I'm looking for Juan.*

BUT

> Estoy buscando un taxi.   *I'm looking for a taxi.*

'Por' and 'para' are hard... but they're really useful to know.

Decide whether you need 'por', 'para' or 'a' in each of these sentences.

1. Esta revista es ____ ti.
2. Visito ____ mi abuelo.
3. ____ la tarde, vemos la tele.
4. Gracias ____ la carta.
5. Juego al fútbol dos veces ____ semana.
6. Lo quiero ____ el fin de semana.

Present Tense	# Verbs in the Present Tense

There's not a lot you can do without verbs — your Spanish won't make very much sense without them.

Verbs are actions

1) A <u>verb</u> is an <u>action word</u> — for example, '<u>speak</u>', '<u>eat</u>' and '<u>live</u>'.

2) Verbs can be put into <u>different tenses</u>, such as the <u>future</u> or <u>past</u>, for example, 'Yesterday, I <u>ate</u> some cake'.

3) To use a verb, you need to know its <u>infinitive</u> — the form you find in a <u>dictionary</u>, e.g. '<u>hablar</u>' (*to speak*).

Forming the present tense

1) Most <u>regular</u> verbs in Spanish end in '-<u>ar</u>', '-<u>er</u>' or '-<u>ir</u>'. To form the <u>present tense</u> of these regular verbs, you need to find the <u>stem</u>. To do this, <u>remove</u> the <u>last two letters</u> from the <u>infinitive</u>.

2) Then <u>add</u> the <u>endings</u> below to the <u>stem</u>.

Infinitive	Remove last two letters	Stem
hablar	ar	habl-

-ar verbs

I speak	hablo	hablamos	we speak
you (inf., sing.) speak	hablas	habláis	you (inf., pl.) speak
he/she/it/you (form., sing.) speak(s)	habla	hablan	they/you (form., pl.) speak

Cantan bien. *They sing well.*

Toca el piano. *He plays the piano.*

-er verbs

I eat	como	comemos	we eat
you (inf., sing.) eat	comes	coméis	you (inf., pl.) eat
he/she/it/you (form., sing.) eat(s)	come	comen	they/you (form., pl.) eat

Bebes té. *You (inf., sing.) drink tea.*

Vendemos uvas. *We sell grapes.*

-ir verbs

I live	vivo	vivimos	we live
you (inf., sing.) live	vives	vivís	you (inf., pl.) live
he/she/it/you (form., sing.) live(s)	vive	viven	they/you (form., pl.) live

Suben la torre. *They go up the tower.*

Kevin interrumpe. *Kevin interrupts.*

When to use the present tense

For another way to say what you're doing now, see p.86.

① Use the <u>present tense</u> for actions taking place <u>now</u>.

Hablo español. *I speak Spanish / I am speaking Spanish.*

② You also need the <u>present tense</u> for things that take place <u>regularly</u>.

Canto todos los días. *I sing every day.*

③ Use the <u>present tense</u> with '<u>desde hace</u>' to say <u>how long</u> you've been doing something.

Toco el violín desde hace cuatro años. *I've been playing the violin for four years.*

④ You can also use the <u>present tense</u> for things that are <u>about to happen</u>.

Mañana vamos al cine. *Tomorrow we are going to the cinema.*

The present? Oh, you really shouldn't have...

Put each of the infinitives into the form given in brackets, and then translate Q8 into Spanish.

1. bailar (yo)
2. beber (nosotros)
3. nadar (vosotros)
4. correr (usted)
5. aprender (él)
6. visitar (ellos)
7. escribir (tú)
8. She has been living here for a year.

Irregular Verbs in the Present Tense

Unfortunately, not all Spanish verbs are regular — and some of the worst offenders are really common verbs...

Radical-changing verbs

These are also known as 'stem-changing verbs'.

1) A <u>radical-changing verb</u> is a verb that <u>changes its spelling</u> in the <u>present tense</u>.

2) Usually, the 'e' in their stem changes to 'ie', or the 'o' or 'u' in their stem to 'ue'. Some <u>verbs</u> like '<u>pedir</u>' (*to order / ask for*), '<u>repetir</u>' (*to repeat*) and '<u>vestirse</u>' (*to get dressed*) change the '<u>e</u>' in their stem to '<u>i</u>'.

3) Their stem <u>changes</u> in every form apart from the '<u>we</u>' and '<u>you (inf., pl.)</u>' forms.

Even though their stems change, their endings are regular.

querer — to want (e to ie)

I want	quiero
you (inf., sing.) want	quieres
he/she/it/you (form., sing.) want(s)	quiere
we want	queremos
you (inf., pl.) want	queréis
they/you (form., pl.) want	quieren

These verbs also change their '<u>e</u>' to '<u>ie</u>'...

cerrar	*to close*	preferir	*to prefer*
comenzar	*to begin*	sentarse	*to sit down*
despertarse	*to wake up*	sentir(se)	*to feel*
empezar	*to begin*	tener	*to have*
pensar	*to think*	venir	*to come*

'Tener' and 'venir' have irregular first person singular forms — 'tengo' and 'vengo'.

poder — to be able to (o to ue)

I can	puedo
you (inf., sing.) can	puedes
he/she/it/you (form., sing.) can	puede
we can	podemos
you (inf., pl.) can	podéis
they/you (form., pl.) can	pueden

These verbs change their '<u>o</u>' or '<u>u</u>' to '<u>ue</u>'...

acostarse	*to go to bed*	encontrar	*to find*
almorzar	*to have lunch*	jugar	*to play*
costar	*to cost*	llover	*to rain*
doler	*to hurt*	morir	*to die*
dormir	*to sleep*	volver	*to return*

Kevin's perspective on life had changed — radically...

Some common irregular verbs

In Spanish, the verbs '<u>to go</u>', '<u>to give</u>', '<u>to do / make</u>' and '<u>to know</u>' are irregular.

To say you know a person, use 'conocer' instead. It also has an irregular 1st person — conozco.

ir — to go

<u>All</u> of the present tense forms of '<u>ir</u>' are <u>irregular</u>.

I go	voy	vamos	we go
you (inf., sing.) go	vas	vais	you (inf., pl.) go
he/she/it/you (form., sing.) go(es)	va	van	they/you (form., pl.) go

saber — to know (something)

I know	sé
you (inf., sing.) know	sabes
he/she/it/you (form., sing.) know(s)	sabe
we know	sabemos
you (inf., pl.) know	sabéis
they/you (form., pl.) know	saben

<u>Only</u> the 'I' form of '<u>saber</u>' is <u>irregular</u>.

<u>Only</u> the 'I' and '<u>you (inf., pl.)</u>' forms of '<u>dar</u>' are <u>irregular</u>.

dar — to give

I give	doy
you (inf., sing.) give	das
he/she/it/you (form., sing.) give(s)	da
we give	damos
you (inf., pl.) give	dais
they/you (form., pl.) give	dan

hacer — to do

<u>Only</u> the 'I' form is <u>irregular</u>.

I do	hago	hacemos	we do
you (inf., sing.) do	haces	hacéis	you (inf., pl.) do
he/she/it/you (form., sing.) do(es)	hace	hacen	they/you (form., pl.) do

'Hacer' can also mean 'to make'.

Radical verbs are just *so* out there...

Find the mistake in each of these Spanish sentences. The subject of the verb is in brackets to help you.

1. Comenza a las tres. (ella)
2. Vís a la tienda. (vosotros)
3. Quieremos leche. (nosotros)
4. Do el libro a Lola. (yo)
5. Podes conducir. (tú)
6. Sabo tu nombre. (yo)

78

Present Tense

'Ser' and 'Estar' in the Present Tense

In Spanish, there are two verbs for 'to be' — 'ser' and 'estar'. They're used differently, so it's really important to know which you need in each situation. Oh, and one more thing — they're irregular too...

Use 'ser' for permanent things

The verb '<u>ser</u>' means '<u>to be</u>'. It's used for <u>permanent things</u>. You need it to...

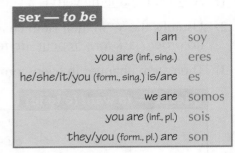

ser — to be	
I am	soy
you are (inf., sing.)	eres
he/she/it/you (form., sing.) is/are	es
we are	somos
you are (inf., pl.)	sois
they/you (form., pl.) are	son

1)   ...talk about <u>nationalities</u>.

> Somos galeses.   *We are Welsh.*

2)   ...say someone's <u>name</u> or say <u>who someone is</u> in relation to you.

> Nerea es mi prima.   *Nerea is my cousin.*

3)   ...talk about someone's <u>job</u>.

> Mi tío es profesor.   *My uncle is a teacher.*

4)   ...describe the <u>physical characteristics</u> of a person or thing.

> Sois altos.   *You (inf., pl.) are tall.*

5)   ...describe someone's <u>personality</u>.

> Son alegres.   *They are cheerful.*   Eres muy amable.   *You are very kind.*

Use 'estar' for temporary things and locations

'<u>Estar</u>' also means '<u>to be</u>'. You use it to...

1)   ...talk about <u>things that might change</u> in the future.

> Estoy bastante enfermo.   *I'm quite ill.*
> (But you might not be ill next week.)

> Estás muy triste hoy.   *You are very sad today.*
> (But you might not be sad tomorrow.)

Alba is positively thrilled with her parents' fashion choices.

estar — to be	
I am	estoy
you are (inf., sing.)	estás
he/she/it/you (form., sing.) is/are	está
we are	estamos
you are (inf., pl.)	estáis
they/you (form., pl.) are	están

2)   ...talk about <u>where someone or something is</u>.

> Madrid está en España.   *Madrid is in Spain.*   Estamos en casa.   *We are at home.*

To be or to be — that's a question worth asking...

Decide whether you need 'ser' or 'estar' in each of these situations.

1. Es / Está muy hablador hoy.
2. Es / Está muy hablador en general.
3. Somos / Estamos de Escocia.
4. Soy / Estoy en Bradford.
5. Este es / está mi hermano.
6. Mi padre es / está médico.

Section 9 — Grammar

Talking About the Past

The preterite tense ('I went' etc.) has quite a few tricky irregular forms — so pay close attention to this page.

I went — *The preterite tense*

To form the preterite tense of regular verbs, find the stem (see p.76) and then add these endings...

-ar verb endings

I	-é	-amos	we
you (inf., sing.)	-aste	-asteis	you (inf., pl.)
he/she/it/you (form., sing.)	-ó	-aron	they/you (form., pl.)

-er and -ir verb endings

I	-í	-imos	we
you (inf., sing.)	-iste	-isteis	you (inf., pl.)
he/she/it/you (form., sing.)	-ió	-ieron	they/you (form., pl.)

Habló con Marcela.
He spoke to Marcela.

Don't forget the accent — without it, you'd be saying 'I speak to Marcela'.

Nací en Japón.
I was born in Japan.

Bebisteis mucho.
You (inf., pl.) drank a lot.

Irregular verbs in the preterite tense

Here are four important irregular verbs in the preterite tense. 'Ser' and 'ir' are the same in the preterite tense.

ser — *to be*; ir — *to go*

I was / went	fui
you (inf., sing.) were / went	fuiste
he/she/it/you (form., sing.) was (were) / went	fue
we were / went	fuimos
you (inf., pl.) were / went	fuisteis
they/you (form., pl.) were / went	fueron

estar — *to be*

I was	estuve
you (inf., sing.) were	estuviste
he/she/it/you (form., sing.) was (were)	estuvo
we were	estuvimos
you (inf., pl.) were	estuvisteis
they/you (form., pl.) were	estuvieron

hacer — *to do / make*

I did / made	hice
you (inf., sing.) did / made	hiciste
he/she/it/you (form., sing.) did / made	hizo
we did / made	hicimos
you (inf., pl.) did / made	hicisteis
they/you (form., pl.) did / made	hicieron

Verbs ending in '-car' change their 'c' to a 'qu' in the 'I' form of the preterite tense — 'tocar' becomes 'toqué'.
Verbs ending in '-zar' change their 'z' to a 'c' in the 'I' form of the preterite tense — 'cruzar' becomes 'crucé'.

Even more irregular verbs

Some verbs change their stem in the preterite tense. If you know what the stem change is, you can predict what the verb is going to be in its other forms.

Infinitive	I	he/she/it
dar (*to give*)	di	dio
decir (*to say*)	dije	dijo
poder (*to be able to*)	pude	pudo
poner (*to put*)	puse	puso
querer (*to want*)	quise	quiso
tener (*to have*)	tuve	tuvo
traer (*to bring*)	traje	trajo
venir (*to come*)	vine	vino

The 'he/she/it/you (form., sing.)' form is sometimes different to what you might expect.

Le dimos un gato.   *We gave him a cat.*

Pero dijiste que te gustó.   *But you (inf., sing.) said you liked it.*

Tuvisteis una idea.   *You (inf., pl.) had an idea.*

Vinieron a mi fiesta.   *They came to my party.*

Irregular verbs are a regular pain...

Put these verbs into the preterite tense. The subject is given in brackets.

1. llorar (ellos)
2. comer (nosotros)
3. escribir (vosotros)
4. cenar (yo)
5. dar (tú)
6. poder (yo)
7. hacer (vosotros)
8. poner (usted)
9. venir (tú)
10. traer (nosotros)

Imperfect Tense	# Talking About the Past

The imperfect tense is used to describe things in the past. It helps you say what you 'were doing', what 'was happening' and what you 'used to do'.

I was going / I used to go — *The imperfect tense*

To form the <u>imperfect tense</u>, find the <u>stem</u> (see p.76) and then <u>add these endings</u>. The 'I' form and the 'he/she/it/you (form., sing.)' form look the <u>same</u>, so you'll have to use the <u>context</u> to tell which is which.

-ar verb endings

I	-aba	-ábamos	we	
you (inf., sing.)	-abas	-abais	you (inf., pl.)	
he/she/it/you (form., sing.)	-aba	-aban	they/you (form., pl.)	

Hablábamos por teléfono.
We were talking / used to talk on the phone.

-er and -ir verb endings

I	-ía	-íamos	we	
you (inf., sing.)	-ías	-íais	you (inf., pl.)	
he/she/it/you (form., sing.)	-ía	-ían	they/you (form., pl.)	

Hacía mucho deporte.
I was doing / used to do a lot of sport.

You can also say what you <u>used to do</u> using the <u>imperfect tense</u> of the verb 'soler' ('solía') and then the <u>infinitive</u>.

Solía viajar mucho. *I used to travel a lot.*

Irregular verbs in the imperfect tense

1) 'Ser', 'ir' and 'ver' are the only three verbs which <u>don't</u> follow the pattern. 'Ser' and 'ir' are <u>irregular</u>...

ser — *to be*

I was	era	éramos	we were	
you (inf., sing.) were	eras	erais	you (inf., pl.) were	
he/she/it/you (form., sing.) was (were)	era	eran	they/you (form., pl.) were	

Mi padre era pintor.
My dad was / used to be a painter.

ir — *to go*

I went	iba	íbamos	we went	
you went (inf., sing.)	ibas	ibais	you went (inf., pl.)	
he/she/it/you (form., sing.) went	iba	iban	they/you (form., pl.) went	

Iba a muchos conciertos.
I went / used to go to lots of concerts.

2) ...but 'ver' is <u>almost regular</u> — just add the '-er' endings onto 've-', e.g. 'veía'.

Veía la tele. *I watched / used to watch TV.*

Había — *there was / there were*

In the <u>present tense</u> 'hay' means 'there is' or 'there are'. The <u>imperfect</u> form of 'hay' is 'había', which means 'there was' or 'there were' — it <u>stays the same</u>, regardless of whether the noun is <u>singular</u> or <u>plural</u>.

Había un mono en el árbol. *There was a monkey in the tree.*

Siempre había muchos niños allí. *There were always lots of children there.*

'Hay' and 'había' come from the verb 'haber'.

Learning the imperfect — a perfect way to spend your time...

Put these verbs into the imperfect tense. The subject is given in brackets.

1. cantar (yo)
2. ser (nosotros)
3. aprender (usted)
4. decir (él)
5. volver (ustedes)
6. seguir (vosotros)
7. nadar (tú)
8. ir (ellos)

Talking About the Past

Choosing which past tense to use can be a tricky business — even for people who have been learning Spanish for ages. Here are some guidelines to get you started — read them carefully.

Use the preterite tense to...

(1) ...talk about a single completed action in the past.

> Fui al cine el jueves.   *I went to the cinema on Thursday.*

(2) ...talk about events that happened during a set period of time.

> Ayer hizo calor.   *Yesterday it was hot.*

Remember to use 'hacer' with nouns such as 'calor', 'frío', 'viento' and 'sol' to say 'it's hot / cold / windy / sunny'. See p.36 for more weather vocabulary.

(3) ...interrupt a description of movement taking place in the imperfect tense.

> Volvía del gimnasio cuando vi a Irene.   *I was coming back from the gym when I saw Irene.*

Use the imperfect tense to...

(1) ...talk about what you used to do repeatedly in the past.

> Iba al cine cada jueves.   *I used to go to the cinema every Thursday.*

(2) ...describe something, like the weather, in the past.

> Hacía calor, pero estaba nublado.   *It was hot, but it was cloudy.*

Camping in the rain was bad enough, but imperfect tents were unforgivable...

(3) ...say where you were going when something else happened. You use the imperfect tense to describe the background situation.

> Volvía del gimnasio cuando vi a Irene.
> *I was coming back from the gym when I saw Irene.*

(4) ...say how long something had been happening for. For this, you also need 'desde hacía', which is the imperfect form of 'desde hace' (see p.76).

> Leía desde hacía una hora cuando me llamó.
> *I had been reading for an hour when he called me.*

You only need to be able to recognise this structure — you don't need to be able to use it.

Preterite or imperfect? It's a very tense business...

In each of the following sentences, choose whether you need the preterite or the imperfect tense.

1. Siempre hizo / hacía mucho viento.
2. Ayer volví / volvía de mis vacaciones.
3. ¿Fuiste / Ibas a la piscina ayer?
4. Fui / Iba al colegio cuando tuve / tenía una idea.

Talking About the Past

The perfect and pluperfect tenses allow you to say what you 'have done' or 'had done'. They're pretty easy to learn and are a useful addition to your magic bag of grammatical tricks.

Finding the past participle

1) In the sentence 'I have done', 'done' is a past participle. You need to know how to form past participles before you get started on the perfect and pluperfect tenses.

2) For '-ar' verbs, remove the 'ar' and add '-ado'.

> esperar (*to wait*) ⟶ esperado (*waited*)

3) For '-er' and '-ir' verbs, remove the 'er' or 'ir' and add '-ido'.

> comer (*to eat*) ⟶ comido (*eaten*)
> elegir (*to choose*) ⟶ elegido (*chosen*)

4) There are some irregular participles that you also need to learn...

Infinitive	Past participle	Infinitive	Past participle
abrir	abierto (*opened*)	leer	leído (*read*)
cubrir	cubierto (*covered*)	poner	puesto (*put*)
decir	dicho (*said*)	romper	roto (*broken*)
escribir	escrito (*written*)	ver	visto (*seen*)
hacer	hecho (*done / made*)	volver	vuelto (*returned*)

In these tenses, the participle stays the same — you don't need to make it feminine or plural.

He hecho — *I have done*

'I have done' is the perfect tense.

To say what you 'have done', you need the present tense of the verb 'haber' and the past participle.

haber — *to have...*

I have...	he	hemos	we have...
you (inf., sing.) have...	has	habéis	you (inf., pl.) have...
he/she/it has... you (form., sing.) have...	ha	han	they have... you (form., pl.) have...

Han jugado al tenis. *They have played tennis.*
¡Ha roto la botella! *He has broken the bottle!*

Me gustaría ir a Roma porque nunca he estado allí. *I'd like to go to Rome because I've never been there.*

Había hecho — *I had done*

'I had done' is the pluperfect tense.

To say what you 'had done', you need the imperfect tense of the verb 'haber' and the past participle.

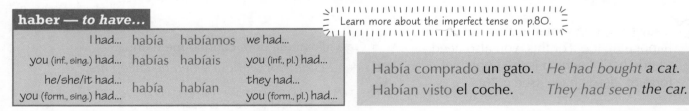

haber — *to have...*

I had...	había	habíamos	we had...
you (inf., sing.) had...	habías	habíais	you (inf., pl.) had...
he/she/it had... you (form., sing.) had...	había	habían	they had... you (form., pl.) had...

Learn more about the imperfect tense on p.80.

Había comprado un gato. *He had bought a cat.*
Habían visto el coche. *They had seen the car.*

No pude ir porque no había hecho mis deberes. *I couldn't go because I hadn't done my homework.*

If only I had learned my past participles...

Translate these sentences into Spanish using the perfect and pluperfect tenses.

1. They had sung. **3.** You have (inf., pl.) learned. **5.** I had drunk. **7.** She has followed.
2. He has travelled. **4.** You have (form., sing.) seen. **6.** We had finished. **8.** You have (inf., sing.) lived.

Talking About the Future

You'll need to talk about things that are going to happen at some point in the future.
There are two ways you can do it — and the first one's a piece of cake...

I'm going to... — *The immediate future*

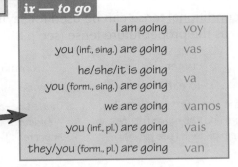

ir — *to go*

I am going	voy
you (inf., sing.) are going	vas
he/she/it is going	va
you (form., sing.) are going	
we are going	vamos
you (inf., pl.) are going	vais
they/you (form., pl.) are going	van

1) The <u>immediate future</u> tense can be used to talk about something that's <u>about to happen</u>, as well as something <u>further</u> on in the future.

2) To form the immediate future, take the <u>present tense</u> of 'ir' (*to go*) that goes with the person you're talking about.

3) Then, add '<u>a</u>' and a verb in the <u>infinitive</u>.

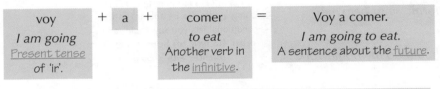

voy	+	a	+	comer	=	Voy a comer.
I am going <u>Present tense</u> of 'ir'.				*to eat* Another verb in the <u>infinitive</u>.		*I am going to eat.* A sentence about the <u>future</u>.

Susana va a leer una revista.   *Susana is going to read a magazine.*

El sábado, vamos a ir a Francia.   *On Saturday, we are going to go to France.*

Put in phrases to say when you're going to do something (p.2-3).

Just a little light reading...

I will... — *The proper future tense*

1) Use the proper <u>future tense</u> to say what will happen.

2) To form it, take the '<u>future stem</u>' of the verb — for most verbs, this is the <u>infinitive</u>.

3) Add the <u>ending</u> that matches the person you're talking about (the endings are the <u>same</u> for <u>all verbs</u>).

Future endings

	I	-é	-emos	we
	you (inf., sing.)	-ás	-éis	you (inf., pl.)
	he/she/it/you (form., sing.)	-á	-án	they/you (form., pl.)

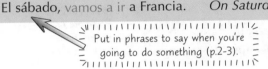

hablar	+	é	=	hablaré
infinitive		*future ending*		*I will talk.*

There are a few verbs that have a special future stem, so you just have to learn them off by heart. These are the most important ones.

Infinitive	'yo' form
decir (*to say*)	diré
haber (*to have...*)	habré
hacer (*to do / make*)	haré
tener (*to have*)	tendré
poner (*to put*)	pondré
querer (*to want*)	querré
saber (*to know*)	sabré
venir (*to come*)	vendré
salir (*to go out*)	saldré
poder (*to be able to*)	podré

Dormirás.   *You will sleep.*

Jugaré al tenis.   *I will play tennis.*

Cogerá el autobús.   *He will take the bus.*

I will win this match...

Venderemos el perro.   *We will sell the dog.*

Predicting the future might be difficult, but talking about it isn't...

Put these present tense verbs into the immediate and proper future tenses, keeping the subject the same.

1. como	**3.** baila	**5.** ponen	**7.** puedes	**9.** queremos
2. tenemos	**4.** doy	**6.** jugáis	**8.** canta	**10.** vivís

Would, Could and Should

Now it's time to talk about what could or would happen in the future.

Future stem + imperfect -er / -ir endings — *The conditional*

1) The <u>conditional</u> tense can be used for saying '<u>would</u>'. It uses the <u>same</u> <u>stems</u> as the proper future tense (see p.83) and adds these endings:

Conditional endings	
I	-ía
you (inf., sing.)	-ías
he/she/it/you (form., sing.)	-ía
we	-íamos
you (inf., pl.)	-íais
they/you (form., pl.)	-ían

comer		comía		comería
to eat	+	*I was eating.*	=	*I would eat.*
This is the <u>infinitive</u>. <u>Not</u> all verbs use the same future stem though (see p.83).		This is the -er / -ir ending of the imperfect tense.		A sentence in the <u>conditional</u>.

Podría ayudarme?	*Could you (form., sing) help me?*

Using 'poder' (to be able to) in the conditional lets you say 'could', and 'deber' (to have to) helps you form sentences with 'should'.

Debería hacer mis deberes.	*I should do my homework.*

2) You can <u>combine</u> the conditional with other tenses to make more <u>complicated</u> sentences:

Bailaría, pero me duelen los pies.	*I would dance, but my feet hurt.*

Les gustaría ir a la playa, sin embargo no pueden ir porque está lloviendo. *They would like to go to the beach, however they can't go because it's raining.*

For more on conjunctions, check out p.73.

3) If you want to seriously <u>wow</u> the examiners, use the <u>conditional</u> tense of '<u>haber</u>' (*to have...*) with the <u>past participle</u> (see p.82) to mean '<u>would have</u>...'.

Habría comprado un libro, pero no tengo dinero.	*I would have bought a book, but I have no money.*

Quisiera — *I would like*

Two really common verbs sometimes get <u>replaced</u> in the conditional by a <u>different form</u>.

1) The conditional form of '<u>querer</u>' (*to want*) is often replaced by '<u>quisiera</u>' — it means '*I would like*'.

Quisiera un coche.	*I would like a car.*		Quisiera una manzana.	*I would like an apple.*

2) You can use 'quisiera' in <u>polite requests</u>.

Quisiera reservar una mesa para tres personas.	*I would like to reserve a table for three.*

3) The conditional of '<u>haber</u>' (*to have...*) can also be replaced by '<u>hubiera</u>'.

Hubiera venido antes.	*I would have come earlier.*

'Quisiera' and 'hubiera' are in the imperfect subjunctive. See p.90 for more.

You can move on to the next topic, on one condition...

... *write these verbs in the conditional. The subject has been given to you in brackets.*

1. ir (tú)
2. cantar (él)
3. venir (nosotros)
4. decir (vosotros)
5. partir (yo)
6. salir (ellos)
7. hablar (usted)
8. tener (nosotros)

Reflexive Verbs

Sometimes you'll have to talk about things you do to yourself — like 'washing yourself' or 'getting yourself up' in the morning. It sounds weird in English, but in Spanish they do it all the time.

Me, te, se... — *Reflexive pronouns*

1) '<u>Se</u>' means '<u>oneself</u>'. Here are all the different ways to say 'self':

myself	me	ourselves	nos
yourself (inf., sing.)	te	yourselves (inf., pl.)	os
himself/herself/oneself yourself (form., sing.)	se	themselves, each other yourselves (form., pl.)	se

You can tell which verbs need 'self' by checking in the dictionary. 'To get washed' in the dictionary would be 'lavarse'.

2) Reflexive verbs follow a straightforward pattern, e.g. '<u>lavarse</u>' = to get washed (literally '<u>to wash oneself</u>'). The <u>reflexive pronoun</u> usually just goes in <u>front</u> of the normal <u>verb</u>.

I get washed	me lavo	we get washed	nos lavamos
you (inf., sing.) get washed	te lavas	you (inf., pl.) get washed	os laváis
he/she/it gets washed you (form., sing.) get washed	se lava	they get washed you (form., pl.) get washed	se lavan

I hope that's p.m...

¿Te sientes **mal**?	*Do you feel ill?*	No me despierto **temprano**.	*I don't wake up early.*

3) There are lots of these verbs, but here are the ones you really <u>should know</u>:

'acostarse', 'sentirse', 'despertarse' and 'vestirse' are all radical-changing verbs (see p.77).

acostarse	*to go to bed*	sentirse	*to feel*	despertarse	*to wake up*	vestirse	*to get dressed*
levantarse	*to get up*	llamarse	*to be called*	irse	*to go away*	ponerse	*to put on*

Putting reflexive verbs in the perfect tense

When you want to use reflexive verbs in the <u>perfect tense</u>, put the <u>reflexive pronoun</u> (e.g. 'me', 'se') in front of the <u>verb</u> as usual:

Me Stick the reflexive pronoun at the start.	+	he puesto Then put the whole of the perfect tense verb (see p.82).	=	Me he puesto el sombrero. *I've put on my hat.*

Use 'se' to make impersonal phrases

The reflexive pronoun '<u>se</u>' is often used in front of a verb that's not reflexive to make it <u>impersonal</u>. It's like saying '<u>one does something</u>' in English. The verb has to be in the '<u>he / she / it</u>' form.

¿Se puede **comer** afuera?	*Can one eat outside?*

For more about impersonal verbs, turn to p.88.

Just me, <u>myself</u> and I revising reflexive verbs...

Write these reflexive verbs in the present and perfect tenses. The subject has been given to you in brackets.

1. llamarse (yo)   **3.** lavarse (él)   **5.** sentirse (nosotros)   **7.** vestirse (usted)
2. levantarse (ellos)   **4.** acostarse (tú)   **6.** irse (vosotros)   **8.** despertarse (tú)

Verbs with '-ing' and 'Just Done'

The continuous tenses are great if you want to specify that something is ongoing at a particular moment.

Use the present continuous for something happening right now

1) <u>Most</u> of the time you'd translate phrases such as 'I am doing' and 'I was doing' with <u>normal tenses</u> — those two would be 'hago' (present tense), and 'hacía' (imperfect tense).

2) If you want <u>to stress</u> that something <u>is happening</u> at the moment, use the <u>present continuous</u>.

> Estoy almorzando.   *I'm having lunch.*

3) To form the present continuous, you need the correct part of '<u>estar</u>' (*to be*) in the <u>present</u> tense...

4) ...and the '<u>-ing</u>' part — also called the <u>present participle</u> or <u>gerund</u>.

estar — *to be*	
I am	estoy
you (inf., sing.) are	estás
he/she/it is you (form., sing.) are	está
we are	estamos
you (inf., pl.) are	estáis
they / you (form., pl.) are	están

5) It's made up of the <u>stem</u> of the verb (p.76), plus the correct <u>ending</u>.

   a) if it's an -<u>ar</u> verb, add '-<u>ando</u>'.

estoy	+	hablar	+	-ando	=	estoy hablando
present of 'estar'		*'hablar' stem*		*-ar ending*		*I am speaking*

   b) if it's an -<u>er</u> or -<u>ir</u> verb, add '-<u>iendo</u>'.

estás	+	comer	+	-iendo	=	estás comiendo
present of 'estar'		*'comer' stem*		*-er ending*		*you (inf., sing.) are eating*

6) There are only a few <u>irregular</u> ones you need to <u>know</u>:

caer (*to fall*)	→	cayendo		servir (*to serve*)	→	sirviendo
leer (*to read*)	→	leyendo		pedir (*to ask for*)	→	pidiendo
oír (*to hear*)	→	oyendo		morir (*to die*)	→	muriendo
construir (*to build*)	→	construyendo		decir (*to say*)	→	diciendo

The imperfect continuous is for saying what was happening

1) If you want <u>to stress</u> that something <u>was happening</u> in the past, use the <u>imperfect continuous</u>.

2) The imperfect continuous is <u>similar</u> to the present continuous, except '<u>estar</u>' has to be in the <u>imperfect</u> tense.

> Estaba durmiendo cuando sonó el teléfono.
> *He / She was sleeping when the telephone rang.*

> The <u>preterite</u> tense is used here to show that a <u>sudden</u> action — the telephone ringing — <u>interrupted</u> an <u>ongoing</u> action in the <u>imperfect continuous</u> — i.e. the person sleeping.

'Acabar de' — *to say that something's just happened*

> 'Acabar' is a regular -ar verb.

To say what's <u>just</u> happened, use the present tense of '<u>acabar</u>', followed by '<u>de</u>' and a verb in the <u>infinitive</u>.

> Acabo de ducharme.   *I have just taken a shower.*

> Acaba de salir.   *She has just left.*

Learning, learning and more learning...

Put these verbs in the present continuous, the imperfect continuous and the 'acabar de' forms.

1. caer (él)	3. saltar (ella)	5. correr (vosotros)	7. dar (tú)	9. servir (ustedes)
2. abrir (tú)	4. decir (ellos)	6. seguir (nosotros)	8. leer (yo)	10. bailar (nosotros)

Negative Forms

No, I'm not going to write anything here about negatives. Nothing at all... except that they're pretty useful.

'No' in front of the verb means 'not'

1) To change a sentence to mean the <u>opposite</u> in Spanish, you have to put '<u>no</u>' in front of the <u>action word</u>:

| Soy profesor. | *I'm a teacher.* | → | No soy profesor. | *I'm not a teacher.* |

| Hablo español. | *I speak Spanish.* | → | No hablo español. | *I don't speak Spanish.* |

2) You can do the <u>same</u> with <u>all of the tenses</u> — look at these examples:

| No vas a leer el libro. | *You're not going to read the book.* | No fui al parque. | *I didn't go to the park.* |

Sometimes you have to say 'no' twice...

1) 'No' in Spanish means both '<u>no</u>' and '<u>not</u>'.

2) This means that if you're answering a <u>question</u>, you may need to say 'no' <u>twice</u>:

| No, no quiero sopa, gracias. | *No, I don't want soup, thanks.* |

| No, Juan no veía la tele. | *No, Juan wasn't watching TV.* |

He wasn't remotely interested in any of the programmes.

Even more negatives...

There are more negatives you need to <u>understand</u> — for top marks you should use them too.

ya no	not any more
no ... nadie	not anybody (nobody)
no ... nunca / jamás	not ever (never)
no ... nada	not anything (nothing)
no ... ni ... ni	neither ... nor
no ... ningún / ninguna	none / not one / not a single (before noun)
no .. ninguno / ninguna	none / not one / not a single one (to replace noun)

Ya no voy a York.
I don't go to York any more.

No hay nadie aquí.
There isn't anybody here. / There's nobody here.

Julia no va nunca al cine.
Julia never goes to the cinema.

No hay nada.
There isn't anything. / There's nothing.

Sam y Clara no van ni a Londres ni a Madrid.
Sam and Clara go to neither London nor Madrid.

No hay ningún plátano. *There is not a single banana.*

No hay ninguna pera. *There is not a single pear.*

Jo no tiene ninguno/a. *Jo doesn't have a single one.*

p.62 has more information on 'ningún'.

On a positive note, that's the negatives finished...

Translate these sentences using negative forms.

1. I didn't go to the cinema.
2. We don't go to the gym any more.
3. You (tú) go to neither Oslo nor Faro.
4. Sally doesn't have a single apple.
5. There's nothing here.
6. There's nobody in the car.

The Passive and Impersonal Verbs

Impersonal verbs and the passive come up occasionally, so it's important that you know a bit about them.

Ser + past participle — *The passive voice*

> You don't need to use the passive, but you do need to be able to recognise it.

1) In an <u>active</u> sentence, the <u>subject does</u> something.　　Lavé la taza.　　*I washed the cup.*

2) In the <u>passive</u> voice, something is <u>done to</u> the <u>subject</u>.　　La taza fue lavada.　　*The cup was washed.*

3) This means you can say something is <u>happening</u> without always saying <u>who</u> is doing it.

4) The passive is formed using '<u>ser</u>' (*to be*) and the <u>past participle</u> (see p.82).

<table>
<tr><td>fueron
they were

This is the <u>preterite tense</u> of 'ser' (*see p.79*). This changes depending on the tense and subject.</td><td>+</td><td>limpiado
cleaned

<u>past participle</u> of the verb '<u>limpiar</u>'</td><td>=</td><td>Las mesas fueron limpiadas.
The tables were cleaned.
A sentence in the <u>passive</u> voice.</td></tr>
</table>

In the passive, the past participle must <u>always</u> match the <u>gender</u> and <u>number</u> of the <u>object</u> that you're talking about. Here 'limpiadas' is used because 'las mesas' are <u>feminine</u> and <u>plural</u>.

5) If you want to add <u>someone</u> or <u>something</u> doing the action, add '<u>por</u>' (*by*) and <u>who / what</u> did it.

El libro será leído por Jo.　　*The book will be read by Jo.*　　Fue escrito por Jordi.　　*It was written by Jordi.*

Se + 3rd person — *Impersonal verbs*

1) You can turn <u>any</u> Spanish verb into an <u>impersonal verb</u> (e.g. '*one does*' rather than '*I do*') by using '<u>se</u>' and the '<u>he / she / it</u>' form of the verb:

¿Se necesita un libro?　　*Does one need a book?*　　¿Se habla francés aquí?　　*Does one speak French here?*

2) If there's a <u>subject</u> in the sentence, use the <u>singular</u> for a single subject, and the <u>plural</u> for plural subjects:

El arroz se cocina durante quince minutos.　　*The rice is cooked for fifteen minutes.*

Las puertas se abren a las nueve.　　*The doors are opened at nine.*

Some more important impersonal verbs...

1) '<u>Hay que</u>' is an impersonal way of saying that '<u>one has to</u> do something'.

Hay que hacer los deberes.　　*Homework has to be done.* ← Literally: *One has to do homework.*

My essay on invisibility.

2) '<u>Parece que</u>' means '*it seems that*':　　Parece que todo ha cambiado.　　*It seems that everything has changed.*

3) <u>Weather</u> verbs are <u>always impersonal</u> — they're written in the '<u>he / she / it</u>' form of the verb.

Llueve.　　*It rains.*　　Está nevando.　　*It's snowing.*　　Truena.　　*It thunders.*

> Tronar (*to thunder*) is a radical-changing verb.

One has to learn this — it's nothing personal...

A) *Decide which of these 4 sentences are in the passive voice.*
1. Comimos la sopa.
2. El poema fue escrito.
3. La mesa es puesta.
4. Cierras la puerta.

B) *Complete using the impersonal form.*
1. .... la bufanda. (comprar)
2. .... los postres. (comer)

The Subjunctive

Oh yes, you're in for a treat — it's time to learn about the Spanish subjunctive...

Forming the present subjunctive

1) Sometimes, the <u>present subjunctive</u> is needed <u>instead</u> of the <u>normal present</u> tense.

2) To <u>form</u> the subjunctive, use the same <u>stem</u> as the 'I' form of the normal <u>present tense</u>.

3) For -<u>ar</u> verbs, add the -<u>er</u> present tense <u>endings</u>. For -<u>er</u> or -<u>ir</u> verbs, add the -<u>ar</u> endings.

infinitive	hablar	comer	vivir
'yo form'	**hablo**	**como**	**vivo**
I	hable	coma	viva
you (inf., sing.)	hables	comas	vivas
he/she/it/you (form., sing.)	hable	coma	viva
we	hablemos	comamos	vivamos
you (inf., pl.)	habléis	comáis	viváis
they/you (form., pl.)	hablen	coman	vivan

Irregular verbs in the present subjunctive

1) Some verbs are <u>irregular</u> in the 'I' form of the <u>present</u> tense, so the <u>subjunctive</u> has to <u>match</u> this.

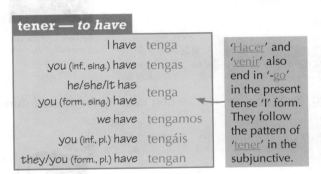

tener — _to have_

I have	tenga
you (inf., sing.) have	tengas
he/she/it has you (form., sing.) have	tenga
we have	tengamos
you (inf., pl.) have	tengáis
they/you (form., pl.) have	tengan

'<u>Hacer</u>' and '<u>venir</u>' also end in '-<u>go</u>' in the present tense 'I' form. They follow the pattern of '<u>tener</u>' in the subjunctive.

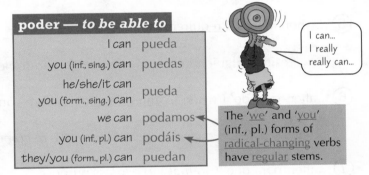

poder — _to be able to_

I can	pueda
you (inf., sing.) can	puedas
he/she/it can you (form., sing.) can	pueda
we can	podamos
you (inf., pl.) can	podáis
they/you (form., pl.) can	puedan

I can... I really really can...

The '<u>we</u>' and '<u>you</u>' (inf., pl.) forms of <u>radical-changing</u> verbs have <u>regular</u> stems.

2) But <u>some verbs</u> are completely <u>irregular</u> in the <u>subjunctive</u>. Here are some of them:

ser — _to be_

I am	sea	seamos	we are
you (inf., sing.) are	seas	seáis	you (inf., pl.) are
he/she/it is you (form., sing.) are	sea	sean	they are you (form., pl.) are

estar — _to be_

I am	esté	estemos	we are
you (inf., sing.) are	estés	estéis	you (inf., pl.) are
he/she/it is you (form., sing.) are	esté	estén	they are you (form., pl.) are

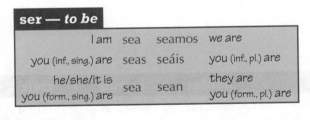

ir — _to go_

I go	vaya	vayamos	we go
you (inf., sing.) go	vayas	vayáis	you (inf., pl.) go
he/she/it goes you (form., sing.) go	vaya	vayan	they go you (form., pl.) go

dar — _to give_

I give	dé	demos	we give
you (inf., sing.) give	des	deis	you (inf., pl.) give
he/she/it gives you (form., sing.) give	dé	den	they give you (form., pl.) give

I want you to revise the subjunctive...

Write these verbs in the present subjunctive. The subject has been given to you in brackets.

1. saltar (tú)
2. escuchar (yo)
3. limpiar (nosotros)
4. abrir (ellos)
5. venir (él)
6. hacer (nosotros)
7. poder (ustedes)
8. tener (vosotros)

The Subjunctive

Now it's time to find out when you need to use the subjunctive. It's a tricky old page so take your time.

Use the present subjunctive...

(1) ...to get <u>someone else</u> to do something:

> Ana quiere que lavemos los platos. *Ana wants us to wash the dishes.*

(2) ...to express a <u>wish</u> or <u>desire</u>:

> Espero que haya fresas en el supermercado. *I hope that there are strawberries in the supermarket.*

(3) ...after expressing an <u>emotion</u> or <u>opinion</u>:

> Es importante que estudiéis. *It's important that you (inf., pl.) study.*

(4) ...to say that something's <u>unlikely</u> to happen:

> No creo que vaya a venir. *I don't believe he's going to come.*

'sepa' is from the verb 'saber' (to know). It's also irregular in the subjunctive — its stem is 'sep'.

Between cooking and the subjunctive, these guys had a lot on their plates.

(5) ...when there's a <u>requirement</u>:

> Necesito a alguien que sepa cocinar. *I need someone who knows how to cook.*

(6) ...after '<u>cuando</u>' ('*when*'), '<u>antes de que</u>' ('*before*') and '<u>aunque</u>' ('*even if*') when talking about the future:

> Vamos al teatro cuando llegue Marta. *We're going to the theatre when Marta arrives.*

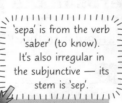

(7) ...after '<u>para que</u>' ('*so that*') to express purpose:

> Van a la tienda para que pueda comprar leche. *They're going to the shop so that he can buy milk.*

If I *were* to go to Spain...

1) The <u>imperfect subjunctive</u> is like the '<u>were</u>' in '*if I <u>were</u> to go to Spain*'. You <u>don't</u> need to use it, but you'll need to <u>recognise</u> it.

2) '<u>Quisiera</u>' ('*I would like*') is a <u>common example</u> of the imperfect subjunctive. See p.84 for more about using it in <u>polite requests</u>.

	hablar	**comer**	**vivir**
I	hablara	comiera	viviera
you (inf., sing.)	hablaras	comieras	vivieras
he/she/it/you (form., sing.)	hablara	comiera	viviera
we	habláramos	comiéramos	viviéramos
you (inf., pl.)	hablarais	comierais	vivierais
they/you (form., pl.)	hablaran	comieran	vivieran

If I were in charge, there would be no exams...

Decide which sentences use the present subjunctive and which use the imperfect subjunctive.

1. Quiere que le des el abrigo.
2. Si tuviera mucho dinero, compraría un coche.
3. Vamos a hacerlo cuando tengamos tiempo.
4. Mi madre pido que mi padre sacara la basura.

Giving Orders

Learn what's on this page and you'll be giving out orders in no time...

Informal commands

1) To form a <u>singular informal</u> command, take the 'tú' part of the <u>present tense</u> verb and <u>take off</u> the 's'.

| escribes *you write* → ¡Escribe! *Write!* | escuchas *you listen* → ¡Escucha! *Listen!* |

2) With commands, <u>pronouns</u> (e.g. *me, them, it*) are placed at the <u>end</u> of the word and you need to <u>add</u> an <u>accent</u> to show where the <u>stress</u> is.

¡Cómelo!   *Eat it!*

3) To tell <u>two or more people</u> what to do in an <u>informal</u> way, take the <u>infinitive</u> and <u>change</u> the final 'r' to a 'd'.

hablar (*to speak*) → ¡Hablad! *Speak!*

leer (*to read*) → ¡Leed! *Read!*

salir (*to go out*) → ¡Salid! *Go out!*

There are a few common irregular imperatives.

Infinitive	Informal Singular
decir (*to say*)	¡Di!
hacer (*to do / make*)	¡Haz!
ir (*to go*)	¡Ve!
poner (*to put*)	¡Pon!
salir (*to go out*)	¡Sal!
ser (*to be*)	¡Sé!
tener (*to have*)	¡Ten!
venir (*to come*)	¡Ven!

Formal commands

1) To <u>politely</u> tell someone what to do, use the <u>formal 'you'</u> form of the <u>present subjunctive</u>.

¡Hable!   *Speak!*

For a reminder of the present subjunctive, head back to p.89.

Siga todo recto.   *Continue straight on.*

Infinitive	Present Subjunctive
dar (*to give*)	dé
haber (*to have...*)	haya
ir (*to go*)	vaya
saber (*to know*)	sepa
ser (*to be*)	sea

2) As always, there are some <u>irregular forms</u> that you just need to <u>learn</u>.

3) When politely telling <u>more than one</u> person what to do, use the <u>formal plural</u> of the <u>subjunctive</u>.

¡Entren!   *Enter!*

Cojan la primera calle a la derecha.   *Take the first street on the right.*

Making commands negative

1) To tell someone <u>not</u> to do something, <u>always</u> use the <u>subjunctive</u>.

¡No escuches!   *Don't listen!*

2) Watch out — any <u>pronouns</u> have to go before the verb:

¡Tócalo!   *Touch it!* → ¡No lo toques!   *Don't touch it!*

Do these exercises — go on...

Write these verbs as positive and negative commands. The type of command is in brackets.

1. cantar (inf., sing.)
2. bailar (form., pl.)
3. tener (inf., sing.)
4. dar (form., sing.)
5. abrir (inf., pl.)
6. venir (inf., pl.)
7. ser (form., sing.)
8. ir (form., pl.)

The Listening Exam

Ah. Your reward for conquering all that grammar is a section about those pesky exams... Sorry about that. But there is some good news — these pages are crammed full of advice to help you tackle them head on.

There are four exams for GCSE Spanish

1) Your Edexcel Spanish GCSE is assessed by four separate exams — Listening, Speaking, Reading and Writing.

2) Each exam is worth 25% of your final mark. You'll get a grade between 1 and 9 (with 9 being the highest).

3) You won't sit all of the papers at the same time — you'll probably have your speaking exam a couple of weeks before the rest of your exams.

The Listening Exam has two sections

If you're sitting foundation tier papers, the format of your exams will be slightly different, but this advice will still be useful.

1) For the listening paper, you'll listen to various recordings of people speaking in Spanish and answer questions on what you've heard.

2) The paper is 45 minutes long (including 5 minutes reading time) and is split into Section A and Section B.

3) Section A is the shorter section — the questions will be multiple choice, with the instructions in Spanish. Section B is longer, but the questions are in English and your answers will be, too.

Read through the paper carefully at the start of the test

1) Before the recordings begin, you'll be given five minutes to read through the paper.

Miguel read 'whole model' instead of 'role model' — it went downhill from there.

2) Use this time to read each question carefully. Some are multiple choice, and others require you to write some short answers — make sure you know what each one is asking you to do.

3) In particular, look at the questions in Section A, which are written in Spanish. Try to work out what the questions mean. There's a list of exam-style Spanish question words and phrases on the inside front cover of this book to help you prepare for this.

4) Reading the question titles, and the questions themselves, will give you a good idea of the topics you'll be asked about. This should help you predict what to listen out for.

5) You can write on the exam paper, so scribble down anything that might be useful.

Make notes while listening to the recordings

1) You'll hear each audio track twice, and then there'll be a pause for you to write down your answer.

2) While you're listening, it's a good idea to jot down a few details — e.g. dates, times, names or key words. But make sure you keep listening while you're writing down any notes.

Listen to the speaker's tone, too — this will hint at their mood, e.g. angry or excited.

3) Listen right to the end, even if you think you've got the answer — sometimes the person will change their mind or add an important detail at the end.

4) Don't worry if you can't understand every word that's being said — just listen carefully both times and try to pick out the vocabulary you need to answer the question.

Don't worry, I'm all ears...

If you've heard a track twice, and you're still not sure of the answer, scribble one down anyway — you never know, it might be the right one. You may as well write something sensible just in case — it's worth a shot.

The Speaking Exam

The Speaking Exam can seem daunting, but remember — no one is trying to catch you out, so try to stay calm.

There are three parts to the Speaking Exam

During your preparation time, you can make notes to take in with you for the first two tasks. You can't keep the notes for the conversation.

1) Your speaking exam will be conducted and recorded by your teacher.

2) The exam is in three parts. Before you start, you'll get 12 minutes to prepare for the first two sections:

① Role play (~2 min.)	② Picture-based task (~3 min.)	③ Conversation (~6 min.)
You'll get a card with a scenario on it. It'll have five bullet points — two will be notes on what to say, in Spanish. The '!' means you'll be asked an unknown question, and '?' shows you have to ask a question about the words next to it. See p.5 for an example.	Before the exam, you'll receive a photo and five bullet points relating to it (there's an example on p.41 for you to have a look at). Your teacher will ask you questions based on the prompts on the picture card, as well as one question you haven't seen.	You and your teacher will have a conversation. The conversation will have two parts. In the first part, you'll talk about the theme that you've chosen. Then, you'll discuss another theme that hasn't been covered in the second task.

3) The role play card will tell you if you need to use 'tú', but otherwise, use 'usted' to talk to your teacher.

Try to be imaginative with your answers

You need to find ways to show off the full extent of your Spanish knowledge. You should try to:

1) Use a range of tenses — e.g. for a question on daily routine, think of when something different happens.

> Pero mañana será diferente porque jugaré al tenis después del instituto.
> *But tomorrow it will be different because I will play tennis after school.*

> If you can't remember a word, just say something suitable that you do know instead, e.g. swap 'tennis' for 'rugby', or 'nephew' for 'sister'.

2) Talk about other people, not just yourself — it's fine to make people up if that helps.

> Me gusta el rugby, pero mi sobrino lo odia.
> *I like rugby, but my nephew hates it.*

3) Give loads of opinions and reasons for your opinions.

> En mi opinión, debemos reciclar más porque producimos demasiada basura.
> *In my opinion, we must recycle more because we produce too much rubbish.*

If you're really struggling, ask for help in Spanish

1) If you get really stuck trying to think of a word or phrase, you can ask for help — as long as it's in Spanish.

2) For example, if you can't remember how to say 'homework' in Spanish, ask your teacher. You won't get any marks for vocabulary your teacher's given you though.

> ¿Cómo se dice 'homework' en español?
> *How do you say 'homework' in Spanish?*

3) If you don't hear something clearly, just ask:

> ¿Puede repetir, por favor?
> *Can you repeat, please?*

> You could also ask this if you're desperately in need of time to think of an answer.

Don't speak too soon — wait for the teacher to tell you to start...

Given that you're only human, you're bound to have a few slip-ups in the speaking exam. Don't panic — it's completely natural. What's important is how you deal with a mistake — just correct yourself and move on.

The Reading Exam

After all that listening and speaking, the Reading Exam offers some nice peace and quiet. Apart from the voice inside your head that screams "WHAT ON EARTH DOES THAT WORD MEAN?!" (Or maybe that's just me...)

Read the questions and texts carefully

1) The higher tier reading paper is 1 hour long, and has three sections.

2) In Sections A and B, you'll be given a variety of Spanish texts and then asked questions about them. The texts could include blog posts, emails, newspaper reports, adverts and literary texts. Section A has questions and answers in English, and Section B has questions and answers in Spanish.

3) Section C is a translation question — you'll have to translate a short passage of text from Spanish into English. See p.96 for more tips on tackling translation questions.

4) In Sections A and B, scan through the text first to get an idea of what it's about. Then read the questions that go with it carefully, making sure you understand what information you should be looking out for.

5) Next, go back through the text. You're not expected to understand every word, so don't get distracted by trying to work out what everything means — focus on finding the information you need.

The inside front cover of this book has a list of common Spanish question words, phrases and instructions.

Don't give up if you don't understand something

1) Use the context of the text to help you understand what it might be saying. You might be able to find some clues in the title of the text or the type of text.

2) Knowing how to spot different word types (e.g. nouns, verbs) can help you work out what's happening in a sentence. See the grammar section (p.59-91) for more.

3) You can guess some Spanish words that look or sound the same as English words, e.g. el problema — *problem*, la música — *music*, el color — *colour*.

Look for words that look like ones you know, e.g. 'la comida basura'. 'La comida' means 'food', and 'basura' means 'rubbish', so you can guess it means 'junk food'.

4) Be careful though — you might come across some 'false friends'. These are Spanish words that look like an English word, but have a completely different meaning:

la nota	*mark*	la carpeta	*folder, file*	la arena	*sand*	la librería	*bookshop*	actual	*present*
el pie	*foot*	la dirección	*address*	el éxito	*success*	sensible	*sensitive*	fatal	*awful*
el campo	*countryside*	el pariente	*relative*	la ropa	*clothes*	largo	*long*	embarazada	*pregnant*

Keep an eye on the time

1) There are quite a few questions to get through in the reading exam, so you need to work at a good speed.

2) If you're having trouble with a particular question, you might want to move on and come back to it later.

Manolo and his colleagues never underestimated the importance of thyme.

3) Don't forget that the last question in the paper (Section C) is a translation — this is worth more marks than any other question, so you should leave plenty of time to tackle it.

4) Make sure you put an answer down for every question — lots of the questions are multiple choice, so even if you can't work out the answer, it's always worth putting down one of the options.

Exams are important — failing can be fatal...

Don't forget, the questions in Section B will be in Spanish. Don't panic if you don't understand them — search for any familiar vocabulary and use any answer lines or boxes to help you guess what you have to do.

The Writing Exam

The Writing Exam is a great way of showing off what you can do — try to use varied vocabulary, include a range of tenses, and pack in any clever expressions that you've learnt over the years.

There'll be three tasks in the Writing Exam

1) The higher tier writing paper is 1 hour and 20 minutes long and has three tasks.

2) Each task is worth a different number of marks, so you should spend more time on the higher-mark tasks.

① Informal writing (20 marks)

There will be two tasks to choose from. You'll be asked to write about 80-90 words in Spanish, based on four bullet points. You'll need to write about each bullet point and give opinions. The scenario for the task will be informal, so use the 'tú' form.

② Formal writing (28 marks)

There will also be two tasks to choose from. You'll need to write about 130-150 words in Spanish, based on four bullet points. Make sure you include some opinions and justify your reasons. You'll need to be more formal in this task, so use the 'usted' form.

③ Translation (12 marks)

You'll be given an English passage to translate into Spanish. The passage could be on any topic you've studied. Make sure you leave plenty of time for this task. There's more advice for doing translations on p.96.

Read the instructions carefully, and spend some time planning

1) Read the instructions for questions 1 and 2 carefully — you'll need to make sure you cover all of the bullet points. You can often use words from the question in your answer too.

2) Spend a few minutes for each question planning out your answer. Decide how you're going to cover everything that's required and in what order you're going to write things.

Try to use varied vocab and a range of tenses.

3) Write the best answer you can, using the Spanish that you know — it doesn't matter if it's not true.

Check through your work thoroughly

Checking your work is really important — even small mistakes can cost marks. Take a look at this checklist:

- Are all the verbs in the right tense?
  Mañana, trabajé en el jardín. ✘   Mañana, trabajaré en el jardín. ✓

- Are the verb endings correct?
  ¿No te gusta las fresas? ✘   ¿No te gustan las fresas? ✓

- Do your adjectives agree with their nouns?
  La camisa es amarillo. ✘   La camisa es amarilla. ✓

- Are your adjectives in the right place?
  Una blanca falda. ✘   Una falda blanca. ✓

- Do your reflexive verbs and pronouns agree?
  A las siete, me levantamos. ✘   A las siete, me levanto. ✓

- Have you spelt everything correctly, including using the right accents?
  El toca la guitar con su tio. ✘   Él toca la guitarra con su tío. ✓

All of the points on this checklist are covered in the grammar section — see p.59-91.

And lastly, don't forget your pen...

When you're nervous and stressed, it's dead easy to miss out something the question has asked you to do. For tasks one and two, try to write about the bullet points in order, and tick them off as you go along.

The Translation Tasks

When you're studying Spanish, you do little bits of translation in your head all the time. For the translation questions, you just need to apply those skills — one sentence at a time — to a couple of short passages.

In the Reading Exam, you'll translate from Spanish to English

1) The final question of the reading paper will ask you to translate a <u>short Spanish passage</u> (about 50 words) <u>into English</u>. The passage will be on a <u>topic you've studied</u>, so most of the vocabulary should be familiar.

2) Here are some <u>top tips</u> for doing your translation:

- Read the whole text <u>before you start</u>. Make some <u>notes in English</u> to remind you of the main ideas.

- Translate the text <u>one sentence at a time</u>, rather than word by word — this will avoid any of the Spanish word order being carried into the English.

Ella compra la manzana roja.	*She buys the apple red.* ✖	*She buys the red apple.* ✔
Salma lo comió.	*Salma it ate.* ✖	*Salma ate it.* ✔

- Keep an eye out for <u>different tenses</u> — there will definitely be a variety in the passage.

- <u>Read through</u> your translation to make sure it sounds <u>natural</u>. Some words and phrases don't translate literally, so you'll need to make sure that your sentences sound like <u>normal English</u>:

  Watch out for adverbs that might suggest a change in tense, e.g. en el futuro — in the future, mañana — tomorrow, ayer — yesterday.

La semana pasada, Irene hizo su maleta.	*The week last, Irene made her suitcase.* ✖	*Last week, Irene packed her suitcase.* ✔

3) Make sure you've translated <u>everything</u> from the original text — you'll lose marks if you miss something.

In the Writing Exam, you'll translate from English to Spanish

1) In the writing paper, you will have to translate <u>a short English passage</u> (about 50 words) <u>into Spanish</u>.

2) Here are <u>some ideas</u> for how you could approach the translation:

- <u>Read</u> through the <u>whole text</u> before you get started so you know exactly what the text is about.

- Tackle the passage <u>one sentence at a time</u> — work slowly and carefully through each one.

- <u>Don't</u> translate things <u>literally</u> — think about what each English sentence means and try to write it in the <u>most Spanish way</u> you know. Don't worry — the translation is likely to include similar sentences to the ones you've learnt.

  Don't try to write a perfect translation first time — do it roughly first, and then write it up properly, crossing out any old drafts. Remember to keep an eye on the time.

- Work on the <u>word order</u> — remember that most Spanish adjectives follow the noun. If you need a <u>double negative</u>, remember to include both bits.

3) Once you've got something that you're happy with, go back through and <u>check that you've covered everything</u> that was in the English.

4) Now <u>check</u> your Spanish text thoroughly using the <u>list from p.95</u>.

Thankfully, none of that got lost in translation...

Elena's translations got the seal of approval.

Congratulations — you've made it to the end of the book. 96 pages is no mean feat, so give yourself a pat on the back. Make sure you still read this page properly though, and take the translation advice on board.

Vocabulary

Section One — General Stuff

Numbers (p.1)

cero	zero
uno (un) / una	one
dos	two
tres	three
cuatro	four
cinco	five
seis	six
siete	seven
ocho	eight
nueve	nine
diez	ten
once	eleven
doce	twelve
trece	thirteen
catorce	fourteen
quince	fifteen
dieciséis	sixteen
diecisiete	seventeen
dieciocho	eighteen
diecinueve	nineteen
veinte	twenty
veintiuno	twenty-one
veintidós	twenty-two
treinta	thirty
treinta y uno	thirty-one
cuarenta	forty
cincuenta	fifty
sesenta	sixty
setenta	seventy
ochenta	eighty
noventa	ninety
ciento (cien)	hundred
ciento setenta y siete	one hundred and seventy-seven
doscientos/as	two hundred
quinientos veintiocho	five hundred and twenty-eight
novecientos noventa y tres	nine hundred and ninety-three
mil	thousand
mil cuatrocientos cincuenta y tres	one thousand four hundred and fifty-three
millón	million
primero / primera	first
segundo/a	second
tercero/a	third
cuarto/a	fourth
quinto/a	fifth
sexto/a	sixth
séptimo/a	seventh
octavo/a	eighth
noveno/a	ninth
décimo/a	tenth
una docena	dozen
el número	number

un par	pair / couple
unos (diez)	about (10)
una cifra	a figure

Times and Dates (p.2-3)

el lunes	Monday
el martes	Tuesday
el miércoles	Wednesday
el jueves	Thursday
el viernes	Friday
el sábado	Saturday
el domingo	Sunday
enero	January
febrero	February
marzo	March
abril	April
mayo	May
junio	June
julio	July
agosto	August
septiembre	September
octubre	October
noviembre	November
diciembre	December
la estación	season
el invierno	winter
el otoño	autumn
la primavera	spring
el verano	summer
a diario	daily / everyday
a eso de ...	at about ...
a fines de ...	at / to the end of ...
a mediados de ...	around the middle of ...
a menudo	often
a partir de	from
a veces	sometimes
ahora	now / nowadays
al mismo tiempo	at the same time
algunas veces	sometimes
anoche	last night
el año	year
anteayer	the day before yesterday
antes (de)	before
ayer	yesterday
breve	brief / short
cada (...) días / horas	every (...) days / hours
casi	nearly
de momento	at the moment / right now
de nuevo	again
de repente	suddenly
de vez en cuando	now and then / from time to time
dentro de (...) días / horas	within (...) days / hours

desde	since
desde hace	since
despacio	slowly
después (de)	after / afterwards
el día	day
durante	during / for
durar	to last
en seguida / enseguida	straightaway
esta noche	tonight
la fecha	date
el fin de semana	weekend
hace (un mes)	a month ago
hace (un mes) que	it's been a month since
hoy	today
lento	slow
los lunes etc.	(on) Mondays etc.
luego	then / afterwards
mañana	tomorrow
la mañana	morning
la medianoche	midnight
el mediodía	noon
el mes	month
mientras tanto	meanwhile
el minuto	minute
mucho tiempo	a long time
la noche	night
otra vez	again
el pasado	past
pasado (adj)	past / last
pasado mañana	the day after tomorrow
pocas veces	seldom / a few times
por año	per year
por fin	at last
por lo general	generally
el porvenir	future
al principio	at the beginning
pronto	soon
próximo	next
que viene (el mes etc.)	next (month etc.)
quince días	fortnight
el rato	while / short time
la semana	week
siempre	always
el siglo	century
siguiente	next / following
sobre	on / around
solo (sólo)	only
tardar	to take time
tarde	late
la tarde	afternoon / evening
la temporada	period / spell / season
temprano	early

tener prisa	to be in a hurry
el tiempo	time
todas (las semanas)	every (week)
todavía	still / yet
todos (los días / meses)	every (day / month)
último	last
una vez	once
dos veces	twice

Questions (p.4-5)

¿(a)dónde?	where (to)?
¿a qué hora?	at what time?
¿cómo?	how?
¿cuál(es)?	which?
¿cuándo?	when?
¿cuánto?	how much?
¿cuánto cuesta(n)?	how much does it / do they cost?
¿cuánto es?	how much is it?
¿cuánto vale(n)?	how much does it / do they cost?
¿cuántos...?	how many?
¿cuántos años tiene(s)?	how old are you?
¿de dónde?	where from?
¿de qué color (es)?	what colour (is it)?
¿de quién?	whose?
¿es...?	is it...?
¿por cuánto tiempo?	for how long?
¿por dónde?	through where?
¿por qué?	why?
¿qué?	what?
¿qué día?	what day?
¿qué fecha?	what date?
¿qué hora es?	what time is it?
¿quién?	who?

Being Polite (p.6-7)

¡Adiós!	Goodbye!
así así	so-so
¡Basta ya!	That's enough!
¡Bienvenido/a!	Welcome!
¡Buen viaje!	Have a good trip!
¡Buena suerte!	Good luck!
¡Buenas noches!	Good night!
¡Buenas tardes!	Good afternoon! / Good evening!
¡Buenos días!	Good morning! / Good day!
¡Claro!	Of course!
¿Cómo está(s)?	How are you?
con permiso	excuse me
¡Cuidado!	Careful! Watch out!
De nada.	You're welcome. / Don't mention it.
¿De veras?	Really?
Encantado/a.	Pleased to meet you.
¡Enhorabuena!	Congratulations!
Este/a es...	This is...
fatal	terrible
¡Felices vacaciones!	Have a good holiday!

¡Felicidades!	Best wishes! / Congratulations!
¡Felicitaciones!	Congratulations!
hasta el (lunes)	till / see you (Monday)
hasta luego	see you later
hasta mañana	see you tomorrow
hasta pronto	see you soon
¡Hola!	Hi! / Hello!
Le presento a...	May I introduce...?
Lo siento.	I'm sorry.
muchas gracias	thank you very much
Mucho gusto.	Pleased to meet you.
(muy) bien	(very) well
no muy bien	not very well
¡Ojo!	Watch out! Careful!
perdón	sorry / excuse me
perdone	sorry / excuse me
por favor	please
¿Puedo...?	May I... ?
¡Qué (+ adjective)!	How... !
¡Qué (+ noun)!	What a... !
¿Qué hay?	What's happening? What's the matter?
¡Que lo pase(s) bien!	Have a good time!
¿Qué pasa?	What's happening? What's the matter?
¿Qué tal?	How are you? How's... ?
¡Qué va!	Come on! Rubbish! Nonsense!
Quisiera...	I would like...
saludar	to greet / say hello
saludos	greetings / best wishes
¡Socorro!	Help!
vale	OK

Opinions (p.8-10)

aburrido	boring / bored
aburrirse	to get bored
adorar	to adore / to love
agradable	pleasant / nice / kind
amable	nice / kind / friendly
antiguo	old / former
aprovechar	to make the most of
aprovecharse (de)	to take advantage (of)
asqueroso	disgusting
barato	cheap
bonito	pretty
bueno	good
la calidad	quality
caro	expensive
creer	to believe
decepcionante	disappointing
decir	to say
desagradable	unpleasant
desear	to wish
la desventaja	disadvantage
disfrutar	to enjoy
distinto	different
divertido	amusing / fun / entertaining

divertirse	to enjoy yourself
dudar	to doubt
duro	hard
emocionante	exciting / thrilling / moving
encantador	charming
encantar	to delight
entretenido	entertaining / amusing
entusiasmado	excited
esperar	to hope
estar a favor	to be in favour of
estar de acuerdo	to agree
estar en contra	to be against
estupendo	fantastic / great
fabuloso	fabulous
fácil	easy
fantástico	fantastic
fastidiar	to annoy / to bother
fatal	awful / fatal
fenomenal	great / fantastic
feo	ugly
genial	brilliant / great
guay	cool
hermoso	beautiful
impresionante	impressive / striking
increíble	incredible
inseguro	unsafe / uncertain
interesante	interesting
interesar(se)	to interest / to be interested in
inútil	useless
malo	bad
maravilloso	marvellous
Me da igual.	I don't mind.
nuevo	new
odiar	to hate
opinar	to think / to give an opinion
parecer	to seem
pasarlo bien / mal	to have a good / bad time
pensar	to think
perfecto	perfect
ponerse de acuerdo	to agree
porque	because
precioso	precious / beautiful
preferir	to prefer
quedar en	to agree
querer decir	to mean
la razón	reason
raro	strange
ridículo	ridiculous
seguro	safe / certain
sencillo	simple / plain / straightforward
sentir(se)	to feel
sorprendido	surprised
tener ganas de hacer algo	to be keen to do something
tonto	silly
tranquilo	peaceful / quiet
único	unique / only

útil	useful
valer la pena	to be worth the trouble
la ventaja	advantage
viejo	old

Comparisons (p.66-68)

bastante	sufficient / enough / quite
comparar	to compare
demasiado	too, too much
igual que	same as
más (que)	more (than)
mayor	main / larger / bigger / greater / older
la mayoría	most / majority
mejor	better / best
menor	smaller / less / least / younger
menos (que)	less (than)
mismo	same
muy	very
parecido a	like / similar to
peor	worse / worst
poco (e.g. poco ruidoso)	not very
tan ... como	as ... as
tanto ... como	as much ... as

Conjunctions (p.73)

a pesar de	in spite of / despite
así que	so / therefore
aun (si)	even (if)
aunque	although / (even) though
como	as / since
cuando	when
de manera que	in such a way that
entonces	then
incluso	even
mientras (que)	while, meanwhile
o / u	or
pero	but
por eso	for that reason / therefore
por lo tanto	therefore
porque	because
pues	then / since
si	if
sin embargo	however
tal vez	maybe / perhaps
también	also
y / e	and
ya (que)	as / since

Prepositions (p.74)

a	to / at
de	from / of
en	in / at
hacia	towards
hasta	until
para	for
por	through / by / in / for / per

según	according to
sin	without

Negative Forms (p.87)

jamás	never
nada	nothing
nadie	nobody
ni ... ni	neither ... nor
ninguno	none / no-one
nunca	never
sino	but (rather) / except
tampoco	neither / not ... either ...
ya no	not any more

Access

abierto	open
abrir	to open
cerrado	closed
cerrar	to close
gratis	free (of charge)
gratuito	free (of charge)
libre	free / unoccupied
ocupado	engaged / occupied
permitir	to allow
prohibido	forbidden
prohibir	to forbid / ban

Colours

amarillo	yellow
azul	blue
blanco	white
claro	light
el color	colour
gris	grey
marrón	brown
naranja	orange
negro	black
oscuro	dark
rojo	red
rosa / rosado	pink
verde	green
vivo	vivid / bright

Common Abbreviations

el AVE	high-speed train
el DNI	ID card
EEUU (Estados Unidos)	USA
ESO	secondary education
Renfe / RENFE	Spanish railways
TALGO	fast train service
UE	European Union

Connectives

además	moreover / besides
aparte de	apart from
claro que	of course
dado que	given that
es decir	in other words / that is to say
por un lado / por otro lado	on the one hand / on the other hand
por una parte / por otra parte	on the one hand / on the other hand

sin duda	obviously / certainly

Correctness

cierto	certain / sure / true
corregir	to correct
equivocado	wrong
equivocarse	to make a mistake
estar equivocado	to be wrong
la falta	error
mal	badly
mentir	to lie
la mentira	lie / untruth
mentiroso	liar
la razón	reason
tener razón	to be right
la verdad	truth
verdadero	true

Dialogues and Messages

el auricular	receiver
con relación a	further to
de hecho	in fact
descolgar el teléfono	to lift the receiver
¿Diga? / ¿Dígame?	Hello? (on the phone)
en contacto con	in communication with
enviado por	sent by
Le paso.	I'll put you through.
Llámeme.	Call me.
marcar el número	to dial the number
Un momento.	One moment.
No cuelgue.	Stay on the line.
el número equivocado	wrong number
el prefijo	area code
el teléfono	telephone
Vuelvo enseguida.	I'll be right back.

Important Verbs

acabar de + infinitivo	to have just (done something)
aceptar	to accept
acompañar	to accompany
aconsejar	to advise
añadir	to add
arrepentirse	to regret
averiguar	to check
caer	to fall
comenzar	to begin
conducir	to drive
contar	to tell / count
continuar	to carry on
dar	to give
darse cuenta (de)	to realise / note
deber	must / have to
decidir	to decide
dejar de (hacer algo)	to stop (doing something)
despedirse	to say goodbye
echar	to throw
echar de menos	to miss
empezar	to begin

Vocabulary

estar	to be
estar a punto de (hacer algo)	to be about to (do something)
estar constipado / resfriado	to have a cold
evitar	to avoid
firmar	to sign
fumar	to smoke
hace(n) falta	to need / to be necessary
hacer	to do / to make
hay	there is / there are
hay que	one must / one has to
intentar	to try
invitar	to invite
ir	to go
ir a (hacer algo)	to be going to (do something)
llamar a la puerta	to knock on the door
llorar	to cry
marcharse	to leave / go away
mejorar	to improve
merecer	to deserve

necesitar	to need
ocurrir	to happen
pasar	to happen / to spend (time)
poder	to be able / can
poner	to put
prevenir	to prevent
querer	to want / to love
quisiera...	I'd like...
romper	to break
saber	to know (a fact / how to do something)
sacar entradas	to buy tickets (for a show)
saltar	to jump
seguir	to continue / to follow
ser	to be
ser capaz de	to be able to
soler	to usually do something
tener	to have / to own
tener cuidado	to be careful

tener éxito	to be successful
tener lugar	to take place
tener prisa	to be in a hurry
tener que	to have to do something
tener sueño	to be sleepy
torcer	to twist / turn
traer	to bring
volver a hacer algo	to do something again

Materials

el algodón	cotton
el cuero	leather
la lana	wool
el lino	linen
el papel	paper
la seda	silk
el terciopelo	velvet
el vidrio	glass

Section Two — About Me

You and Your Family (p.11-12)

el/la abuelo/a	grandfather / grandmother
el/la adolescente	adolescent
adoptado	adopted
el apellido	last name
el apodo	nickname
el bebé	baby
cuidar	to look after
el cumpleaños	birthday
cumplir años	to have a birthday
la edad	age
el/la familiar	relative
el/la gemelo/a	twin
la gente	people
el/la hermanastro/a	stepbrother / stepsister
el/la hijo/a (único/a)	(only) child
los hijos	children
el hogar	home
llamarse	to be called
la madrastra	stepmother
la madre	mother
la mamá	mum
el marido	husband
menor de edad	underage
el miembro	member
la mujer	wife
nacer	to be born
nacido	born
el nacimiento	birth
la nacionalidad	nationality
el/la nieto/a	grandchild
el/la niño/a	child
el nombre (de pila)	(first) name

la nuera	daughter-in-law
el padrastro	stepfather
el padre, los padres	father, parents
el papá	dad
los parientes	relatives
el/la primo/a	cousin
el/la sobrino/a	nephew / niece
tener ... años	to be ... years old
el/la tío/a	uncle / aunt
el/la vecino/a	neighbour
el yerno	son-in-law

Describing People (p.13-14)

alegre	happy
alto	tall
(de) altura mediana	(of) medium height
amable	kind
el/la anciano/a	old person
animado	lively
antipático	unpleasant
el aspecto	appearance / looks
atrevido	daring / cheeky
autoritario	bossy
bajo	short (height)
la barba	beard
barbudo	bearded
el bigote	moustache
callado	quiet / reserved
calvo	bald
la cara	face
la característica	character trait
cariñoso	affectionate / tender
castaño	chestnut / brown
celoso	jealous
comprensivo	understanding

cortés	polite
corto	short (length)
débil	weak
delgado	slim
deportista	sporty
deprimido	depressed
egoísta	selfish
encantador	charming
engreído	conceited
equilibrado	well-balanced
feliz	happy
flaco	thin
fuerte	strong
las gafas	glasses
generoso	generous
gordo	fat
gracioso	funny
el grano	spot / pimple
guapo	good-looking
hablador	chatty / talkative
honrado	honest
joven	young
el/la joven	young person
la juventud	youth / young people
lacio	straight / lank (hair)
largo	long
leal	loyal
liso	straight (hair)
loco	mad
maduro	mature
maleducado	rude
mono	pretty
moreno	dark (-haired / -skinned)

Vocabulary

el ojo	eye
parecerse a	to look like
las pecas	freckles
el/la pensionista	pensioner
pelirrojo	red-haired
el pelo	hair
perezoso	lazy / idle
la persona mayor	adult
la personalidad	personality
pretencioso	pretentious
racista	racist
razonable	reasonable
rico	wealthy / rich
rizado	curly
rubio	blonde
seguro de sí mismo	self-confident
sensible	sensitive
el sentido del humor	sense of humour
serio	serious / responsible
sexista	sexist
simpático	kind / nice / pleasant
tacaño	mean / stingy
terco	stubborn
tímido	shy
torpe	clumsy
travieso	naughty / mischievous
triste	sad
valiente	brave / bold
la vejez	old age
viejo	old

Pets (p.15)

el animal doméstico	pet
el cobayo / el conejillo de Indias	guinea pig
el conejo	rabbit
fiel	loyal
el gato	cat
el hámster	hamster
mandón	bossy / demanding
la mascota	pet
el olor	smell
el perro	dog
el pez de colores	goldfish
el pez tropical	tropical fish
la serpiente	snake
la tortuga	tortoise

Style and Fashion (p.16)

el abrigo	coat
afeitarse	to shave
ajustado	tight
el anillo	ring
anticuado	old-fashioned
la barra de labios	lipstick
la bata	dressing gown
el bolso	handbag
las botas	boots
la bufanda	scarf
los calcetines	socks
la camisa	shirt

el camisón	nightdress
ceñido	tight
la chaqueta	jacket
la chaqueta de punto	cardigan (knitted)
el cinturón	belt
el collar	necklace
cortarse el pelo	to have your hair cut
de estilo retro	vintage style
de lunares	spotty
de rayas / rayado	striped
elegante	smart / elegant
estar de moda	to be in fashion (thing)
estar en la onda	to be fashionable (person)
el estilo	style
la falda	skirt
el/la famoso/a	celebrity
la gorra	cap
los guantes	gloves
holgado	loose / baggy
ir vestido a la moda	to dress fashionably
el jersey	jumper
las joyas	jewellery
el maquillaje	make-up
maquillarse	to put make-up on
la marca	brand
el/la modelo	model
el paraguas	umbrella
pasado de moda	out of fashion
los pendientes	earrings
el perfume	perfume
el piercing	body piercing
pintarse	to put make-up on
el polo	polo shirt
la pulsera	bracelet
la rebeca	cardigan
el reloj	watch
la ropa de deporte	sports kit
el sombrero de paja	straw hat
la sudadera	sweatshirt
suelto	loose
el tatuaje	tattoo
tatuarse	to get a tattoo
teñido	dyed
el traje	suit
el traje de baño	swimming costume / trunks
los vaqueros	jeans
vestido de	dressed in
la zapatería	shoe shop
las zapatillas	slippers
las zapatillas de deporte	trainers

Relationships (p.17-19)

acosar	to bully
aguantar	to bear / to put up with
la amistad	friendship
apoyar	to support
la barrera generacional	generation gap

besar	to kiss
el beso	kiss
la boda	wedding
casado	married
el casamiento	wedding
casarse	to get married
el/la compañero/a	friend / colleague
comprometerse	to get engaged
el compromiso	engagement
confiar en	to trust
conocer	to know / be familiar with / get to know
el/la conocido/a	acquaintance
el cura	priest
de buen humor	in a good mood
la discusión	argument
discutir	to argue
divorciado	divorced
divorciarse	to get divorced
echar de menos	to miss (someone)
enamorado	in love
enamorarse	to fall in love
enfadarse	to get angry
el/la esposo/a	husband / wife
fastidiar	to annoy / to bother
la fe	faith
hacer amigos	to make friends
el hombre	man
insoportable	unbearable
intimidar	to bully
juntos	together
llevarse bien / mal con	to get on well / badly with someone
el marido	husband
el matrimonio	marriage / married couple
mimado	spoilt
el modelo de conducta	role model
molestar	to bother
la mujer	wife / woman
el noviazgo	engagement
el/la novio/a	boy/girlfriend / fiancé(e)
optimista	optimistic
la pandilla	gang
pasarlo bien	to have a good time
la pelea	argument
pelearse	to fight
perdonar	to forgive
reírse	to laugh
relacionarse con	to be in contact with
la religión	religion
reñir	to quarrel
respetar	to respect
el sacerdote	priest
salir	to go out
separado	separated
separarse	to separate
el sentimiento	feeling
solo	alone
soltero	single (not married)
sonreír	to smile

Vocabulary

Section Three — Daily Life

Everyday Life (p.20)

acostarse	to go to bed
la almohada	pillow
arreglar	to tidy / to repair
ayudar	to help
el bricolaje	DIY
cortar el césped	to mow the lawn
despertarse	to wake up
el dinero de bolsillo	pocket money
dormirse	to go to sleep
ducharse	to have a shower
fregar los platos	to do the washing up
hacer de canguro	to babysit
hacer la cama	to make the bed
hacer las compras	to do the shopping
el lavaplatos	dishwasher
lavarse la cara	to wash your face
levantarse	to get up
limpiar	to clean
limpio	clean
la paga	pocket money
pasar la aspiradora	to do the vacuuming
pasear al perro	to walk the dog
planchar	to iron
poner la mesa	to lay the table
quitar la mesa	to clear the table
la sábana	sheet
sacar la basura	to take out the rubbish
la tarea doméstica	chore
vestirse	to get dressed

Food and Drink (p.21)

el aceite	oil
el agua mineral (con / sin gas) (f)	(fizzy / still) mineral water
el ajo	garlic
el albaricoque	apricot
las albóndigas	meatballs
la alcachofa	artichoke
el alimento	type of food
el aliño	dressing (for salad)
almorzar	to have lunch
el almuerzo	lunch
el apetito	appetite
el arroz	rice
el atún	tuna
el azúcar	sugar
la barra (de pan)	loaf (of bread)
beber	to drink
la bebida	drink
el bistec	steak
el bocadillo	sandwich
la brocheta	kebab
el café	coffee
la cafetera	coffee pot
la cafetería	café
los calamares	squid
el caramelo	boiled sweet

la carne	meat
de cerdo	pork
de cordero	lamb
de ternera	veal
de vaca	beef
la carne picada	mince
la cebolla	onion
la cena	dinner
cenar	to have the evening meal
los cereales	cereal
la cereza	cherry
la cerveza (de barril)	(draught) beer
el champán	champagne
los champiñones	mushrooms
el chorizo	Spanish sausage
la chuleta	chop (e.g. pork)
los churros	long doughnuts
la ciruela	plum
cocinar	to cook
la col	cabbage
las coles de Bruselas	Brussels spouts
la coliflor	cauliflower
comer	to eat
la comida	meal / lunch
la comida (basura / rápida)	junk / fast food
la comida precocinada	ready meal
desayunar	to have breakfast
el desayuno	breakfast
la ensalada	salad
los espaguetis	spaghetti
las espinacas	spinach
el filete	steak
la frambuesa	raspberry
la fresa	strawberry
la galleta	biscuit
las gambas	prawns
el gazpacho	cold soup
la grasa	fat
los guisantes	peas
la hamburguesa	hamburger
el helado	ice cream
el hielo	ice
el huevo	egg
el huevo frito	fried egg
los huevos revueltos	scrambled eggs
el jamón	ham
las judías verdes	green beans
la leche	milk
la leche (semi) desnatada	(semi-)skimmed milk
la leche entera	full fat milk
la lechuga	lettuce
las legumbres	vegetables / pulses
el limón	lemon
la limonada	lemonade
la mantequilla	butter

la manzana	apple
los mariscos	seafood
el melocotón	peach
el melón	melon
merendar	to have an afternoon snack / picnic
la merienda	afternoon snack / picnic
la mermelada	jam
la miel	honey
la mostaza	mustard
la naranja	orange
la nata	cream
el pastel	cake / pie
los pastelitos	pastries
la patata	potato
las patatas fritas	chips
el pato	duck
el pavo	turkey
el pepino	cucumber
la pera	pear
el pescado	fish
la pimienta	pepper (seasoning)
el pimiento	pepper (vegetable)
la piña	pineapple
el plátano	banana
el pollo	chicken
el pomelo	grapefruit
el puerro	leek
el queso (de cabra)	(goat's) cheese
el rábano	radish
el refresco	refreshment
la sal	salt
la salchicha	sausage
el salmón	salmon
la salsa	gravy / sauce
la seta	mushroom
la sidra	cider
la sopa	soup
las tapas	nibbles / bar snacks
la tarta	tart / cake
el té	tea
la tisana	herbal tea
la tortilla	omelette
la tostada	toast
la trucha	trout
las uvas	grapes
la vainilla	vanilla
las verduras	vegetables
el vinagre	vinegar
el vino	wine
el yogur	yoghurt
la zanahoria	carrot
el zumo (de fruta)	(fruit) juice

Shopping (p.22-23)

a mitad de precio	half-price
el agujero	hole
Aquí lo tienes.	Here you are.
bastante	enough

Vocabulary

la bolsa	paper / plastic bag	el servicio de reparto a domicilio	home delivery service	el disco duro	hard disk /drive
la caja	box / till	suficiente	enough	en línea	online
cambiar	to change	la talla	size (clothes)	enviar	to send
la cantidad	quantity	la tarjeta de crédito	credit card	escribir a máquina	to type
el cartón	carton	el tarro	jar	funcionar	to work / function
el centro comercial	shopping centre	el tercio	third	grabar	to record / burn (a disk)
el chándal	tracksuit	la tienda de comestibles	grocery shop		
el/la cliente	customer			guardar	to save
la corbata	tie	el trozo	slice, piece	hablar	to speak / talk
el/la dependiente/a	sales assistant	vacío	empty	hacer clic	to click
el descuento	discount	varios/as	several	la herramienta	tool
devolver	to return	el vestido	dress	la impresora	printer
el dinero	money			imprimir	to print
en efectivo	(in) cash			el/la internauta	Internet user

Technology (p.24-27)

el escaparate	shop window	acceder	to access	mandar	to send
exactamente	exactly	el acoso cibernético	cyber bullying	el mensaje (de texto)	(text) message
el gramo	gram	adjuntar	to attach		
los grandes almacenes	department store	el archivo	file	el móvil	mobile phone
		arroba	@	el muro	wall
el hipermercado	hypermarket	la barra	forward slash	el navegador	browser
el kilo	kilogram	el blog	blog	navegar	to surf
la lata	tin	borrar	to erase / delete	el ordenador	computer
el litro	litre	el buscador	search engine	la pantalla (táctil)	(touch) screen
lleno	full	el buzón	inbox / mailbox	el portátil	laptop
el número (de zapato)	shoe size	cargar	to load	el/la programador/a	programmer
		charlar	to chat	publicar	to publish
pagar	to pay	el chat	chat room	el ratón	mouse
el paquete	packet	colgar	to post (photos on social media, etc.)	recibir	to receive
el pedazo	piece			la red	network / Internet
pesar	to weigh	la conexión	connection	la red social	social network
los probadores	changing rooms	la consola de juegos	games console	el riesgo	risk
quejarse	to complain			la seguridad	security
la ración	portion	la contraseña	password	el servidor de seguridad	firewall
rasgado	ripped	el correo basura	spam		
las rebajas	the sales	el correo electrónico	email	el sitio web	website
la rebanada	slice			subir	to upload
el recibo	receipt	crear	to create	el teclado	keyboard
reembolsar	to refund	la cuenta	account	usar	to use
reemplazar	to replace	desactivar	to deactivate / block	el/la usuario/a	user
roto	broken	descargar	to download	utilizar	to use
		digital	digital	el videojuego	video game

Section Four — Free-Time Activities

Celebrations and Festivals (p.28-29)

el Año Nuevo	New Year	¡Feliz Navidad!	Merry Christmas!	el paso	statue paraded at Easter
celebrar	to celebrate	festejar	to celebrate		
la corrida	bullfight	la fiesta	festival / party	la plaza de toros	bullring
la costumbre	custom / way	el Hannukah	Hannukah	la procesión	procession
cristiano	Christian	judío	Jewish	religioso	religious
la Cuaresma	Lent	el juguete	toy	los Reyes Magos	the Three Kings
el desfile	procession / parade	el Lunes de Pascua	Easter Monday	el santo	saint's day
el Día de la Madre	Mother's Day	el/la muerto/a	dead (person)	la Semana Santa	Easter week
el Día de los Muertos	Day of the Dead	musulmán	Muslim	tener suerte	to be lucky
		Navidad	Christmas	la Tomatina	tomato-throwing festival
el Día de Reyes / Epifanía	Epiphany / 6 January	Nochebuena	Christmas Eve		
		Nochevieja	31 December	el toro	bull
el día festivo	public holiday	el panecillo de Pascua	hot cross bun	la tradición	tradition
el Eid al-Fitr	Eid al-Fitr			el turrón	Spanish nougat
¡Feliz cumpleaños!	Happy Birthday!	Papá Noel	Father Christmas	la vela	candle
		la Pascua	Easter	el Viernes Santo	Good Friday
				el villancico	Christmas carol

Vocabulary

Books and Reading (p.30)

el lector de libros electrónicos	e-reader
la lectura	reading
leer	to read
el libro	book
el libro electrónico	e-book
la novela	novel
la novela de suspense	thriller
el periódico	newspaper
la prensa	the press
la revista	magazine
el tebeo	comic strip

Music, Film and TV (p.31-32)

el actor	actor
la actriz	actress
el anuncio (publicitario)	advert
el/la artista	artist
la banda sonora	soundtrack
la batería	drums
la cadena	channel
el canal	channel
la canción	song
el/la cantante	singer
cantar	to sing
la ciencia ficción	science fiction
el clarinete	clarinet
la comedia	sitcom
la comedia musical	musical comedy (musical)
el concierto	concert
el culebrón	soap opera
los dibujos animados	cartoons
el documental	documentary
el drama	drama
en directo	live
la entrada	ticket
el entretenimiento	entertainment
el equipo de música	stereo system
el espectáculo	show
la flauta	flute
la flauta dulce	recorder
el género	genre
la gira	tour
el grupo	band
la guitarra	guitar
la letra	song lyrics
el mando a distancia	remote control
los medios de comunicación	the media
la melodía	melody / tune
el/la músico/a	musician
la música clásica	classical music
la música folklórica	folk music
la música pop	pop music
la música rap	rap music
la música rock	rock music

las noticias	news
la orquesta	orchestra
el papel	role
la película	film
la película de aventuras	adventure film
la película de fantasía	fantasy film
(la película) doblada	dubbed (film)
la película romántica	romantic film
el piano	piano
policíaco	detective (adj.)
el programa	programme
el programa concurso	quiz show
el reparto	cast
el saxofón	saxophone
la serie	series
los subtítulos	subtitles
la telenovela	soap opera
el telespectador	TV viewer
la televisión por cable	cable TV
el televisor	TV set
tocar	to play (an instrument)
la trama	plot
la trompeta	trumpet
la versión original	original version
el violín	violin

Sport (p.33)

(el/la) aficionado/a	enthusiast
al aire libre	outdoors
el alpinismo	mountaineering
andar	to walk
el/la árbitro/a	referee
las artes marciales	martial arts
el atletismo	athletics
el bádminton	badminton
bailar	to dance
el baile	dancing
el balón	ball
el baloncesto	basketball
la bicicleta / bici	bicycle / bike
la bicicleta de montaña	mountain bike
el boxeo	boxing
la cama elástica	trampoline
el campeonato	championship
la caña de pescar	fishing rod
la carrera	race
el ciclismo	cycling
el concurso	contest / competition
correr	to run
el culturismo	body building
el deporte	sport
los deportes extremos	extreme sports
deportista	sporty
el/la deportista	sportsperson
el descanso	half-time

entrenar	to train
el equipo	team / equipment
la equitación	horse riding
la escalada en roca	rock climbing
la esgrima	fencing
el estadio	stadium
el fútbol	football
ganar	to win
la gimnasia	gymnastics
el gol	goal
hacer ejercicio	to do exercise
el hockey	hockey
ir a la bolera	to go ten pin bowling
el judo	judo
el juego	game
los Juegos Olímpicos	Olympic Games
el/la jugador/a	player
jugar	to play
el karate	karate
la liga	league
marcar (un gol)	to score (a goal)
el monopatinaje	skateboarding
el montañismo	mountaineering
montar (a caballo / en bici)	to ride (horse / bike)
nadar	to swim
la natación	swimming
el ocio	leisure
el parapente	paragliding
el patinaje	skating
el patinaje sobre hielo	ice skating
patinar	to skate
patinar sobre ruedas	to roller-skate
la pelota	ball
perder	to lose
la pesca	fishing
pescar	to fish
el piragüismo	canoeing
la pista de hielo	ice rink
el remo	rowing
el rugby	rugby
ser aficionado a	to be fond of / a fan of (activity)
el/la socio/a	member
el squash	squash
el submarinismo	scuba diving
el surf	surfing
el tenis (de mesa)	(table) tennis
el tiro con arco	archery
el torneo	tournament
la vela	sail / sailing
el velero	sailing boat
el vóleibol	volleyball

Section Five — Where You Live

Where You Live (p.34-35)

las afueras	outskirts
la aldea	village
la alfombra	rug
alquilar	to rent / to hire
el alquiler	rent
los alrededores	surrounding area
amueblado	furnished
el aparcamiento	parking
el apartamento	flat
el armario	wardrobe / cupboard
el ascensor	lift
el aseo	toilet
el asilo de ancianos	old people's home
el ático	attic
el ayuntamiento	town hall
el banco	bank
el baño	bathroom / bath
el barrio	neighbourhood
la biblioteca	library
el bloque de pisos	block of flats
la bolera	bowling alley
la butaca	armchair
la calefacción	heating
la calle	street
la cama	bed
el campo	countryside
la cancha (de tenis)	(tennis) court
la carnicería	butcher's
la casa (adosada)	(semi-detached) house
el centro	centre
el cine	cinema
la ciudad	city
el club (de jóvenes)	(youth) club
el club nocturno	night club
la cocina	cooker / kitchen
la colina	hill
el comedor	dining room
la comisaría	police station
cómodo	comfortable
compartir	to share
concurrido	busy / crowded
construir	to build
Correos	Post Office
el cuarto de baño	bathroom
de lujo	luxury
el desván	attic
la dirección	address
el dormitorio	bedroom
la ducha	shower
el edificio	building
los electrodomésticos	electrical appliances
la entrada	entrance
entrar	to go in / enter
la escalera	stairs
el espacio	space
el espejo	mirror

el estanco	tobacconist's
la estantería	shelves
la fábrica	factory
la farmacia	chemist's
el fregadero	kitchen sink
el garaje	garage
la granja	farm
la habitación	room
el/la habitante	inhabitant
el hogar	home
el horno	oven
la iglesia	church
industrial	industrial
el jardín	garden
la joyería	jeweller's
el lago	lake
el lavabo	washbasin
la librería	bookcase / bookshop
la llave	key
el lugar de residencia	place of residence
la luz	light
el mercado	market
la mesa	table
la mezquita	mosque
mudarse (de casa)	to move (house)
los muebles	furniture
el museo	museum
el negocio	business
la nevera	fridge
el paisaje	landscape / scenery
la panadería	bakery
la papelería	stationery shop
la pared	wall
el parque	park
la pastelería	pastry shop
la peluquería	hairdresser's
la pescadería	fishmonger's
el piso	flat / floor (of room)
la planta	floor / plant
la planta baja	ground floor
la plaza de toros	bullring
el polideportivo	sports centre
el pueblo	town / village / people / nation
el puente	bridge
la puerta	door
el puerto	port / harbour
el quiosco de periódicos	newspaper stall
el río	river
el ruido	noise
ruidoso	noisy
la sala de estar	living room / lounge
el salón	living room / lounge
la segunda planta	second floor
la silla	chair
el sillón	armchair
el sofá	sofa

el sótano	basement / cellar
subir	to go up
el suelo	floor
el teatro	theatre
el/la vecino/a	neighbour
la ventana	window
la zona peatonal	pedestrian zone / area

Weather (p.36)

el boletín meteorológico	weather report
brillar	to shine (sun)
buen / mal tiempo	good / bad weather
el calor	heat
caluroso	hot / warm
el chubasco	shower
el cielo	sky
el clima	climate
despejarse	to brighten up
fresco	fresh
el grado	degree
granizar	to hail
¡Hace un frío que pela!	It's freezing!
hacer (frío / calor etc.)	to be (cold / hot etc.)
helar	to freeze
el hielo	ice
llover	to rain
la lluvia	rain
máximo	maximum
mejorar	to improve
mínimo	minimum
la neblina	mist
nevar	to snow
la niebla	fog
la nieve	snow
la nube	cloud
nublado	cloudy / overcast
el período soleado	bright spell
la precipitación	rainfall
el pronóstico del tiempo	weather forecast
el relámpago	lightning
seco	dry
el sol	sun
soleado	sunny
tener (frío / calor)	to feel (cold / hot)
el tiempo	weather
la tormenta	storm
tormentoso	stormy
el trueno	thunder
variable	changeable
el viento	wind

Section Six — Travel and Tourism

Where to Go (p.37)

África	Africa
Alemania	Germany
alemán	German
América Latina	Latin America
latinoamericano	Latin American
Andalucía	Andalusia
Argentina	Argentina
argentino	Argentinian
Asia	Asia
Australia	Australia
Bélgica	Belgium
belga	Belgian
Brasil	Brazil
brasileño	Brazilian
Canadá	Canada
canadiense	Canadian
el canal de la Mancha	English Channel
la capital	capital (city)
Cataluña	Catalonia
el centro turístico costero	seaside resort
Chile	Chile
chileno	Chilean
Colombia	Colombia
colombiano	Colombian
la colonia de vacaciones	summer camp
la comunidad autónoma	autonomous community
la costa	coast
Cuba	Cuba
cubano	Cuban
Dinamarca	Denmark
danés	Danish
Escocia	Scotland
escocés	Scottish
España	Spain
español	Spanish
los Estados Unidos	United States
estadounidense	from the US
Europa	Europe
europeo	European
en el / al extranjero	abroad
Francia	France
francés	French
Galicia	Galicia
Gran Bretaña	Great Britain
británico	British
Grecia	Greece
griego	Greek
la India	India
indio	Indian
Inglaterra	England
inglés	English
Irlanda	Ireland
irlandés	Irish
la isla	island

Italia	Italy
italiano	Italian
Londres	London
el mar	sea
el mar Mediterráneo	Mediterranean Sea
México	Mexico
mexicano	Mexican
la montaña	mountain
el mundo	world
el Océano Atlántico	Atlantic Ocean
el país	country
País de Gales	Wales
galés	Welsh
el País Vasco	the Basque Country
los Países Bajos	the Netherlands
holandés	Dutch
Pakistán	Pakistan
pakistaní	Pakistani
Perú	Peru
peruano	Peruvian
los Pirineos	the Pyrenees
pintoresco	picturesque
la playa	beach
la provincia	province
Rusia	Russia
ruso	Russian
Sudamérica	South America
sudamericano	South American
Suecia	Sweden
sueco	Swedish
Turquía	Turkey
turco	Turkish
las vacaciones de invierno / de esquí	winter / skiing holiday

Preparation (p.38-39)

la agencia (de viajes)	(travel) agent's
el aire acondicionado	air-conditioning
el albergue juvenil	youth hostel
el alojamiento	accommodation
alojarse	to lodge / stay
el balcón	balcony
buscar	to look for
la cama de matrimonio	double bed
cambiar	to change
el camping	campsite
la caravana	caravan
el carné / carnet de identidad	identity card
la crema solar	sun cream
disponible	available
DNI	ID card
el equipaje	luggage
la ficha	registration form
el formulario	registration form

el folleto	leaflet / pamphlet
(no) fumador	(non) smoking
el/la guía	guide
la guía	guidebook
la habitación (doble / individual)	(double / single) room
informarse	to find out
las instalaciones	facilities
irse de camping	to go camping
libre	available
llevar	to take
el lugar	place
la maleta	suitcase
el mapa	map
la máquina fotográfica	camera
media pensión	half board
el papel higiénico	toilet paper
el pasaporte	passport
la pensión	boarding house (B&B)
pensión completa	full board
perder	to lose
el permiso de conducir	driving licence
la piscina (cubierta)	(indoor) swimming pool
por adelantado	in advance
la posada	inn
quedarse	to stay
la recepción	reception
el/la recepcionista	receptionist
recordar	to remember
el regreso	return
la reserva	reservation
reservar	to book / reserve
el saco de dormir	sleeping bag
la sala de juegos	games room
el sitio	space / room / place / site
la tienda	tent
las vacaciones	holidays
el viaje organizado	package holiday
la vista	view

How to Get There (p.40)

a pie	on foot / walking
la aduana	customs
el aeropuerto	airport
el andén	platform
aparcar	to park
el asiento	seat
aterrizar	to land (plane)
el autocar	coach
la autopista	motorway
el avión	aeroplane
el barco	boat
el billete (de ida / de ida y vuelta)	(single / return) ticket

el cinturón de seguridad	seat belt
el coche	car
el código postal	postcode
coger	to take / catch
el compartimento	compartment
conducir	to drive / lead
el/la conductor/a	driver
el cruce	crossroads
cruzar	to cross
despegar	to take off (plane)
embarcar	to board (plane / train)
esperar	to wait
la estación (de autobuses / autocares / trenes)	(bus / coach / train) station
la estación de servicio	service station
la red de ferrocarril	railway network
el ferry	ferry
la gasolina (sin plomo)	(unleaded) petrol
hacer transbordo	to change / transfer
la llegada	arrival
llegar	to arrive
el metro	underground
la moto	motorbike
la parada	stop
parar	to stop
el/la pasajero/a	passenger
pasar (por)	to go (through) / pass
el peaje	toll
perder (vuelo etc.)	to miss (flight etc.)
perderse	to get lost
el retraso	delay
la sala de espera	waiting room
la salida	exit
la señal	sign / signal
tardar	to take (time)
el tranvía	tram
el vagón	carriage (train)
venir	to come
la vía	track / platform
la vía para bicicletas	cycle lane
viajar	to travel
el viaje	trip / journey
el/la viajero/a	traveller
volver	to return
el vuelo	flight

What To Do (p.41)

bañarse	to bathe / swim
broncearse	to get a tan
caminar	to walk
el camino	path / road
los deportes acuáticos	water sports
descansar	to rest
el descanso	rest / pause
la entrada	entry / admission

el esquí	skiing
esquiar	to ski
estar de vacaciones	to be on holiday
la excursión	trip / excursion
la exposición	exhibition
la galería de arte	art gallery
el lago	lake
el mar	sea
la montaña	mountain
el museo	museum
la naturaleza	nature
el parque de atracciones	fairground
el parque temático	theme park
el parque zoológico	zoo
pasar (tiempo)	to spend (time)
la playa	beach
la postal	postcard
el recorrido	tour
el recuerdo	souvenir
relajarse	to relax
el río	river
sacar fotos	to take photos
la tarjeta (postal)	card / (post)card
tomar el sol	to sunbathe
el/la turista	tourist
ver	to see

Eating Out (p.42)

a la plancha	grilled
ahumado	smoked
amargo	bitter
apetecer	to fancy / to feel like
apetitoso	appetising
apto	suitable
asado	roast(ed)
de autoservicio	self-service
la bandeja	tray
la bebida	drink
bien cocido	well-done (steak)
el/la camarero/a	waiter / waitress
la carta	menu
la cocina	cuisine / cooking
crudo	raw
la cuchara	spoon
la cucharita / la cucharadita	teaspoon
el cuchillo	knife
la cuenta	bill
dulce	sweet
elegir / escoger	to choose
la entrada	starter
la especialidad	speciality
frito	fried
la heladería	ice cream parlour
hervido	boiled
incluido	included
el mantel	table cloth
nada más	nothing else
pedir	to order / ask for
picante	spicy

la pizzería	pizzeria
el platillo	saucer
el plato (combinado)	(set) dish
el plato principal	main course
poco hecho	rare (steak)
el postre	dessert
probar	to taste / to try
la propina	tip
rico	tasty
sabroso	tasty
salado	salty
el salón de té	tearoom
los servicios	toilets
la servilleta	napkin
la taza	cup
el tenedor	fork
tener hambre	to be hungry
tener sed	to be thirsty
tomar	to have / to take
traer	to bring
el vaso	glass
el/la vegetariano/a	vegetarian

Practical Stuff (p.43)

asegurar	to insure
la avería	breakdown
el cajero automático	ATM / cashpoint
el camión	lorry
la cartera	wallet
chocar	to crash
la colisión	crash
la comisaría	police station
confirmar un billete	to validate a ticket
la consigna automática	left luggage locker
el desvío	diversion
la factura	bill (invoice)
el garaje	garage
la gasolina	petrol
gratis	free
gratuito	free
el monedero	purse
perder	to lose
prohibido	forbidden
el/la revisor/a	ticket inspector
robar	to steal / rob

Directions (p.44)

a un paso (de)	a few steps away (from)
abajo (de)	under / below
la acera	pavement
afuera (de)	outside
ahí	(just) there
aislado	isolated
al final (de)	at the end (of)
allá	(over) there
allí	(over) there
alrededor (de)	around
aquí	here
arriba (de)	above / on top (of)

Vocabulary

atrás	behind	en el / al fondo	at the back / at the bottom	lejano	far away / distant / remote
atravesar	to cross	en la esquina	on the corner	lejos (de)	far (from)
la calle mayor	main street	encima (de)	above / on top / overhead	el lugar	place
cerca (de)	near			en (el) medio (de)	in the middle of
cercano	nearby	encontrarse	to be situated	el norte	north
contra	against	enfrente (de)	opposite	el oeste	west
cruzar	to cross	entre	between	el paso de peatones	pedestrian crossing
debajo (de)	under	estar situado	to be situated		
delante (de)	in front of	el este	east	seguir	to follow / continue
dentro (de)	inside	fuera (de)	outside	el semáforo	traffic lights
a la derecha	on / to the right	la glorieta	roundabout	el sitio	place
(todo) derecho	straight ahead	a la izquierda	on / to the left	el sur	south
detrás (de)	behind	al lado (de)	next to	todo recto	straight ahead
en / por todas partes	everywhere			tomar	to take (a road)

Section Seven — Current and Future Study and Employment

School Subjects (p.45)

el alemán	German
el arte dramático	drama
la asignatura	school subject
la biología	biology
las ciencias	science
la cocina	food technology
el comercio	business studies
el curso	school year
el dibujo	art
la economía	economics
la educación física	PE
las empresariales	business studies
enseñar	to teach
el español	Spanish
la física	physics
el francés	French
la geografía	geography
la gimnasia	gymnastics
la historia	history
las humanidades	humanities
el idioma	language
la informática	IT
el inglés	English
el latín	Latin
la lengua	language / tongue
las matemáticas	maths
la materia	school subject
la música	music
optar	to choose / opt for
optativo	optional
la química	chemistry
la religión	RE
la sociología	sociology
la tecnología	technology
los trabajos manuales	handicrafts

School Life (p.46-48)

el acoso (escolar)	(school) bullying
la agenda	diary
el/la alumno/a	pupil / student

apoyar	to support / back / help
el apoyo	support / backing / help
aprender	to learn
aprobar	to approve / pass (an exam)
el aula (f)	classroom
los auriculares	earphones
ausente	absent
la ayuda	help
el bloc de notas	notebook
el bolígrafo	pen
la calculadora	calculator
la cantina	canteen
la carpeta	folder / file
el cartucho de tinta	ink cartridge
castigar	to punish
el chicle	chewing gum
la clase	lesson
el colegio mixto	mixed school
el colegio privado	private school
el colegio público	state school
el colegio religioso	religious school
el comportamiento	behaviour
comportarse	to behave
el/la conserje	caretaker
contestar	to answer
copiar	to copy
la corbata	tie
el coro	choir
corregir	to correct
el cuaderno	exercise book
los deberes	homework
deletrear	to spell (out)
el despacho	office
el día escolar	school day
dibujar	to draw
el diccionario	dictionary
el/la director/a	head teacher / principal
diseñar	to design

dotado	gifted
la educación	education
educativo	educational
el ensayo	essay
la enseñanza	teaching / education
enseñar	to teach
entender	to understand
el equipo	team
escribir	to write
la escuela (primaria)	(primary) school
estresante	stressful
estricto	strict
el estuche	pencil case
la evaluación	test / assessment
el examen	exam
el éxito	success
el experimento	experiment
explicar	to explain
extraescolar	extracurricular
la falta	mistake / absence
femenino	feminine
fracasar	to fail
el fracaso	failure
el gimnasio	gymnasium
golpear	to hit
la goma	rubber
hacer novillos	to play truant
la hoja de ejercicios	work sheet
la hora de comer	lunchtime
el horario	timetable
el instituto	secondary school / institute
el internado	boarding school
la intimidación	bullying
el lápiz	pencil
la lección	lesson
la letra	letter of the alphabet
levantar la mano	to put your hand up
el libro	book
el libro de texto	textbook
listo	clever
masculino	masculine

Vocabulary

mirar	to look
la mochila	rucksack / school bag
molestar	to annoy / bother
la norma	rule
la nota	mark
obligatorio	compulsory
oír	to listen / hear
olvidar	to forget
la página	page
la palabra	word
el parvulario	nursery school
pasar (la) lista	to call the register
el patio	playground
pedir prestado	to borrow
el pegamento	glue
el permiso	permission
la pizarra interactiva	smart board
la pregunta	question
preguntar	to ask a question
la presión	pressure
prestar atención	to pay attention
privado	private
el proyector	projector
la prueba	test / proof
el pupitre	desk
el recreo	break
la regla	rule / ruler
repasar	to revise
repetir	to repeat
la respuesta	answer
el rotulador	felt tip
la rutina	routine
el sacapuntas	pencil sharpener
sacar buenas / malas notas	to get good / bad marks
la sala de profesores	staffroom
el salón de actos	assembly room
sobresaliente	outstanding
suspender	to fail (exam / subject)
el taller	workshop
la tarea	task / piece of homework
el tema	topic / theme
tener miedo	to be afraid
terminar	to finish
las tijeras	scissors
trabajador	hard-working
el trabajo	work
el trimestre	(school) term
el uniforme	uniform
los vestuarios	changing rooms

School Events (p.49)

el/la amigo/a por correspondencia	penfriend
el autobús escolar	school bus
el día de disfraces	fancy dress day
la entrega de premios	prize-giving
la excursión (del colegio)	school trip
(al) extranjero	abroad
el grupo escolar	school group
el intercambio	exchange
participar en	to participate in
el rendimiento	achievement / performance
la reunión de padres	parents' evening
la venta de pasteles	cake sale
la visita guiada	guided tour
la vuelta al colegio	first day back at school

Education Post-16 (p.50)

a distancia	distance (i.e. distance learning)
la academia	academy / school post-16 (for certain careers)
la ambición	ambition
el/la aprendiz/a	apprentice
el aprendizaje	apprenticeship / training / learning
el bachillerato	school leaving exam (e.g. A-levels)
calificado	competent / skilled
la capacitación	training
la carrera	career / profession
el conocimiento	knowledge
conseguir	to get / achieve
dejar	to leave
Derecho	law (at university)
esperar	to hope / expect
la experiencia laboral	work experience
la formación (profesional)	vocational training
la licenciatura	degree
lograr	to achieve
las perspectivas laborales	employment prospects
la práctica	work placement
el título	qualification
tomarse un año libre / sabático	to take a gap year
la universidad	university
útil	useful

Career Choices (p.51)

a tiempo completo	full time
a tiempo parcial	part time
el/la abogado/a	lawyer / solicitor
el/la arquitecto/a	architect
el/la bombero/a	firefighter
el/la cajero/a	bank-teller / cashier
el/la carnicero/a	butcher
el/la cocinero/a	cook
el/la constructor/a	builder
el/la contable	accountant
desafiante	challenging
el/la electricista	electrician

el/la empleado/a	employee / worker
el empleo	job / employment
la empresa	company
encontrar	to find
el/la enfermero/a	nurse
el/la escritor/a	writer
estar en paro	to be unemployed
estimulante	stimulating
el/la fontanero/a	plumber
el/la funcionario/a	civil servant
ganar	to earn
el/la gerente	manager
el/la granjero/a	farmer
gratificante	rewarding
el hombre / la mujer de negocios	businessman / businesswoman
el/la ingeniero/a	engineer
el/la jefe	boss
laboral	working
llegar a ser	to become
el/la mecánico/a	mechanic
el/la médico/a	doctor
el objetivo	aim / objective
obtener	to get / obtain
el/la oficial de policía	police officer
el/la orientador/a	careers adviser
el/la panadero/a	baker
parado	unemployed
el paro	unemployment
el/la peluquero/a	hairdresser
el periodismo	journalism
el/la periodista	journalist
probar	to have a go / try
pronto	ready
el sueldo	salary
el/la técnico/a	technician
el/la trabajador/a	worker
trabajar	to work
el trabajo	work / job
el/la traductor/a	translator
triunfar	to triumph / succeed
variado	varied
el/la veterinario/a	veterinary surgeon

Languages for the Future (p.52)

el/la auxiliar de lengua	language assistant
el/la azafato/a	flight attendant
el castellano	Castilian (Spanish spoken in Spain)
comunicarse	to communicate
conocer a alguien	to get to know someone
expresarse	to express yourself
el idioma	language
internacional	international
el laboratorio de idiomas	language lab
la lengua	language
multicultural	multicultural

pronunciar	*to pronounce*	la cita	*appointment*	las posibilidades de promoción	*promotion prospects*
traducir	*to translate*	con experiencia	*experienced*	rellenar	*to fill in*
viajar por el mundo	*to travel the world*	las condiciones de empleo	*terms of employment*	solicitar un puesto de trabajo	*to apply for a job*

Applying for Jobs (p.53)

adjuntar	*to attach*	el currículum	*CV*	la solicitud	*appliciation form*
el anuncio de trabajo	*job advertisement*	despedir	*to dismiss*	el sueldo	*salary*
		el/la director/a	*boss*	la vacante	*vacancy*
bien pagado	*well-paid*	la entrevista	*interview*		
la carta de solicitud	*application letter*	la habilidad	*skill*		
		por hora	*per hour*		

Section Eight — Global Issues

The Environment (p.54-56)

el abono	*compost*
el agua dulce	*fresh water*
el agua potable	*drinking water*
amenazar	*to threaten*
apagar	*to turn off (lights etc.)*
la atmósfera	*atmosphere*
la basura	*rubbish*
el bosque	*forest*
el calentamiento global	*global warming*
el cambio climático	*climate change*
el carbón	*coal*
el cartón	*cardboard*
combatir	*to fight / combat*
el combustible	*fuel*
los combustibles fósiles	*fossil fuels*
el comercio justo	*fair trade*
contaminar	*to pollute*
el cubo de basura	*rubbish bin*
la culpa	*fault / blame / guilt*
dañar	*to harm / damage*
desaparecer	*to disappear*
el desastre	*disaster*
los desechos	*rubbish / waste*
ducharse	*to have a shower*
echar la culpa	*to blame*
ecológico	*environmentally friendly*
el efecto invernadero	*greenhouse effect*
la electricidad	*electricity*
encender	*to turn on (lights etc.)*
la energía (solar)	*(solar) power*
ensuciar	*to make dirty / soil / make a mess*
el envase	*wrapping / packaging / container*
la escasez	*shortage / lack*
la especie	*species*
la falta	*lack*
faltar	*to be missing*
el fuego	*fire*
el gas	*gas*

el hambre (f)	*famine*
el huracán	*hurricane*
el incendio	*fire*
la inundación	*flood*
el medio ambiente	*environment*
medioambiental	*environmental*
morir	*to die*
el mundo	*world*
la naturaleza	*nature*
nocivo	*harmful*
el petróleo	*oil*
la pila	*battery*
el planeta	*planet*
la polución	*pollution*
preocupante	*worrying*
preocuparse	*to worry*
la protección	*protection*
proteger	*to protect*
la protesta	*protest*
recargable	*rechargeable*
el reciclaje	*recycling*
reciclar	*to recycle*
los recursos naturales	*natural resources*
renovable	*renewable*
los residuos	*refuse / waste / rubbish*
reutilizar	*to reuse*
salvar	*to save*
la selva (tropical)	*(rain) forest*
separar	*to separate*
la sequía	*drought*
sobrevivir	*to survive*
solucionar	*to solve / resolve*
sucio	*dirty*
el terremoto	*earthquake*
la Tierra	*Earth*
tirar	*to throw (away)*
el uso	*use / usage*
utilizar	*to use*
la ventaja	*advantage*
el vertedero	*rubbish dump / tip*
el volcán	*volcano*

Problems in Society (p.57)

la culpa	*fault / blame / guilt*
los derechos	*rights*
el desempleo	*unemployment*
la desigualdad	*inequality*
la discriminación	*discrimination*
estar en paro	*to be unemployed*
el gobierno	*government*
grave	*serious*
la guerra	*war*
la igualdad	*equality*
inquietante	*worrying / disturbing*
inquietar(se)	*to worry*
justo	*just / fair*
la ley	*law*
la libertad	*liberty / freedom*
luchar	*to fight / struggle*
los necesitados	*needy people*
el peligro	*danger*
peligroso	*dangerous*
pobre	*poor*
la pobreza	*poverty*
el prejuicio	*prejudice*
el/la refugiado/a	*refugee*
los "sin techo"	*homeless people*
el/la testigo	*witness*
la tienda benéfica	*charity shop*
la violencia	*violence*

Global Events (p.58)

a beneficio de	*in aid of*
asistir a	*to attend*
la campaña	*campaign*
estar en desventaja	*to be disadvantaged*
el evento	*event*
el festival (de música)	*(music) festival*
los Juegos Olímpicos	*Olympic Games*
llamar la atención	*to attract attention*
el Mundial	*World Cup (football)*
la organización caritativa	*charitable organisation*
recaudar dinero	*to raise money*

Answers

The answers to the translation questions are sample answers only, just to give you an idea of one way to translate them. There may be different ways to translate these passages that are also correct.

Section 1 — General Stuff

Page 1: Numbers

1) Tiene diecisiete años.
2) Tiene ochenta y ocho años.
3) Vive en la segunda calle a la derecha.

Page 3: Times and Dates

1) a) the day before yesterday   b) London   c) Friday

Page 9: Opinions

1) Luis prefers watching films at home.
2) No, he doesn't. He thinks they're boring.
3) Elena thinks sometimes they're ridiculous.

Page 10: Putting it All Together

1 (i) a) escuchar música   b) divertido   c) interesantes
  (ii) a) relajarse   b) guay

Section 2 — About Me

Page 12: Your Family

I live with my mother, my older sister and my two younger sisters. They are twins. For me, it's important to have brothers and sisters because you always have someone to go out with. At the weekend, I visit my father, his wife and my stepbrother. He was born last year and he is only six months old. I would like to spend more time there with them because it's great fun / entertaining.

Page 13: Describing People

Descripción 1 = foto b   Descripción 3 = foto a
Descripción 2 = foto d   Descripción 4 = foto c

Page 15: Pets

I have a bird as a pet. He has always been very chatty — he repeats what you say and it's very funny when he says rude things. The good thing about birds is that they eat fruit, vegetables and cereals, so their food doesn't cost much. However, next weekend I have to take him to the vet and I think it will cost a lot of money.

Page 16: Style and Fashion

1) A   2) C

Page 19: Partnership

1 a) False   b) True   c) False
2) Jerez

Section 3 — Daily Life

Page 20: Everyday Life

I believe it's important to help at home, but I don't think it's fair if I do a lot and my younger brother does very little. I love walking the dog. My dad gives me money if I mow the lawn, so I will do it next Sunday. Last week I had to clean the bathroom. How disgusting!

Page 21: Food and Drink

The true sentences are b and c.

Page 23: Shopping

1) a) half a kilo   c) he's just sold the last bottle
   b) salt   d) €6.50

Page 25: Technology

No podría vivir sin la tecnología porque es muy útil. Me gusta jugar a los videojuegos en la red con mi hermano. Hablamos con internautas en otros países. Ayer, jugué con un chico en Chile, pero para proteger mi identidad, no uso nunca mi nombre. Lo mejor de los móviles es que no tienes que estar en casa para usar la red. En el futuro, pienso que los niños tendrán móviles cuando tengan dos o tres años.

Page 26: Social Media

1) V   2) V   3) F   4) F

Section 4 — Free-Time Activities

Page 28: Celebrations and Festivals

The true statements are C and E.

Page 31: Music

1) a) the saxophone
   b) It's very quick to get songs.
      It's cheaper than going to a shop and buying a CD.
   c) Live music is always very exciting.

Page 32: Film and TV

Me encantan las películas. En mi opinión, las películas policíacas son las mejores. Son las películas más divertidas porque tienes que pensar en la trama. La semana pasada, vi una película muy divertida. Me gusta ver películas con mis amigos los fines de semana. En el futuro, me encantaría ser actriz.

Section 5 — Where You Live

Page 35: The Home

The true statements are C and E.

Page 36: Weather

1) the south
2) in the west (near Portugal)
3) It'll be good weather.
4) The temperatures will drop.
5) There might be storms.

Section 6 — Travel and Tourism

Page 37: Where to Go

1) Está en la costa del océano Atlántico en el norte de España.
2) Es famosa por su catedral y sus peregrinaciones.
3) Se puede nadar en uno de los ríos.

Page 38: Accommodation

modern; elegant; live

Page 40: How to Get There

My city has many types of transport. The underground, which opened in 1924, is very clean and fast. Moreover, there is a tram network by which you can visit the majority of the neighbourhoods of the city. From the airport, it is possible to fly to all the important cities in Europe and it's not very far from the centre. Soon, they're going to improve the bus network, which will be great.

Page 44: Giving and Asking for Directions

1) a) este   b) menos   c) enfrente   d) derecha

112

Section 7 — Current and Future Study and Employment

Page 46: School Routine
1) a) C   b) A   c) C

Page 47: School Life
Statements B, E and F are true.

Page 50: Education Post-16
Cuando era joven, pensaba que me gustaría ser profesor/a. Mis padres son profesores y aunque encuentran el empleo interesante, mi padre dice que es bastante estresante. Ahora he decidido que voy a ir a una academia para estudiar fotografía. ¡Me encantaría sacar fotos de bodas!

Page 51: Career Choices and Ambitions
"When I was fifteen, it was difficult to get a job," said my mother. "Yes, but a lot has changed in recent years," I replied. "I want to be a lawyer. They earn a good salary and I would like to help people. The work would be so varied!"

Page 52: Languages for the Future
1) know at least three languages
2) start going to German evening classes
3) it will have language labs
4) the pronunciation

Section 8 — Global Issues

Page 55: Environmental Problems
El cambio climático me preocupa mucho. Las fábricas y los coches contribuyen al efecto invernadero. Para mí, lo peor es que la gente en algunos países pobres sufre debido a las inundaciones y las sequías. No es justo. Creo que deberíamos trabajar juntos para reducir los efectos del cambio climático, pero será muy difícil.

Page 57: Problems in Society
1) a) economic problems
   b) very difficult
   c) prejudice
   d) lazy
   e) work together

Page 58: Global Events
Este año, hemos trabajado con una organización caritativa que ayuda a niños en desventaja en Asia. Organizamos un concierto y escribimos a unos cantantes para preguntarles si nos apoyarían. Tres de ellos vinieron y todo el mundo lo pasó bien. En el futuro, me encantaría ir al Mundial. Creo que sería muy divertido.

Section 9 — Grammar

Page 59: Words for People and Objects
1) el; los sombreros
2) el; los problemas
3) la; las tradiciones
4) el; los viernes
5) el; los porcentajes
6) el; los franceses
7) la; las tensiones
8) la; las dificultades
9) la; las ciudades
10) el; los mapas

Page 60: 'The', 'A', 'Some' and Other Little Words
1) Me gusta el chocolate.
2) No tengo agua.
3) Es profesora.
4) Quiere unas patatas.
5) Quiero hablar con la señora López.
6) Cada persona tiene dos perros.

Page 61: Words to Describe Things
1) el perro feliz
2) siete faldas rojas
3) los coches azules
4) dos mujeres bajas
5) cinco gatos pequeños
6) nueve sillas violeta
7) cuatro libros beis
8) una persona triste

Page 62: Words to Describe Things
1) Hay muchos gatos.
2) el primer día
3) el mismo perro
4) los otros alumnos
5) Algunas personas creen que... / Alguna gente cree que...
6) Es un gran profesor.

Page 63: Words to Describe Things
1) Sus libros son nuevos. / Los libros suyos son nuevos.
2) Quiero esa manzana.
3) Aquel león está comiendo.
4) Estas peras son buenas.
5) Ese hombre, cuya mujer es española, es alto.
6) Lucas es el chico cuyos padres son simpáticos.

Page 64: Words to Describe Actions
1) Lloran ruidosamente.
2) Vive saludablemente.
3) Habla claramente.
4) Hablamos inteligentemente.
5) El bebé duerme bien.
6) Corro rápidamente / deprisa.
7) Bailas / Bailáis mal.
8) Leo lentamente / despacio.

Page 65: Words to Describe Actions
1) Mis zapatos están aquí.
2) Quiero hacerlo de nuevo. / Lo quiero hacer de nuevo.
3) Lo hice con paciencia.
4) Vivimos lejos.
5) Lo hizo en seguida.
6) Bailó con entusiasmo.

Page 66: Words to Compare Things
1) Mi gato es el más gordo.
2) Soy tan alto/a como mi padre.
3) Juan es mayor que Marta.
4) Fue el peor día de la semana.
5) La película es mejor que el libro.
6) Nuestra revista es la más interesante.

Page 67: Words to Compare Actions
1) Carmen come más rápidamente.
2) Luis canta tan bien como Adela.
3) Selina es la que mejor conduce.
4) Estudio mejor que mis amigos.
5) Andamos / Caminamos más lentamente / más despacio que Rob.
6) Ed es el que peor corre.

Page 68: Words to Say How Much
1) Hay demasiados gatos aquí.
2) Es bastante interesante.
3) Tengo muchos amigos.
4) Hablan demasiado lentamente / despacio.
5) Hay tantas playas en España.
6) El libro es buenísimo.

Page 69: I, You, We
1) ellos
2) ella
3) nosotros
4) vosotros
5) él
6) ustedes
7) ellas
8) ellos

Page 70: Me, You, Them
1) La rompe.
2) La bebo.
3) Le compró una falda.
4) Le envío / mando un correo electrónico.
5) Quiero hacerlo. / Lo quiero hacer.
6) Nos lo dijo.

Answers

Page 71: More Pronouns

1) Mi hermana, que tiene siete años, es baja.
2) Fui a Madrid, que es la capital de España.
3) ¿Cuál es tu dirección?
4) ¿Con quién vives?
5) ¿De quién es este perro?
6) ¿Cuál prefieres?

Page 72: More Pronouns

1) Son los míos.
2) ¿Qué es aquello?
3) Esta cama es más grande que aquella.
4) Este libro es más interesante que ese.
5) ¿Es el vuestro?
6) Alguien está hablando tranquilamente.

Page 73: Conjunctions

1) La geografía es divertida, pero es difícil.
2) Me gusta la historia porque es fácil.
3) Como estoy enfermo/a, me quedo en casa.
4) Voy al parque cuando hace calor.
5) Hablo francés e italiano.
6) ¿Prefieres azul o amarillo?

Page 74: Prepositions

1) La casa está enfrente del banco.
2) El tren va hasta Italia.
3) Lo escuché en la radio.
4) Entro en el supermercado.
5) Soy de Hull, pero vivo en Crewe.
6) A partir de septiembre, tendré un trabajo.

Page 75: 'Por', 'Para' and the Personal 'a'

1) para 3) Por 5) por
2) a 4) por 6) para

Page 76: Verbs in the Present Tense

1) bailo 4) corre 7) escribes
2) bebemos 5) aprende 8) Vive aquí desde hace un año.
3) nadáis 6) visitan

Page 77: Irregular Verbs in the Present Tense

1) Comienza 3) Queremos 5) Puedes
2) Vais 4) Doy 6) Sé

Page 78: 'Ser' and 'Estar' in the Present Tense

1) Está 3) Somos 5) es
2) Es 4) Estoy 6) es

Page 79: Talking About the Past

1) lloraron 6) pude
2) comimos 7) hicisteis
3) escribisteis 8) puso
4) cené 9) viniste
5) diste 10) trajimos

Page 80: Talking About the Past

1) cantaba 3) aprendía 5) volvían 7) nadabas
2) éramos 4) decía 6) seguíais 8) iban

Page 81: Talking About the Past

1) hacía 2) volví 3) Fuiste 4) Iba; tuve

Page 82: Talking About the Past

1) Habían cantado. 5) Había bebido.
2) Ha viajado. 6) Habíamos terminado.
3) Habéis aprendido. 7) Ha seguido.
4) Ha visto. 8) Has vivido.

Page 83: Talking About the Future

1) voy a comer; comeré
2) vamos a tener; tendremos
3) va a bailar; bailará
4) voy a dar; daré
5) van a poner; pondrán
6) vais a jugar; jugaréis
7) vas a poder; podrás
8) va a cantar; cantará
9) vamos a querer; querremos
10) vais a vivir; viviréis

Page 84: Would, Could and Should

1) irías 5) partiría
2) cantaría 6) saldrían
3) vendríamos 7) hablaría
4) diríais 8) tendríamos

Page 85: Reflexive Verbs

1) me llamo; me he llamado
2) se levantan; se han levantado
3) se lava; se ha lavado
4) te acuestas; te has acostado
5) nos sentimos; nos hemos sentido
6) os vais; os habéis ido
7) se viste; se ha vestido
8) te despiertas; te has despertado

Page 86: Verbs with '-ing' and 'Just Done'

1) está cayendo; estaba cayendo; acaba de caer
2) estás abriendo; estabas abriendo; acabas de abrir
3) está saltando; estaba saltando; acaba de saltar
4) están diciendo; estaban diciendo; acaban de decir
5) estáis corriendo; estabais corriendo; acabáis de correr
6) estamos siguiendo; estábamos siguiendo; acabamos de seguir
7) estás dando; estabas dando; acabas de dar
8) estoy leyendo; estaba leyendo; acabo de leer
9) están sirviendo; estaban sirviendo; acaban de servir
10) estamos bailando; estábamos bailando; acabamos de bailar

Page 87: Negative Forms

1) No fui al cine.
2) Ya no vamos al gimnasio.
3) No vas ni a Oslo ni a Faro.
4) Sally no tiene ninguna manzana.
5) No hay nada aquí.
6) No hay nadie en el coche.

Page 88: The Passive and Impersonal Verbs

A) Sentences 2 and 3 are written in the passive voice.
B) 1) Se compra 2) Se comen

Page 89: The Subjunctive

1) saltes 5) venga
2) escuche 6) hagamos
3) limpiemos 7) puedan
4) abran 8) tengáis

Page 90: The Subjunctive

1) present subjunctive 3) present subjunctive
2) imperfect subjunctive 4) imperfect subjunctive

Page 91: Giving Orders

1) ¡Canta!; ¡No cantes! 5) ¡Abrid!; ¡No abráis!
2) ¡Bailen!; ¡No bailen! 6) ¡Venid!; ¡No vengáis!
3) ¡Ten!; ¡No tengas! 7) ¡Sea!; ¡No sea!
4) ¡Dé!; ¡No dé! 8) ¡Vayan!; ¡No vayan!

Answers

Transcript

Section 1 — General Stuff

Track 1 — p.3

E.g. **M1:** ¡Hola! Soy Carlos. Voy al gimnasio todos los días y los jueves juego al fútbol.

1) **F1:** ¡Buenos días! Me llamo Anabel. Celebré mi cumpleaños anteayer y fui a un restaurante con mi familia y mis amigos. Ayer, fuimos de compras a Londres, pero mañana por la mañana, iremos a Oxford. Me encantan las cafeterías en Oxford.

   F2: ¡Hola! Me llamo Julia. Mañana voy a ir al cine con mis amigas, y el viernes vamos a ir al teatro.

Track 2 — p.10

1) (i) **M1:** ¿Qué te gusta hacer los fines de semana, Carolina?

   F1: Me encanta ir a la piscina. Y tú Antonio, ¿qué te gusta hacer los fines de semana?

   M1: A mí me gusta ir de compras, pero no me gusta escuchar música. Me gusta ir de compras porque es muy divertido y las tiendas en mi ciudad son estupendas. Alguna gente cree que ir de compras es para chicas, pero eso no es verdad. Mucha gente adora la música, pero a mí nunca me ha interesado. Prefiero leer. Acabo de terminar una novela fenomenal. Las novelas y los periódicos sí que son interesantes porque se puede aprender mucho. ¿Estás de acuerdo?

   (ii) **F1:** Sí, estoy de acuerdo. Me encanta leer porque es relajante, pero me gusta escuchar música también. Prefiero los grupos de música pop porque la música pop me parece guay.

Section 2 — About Me

Track 3 — p.13

1) **F2:** Esta persona parece bastante baja. Tiene el pelo liso y castaño, pero no lo tiene especialmente largo. Lleva unas gafas bastante grandes. Es una persona joven.

   M1: Tiene el pelo negro, pero no es ni liso ni rizado. Creo que tiene los ojos marrones y que es una persona bastante alta. No lleva gafas.

   F2: Esta persona no tiene ni barba ni bigote. Tiene el pelo largo y moreno, y creo que es bastante delgada. Lleva maquillaje y no tiene pecas.

   M1: No es totalmente calvo, pero no tiene mucho pelo. Tiene el pelo gris, y tiene barba. No sé el color de sus ojos. No es joven — la verdad, parece bastante viejo.

Section 3 — Daily Life

Track 4 — p.21

E.g. **M1:** ¡Hola! Soy Joaquín. Cuando era pequeño, me gustaba comer muchos caramelos y helados y odiaba las verduras. ¡No me importaba para nada la salud!

1) **M1:** Ahora como de todo — mariscos, legumbres y carne. Odio la comida basura porque no solo engorda, sino que suele llevar cantidades enormes de sal y azúcar. ¿Qué te gusta comer, Alejandra?

   F1: Creo que comes mejor que yo, Joaquín. Si pudiera comer caramelos todos los días, lo haría. Sería mejor si comiera más fruta, pero no me gusta mucho. Mis padres me dicen que bebo demasiado café, así que ahora estoy intentando beber más agua.

   F2: Me llamo Raquel. No como ni pescado ni carne — soy vegetariana. Normalmente es bastante fácil evitar la carne porque me gustan las legumbres. Sin embargo, cuando voy a restaurantes con mis amigos, es más difícil porque hay pocos platos sin carne. Por otro lado, los platos vegetarianos suelen ser más baratos que los que contienen carne o pescado.

Track 5 — p.23

E.g. **F2:** ¡Hola! Quiero hacer una tortilla española para una fiesta de cumpleaños y necesito unos ingredientes. ¿Me puede ayudar?

   M1: Sí, claro. ¿Qué le hace falta?

1) **F2:** Pues primero, necesito un kilo de patatas. Y póngame también medio kilo de cebollas.

   M1: Claro. ¿Algo más?

   F2: Sí, deme seis huevos, pero no necesito sal, porque ya la tengo en casa.

   M1: Aquí tiene.

   F2: ¡Ay, casi se me ha olvidado! Necesito también una botella de aceite de oliva.

   M1: Desafortunadamente, no tengo aceite de oliva. Acabo de vender la última botella.

   F2: ¡Qué pena! Tendré que ir a otra tienda. ¿Cuánto cuesta todo?

   M1: Cuesta seis euros cincuenta.

   F2: Vale, gracias. Aquí tiene. ¡Adiós!

   M1: Gracias. ¡Adiós!

Transcript

Section 4 — Free-Time Activities

Track 6 — p.31

E.g. **F2:** Diría que mi género preferido es la música rap porque creo que es la música más original y distinta. Me encanta la música clásica también porque es relajante. Sin embargo, según mi hermana menor, la música más importante para nuestra generación sería la música pop.

1) **F2:** Cuando era más joven, tocaba el piano, pero en este momento, no tengo suficiente tiempo para practicar. Me encantaría aprender a tocar el saxofón porque es un instrumento fenomenal y porque el jazz es un tipo de música que siempre me ha fascinado. Me gusta escuchar música por Internet, porque es muy rápido descargar canciones y cuesta menos que ir a una tienda para comprar un CD. Me encanta ir a conciertos también, porque la música en directo es siempre muy emocionante.

Section 6 — Travel and Tourism

Track 7 — p.44

1) **M1:** ¡Hola! Te voy a hablar de mi barrio. El teatro está en la parte este del barrio donde también hay muchos restaurantes. Está al lado de un museo muy impresionante. En la plaza hay un bar que es muy popular tanto con los jóvenes como con los jubilados. Había tres supermercados hace un par de años, pero ahora solo hay uno. Se puede encontrar el supermercado al fondo de la calle San Felipe, enfrente de la comisaría. Luego, si sigues esa calle y tomas la segunda calle a la derecha, encontrarás la iglesia.

Section 7 — Current and Future Study and Employment

Track 8 — p.46

1) **M1:** ¡Ay, Marta! Odio los lunes.

 F1: ¿Por qué?

 M1: ¿No es obvio? Tenemos matemáticas, comercio y después del recreo, inglés. Es horrible.

 F1: Pero los martes son mejores, ¿no? Me gustan las ciencias y el dibujo.

 M1: ¿Y el francés?

 F1: No me emociona mucho. Prefiero las asignaturas más prácticas.

 M1: Estoy de acuerdo. Yo prefiero los miércoles. Es una oportunidad para ser creativo. Por ejemplo, empezamos con los trabajos manuales. Después hay el español y a las diez y media, tenemos música. Es mi día preferido.

Section 8 — Global Issues

Track 9 — p.57

E.g. **F2:** Desafortunadamente, hay miles de personas sin techo en España.

1) **F2:** Debido a los problemas económicos que tenemos, muchas personas han perdido su trabajo y no tienen suficiente dinero para pagar el alquiler. Algunos pueden pedir ayuda a sus padres o amigos, pero otros acaban en la calle. Lo que todos tienen en común es que tienen una vida dificilísima. Sin embargo, lo peor es que frecuentemente son víctimas del prejuicio, lo que les puede dificultar la vida bastante. Este prejuicio existe porque mucha gente cree que los sin techo no pueden pagar su alquiler porque son perezosos. Si queremos cambiar la situación de estas personas, tenemos que trabajar juntos — es la única manera de hacerlo.

Index